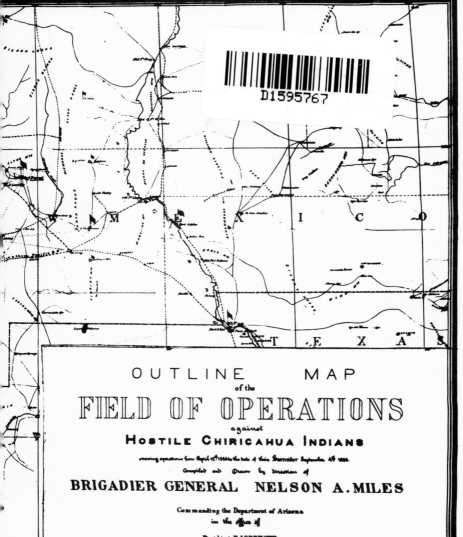

OUTLINE MAP

of the

FIELD OF OPERATIONS

against

HOSTILE CHIRICAHUA INDIANS

showing operations from April 1st 1886 to the date of their Surrender September 4th 1886.

Compiled and Drawn by direction of

BRIGADIER GENERAL NELSON A. MILES

Commanding the Department of Arizona

in the Office of

First Lieut. E.I.SPENCER.

Corps of Engineers.

ENGINEER OFFICER OF THE DEPARTMENT.

Oskar Huber,   Top. Assistant

Charleston Troop I   4th Cavalry

Scale 1 inch : 12 Miles.

LEGEND

Department Headquarters. — Wagon Roads and Trails practicable for Wagons

Military Posts (garrisons) — Trails practicable for Packmules.

Military Posts (unoccupied) — International Boundary.

Camp for Scouting Observation. — State & territorial Boundaries.

Heliograph Stations   and Boundaries of Indian Military Reservations

Heliograph communications

Telegraph Lines. — On U.S. Limits of Districts of Observation under command of senior officers therein.

Indian fights - Indian

Rail Roads

Creek (dry) — Sta. Maria Prefecture Limits.

Authorities

Territories of New Mexico & Arizona .... Capt. G.M. Wheeler   South Eastern Arizona, ... Lt. E.J. Spencer

South Western   New Mexico .... Powell & Kingman   Official Map of the State of Sonora, ... H.W. Herbert

ON THE BLOODY TRAIL OF GERONIMO
WESTERNLORE GREAT WEST AND INDIAN SERIES XII

(A facsimile re-issue)

On the Bloody Trail of Geronimo

Lt. John Bigelow, Jr.

with the original illustrations of
HOOPER, McDOUGALL, CHAPIN, HATFIELD
and FREDERIC REMINGTON

Foreword, Introduction and Notes
by ARTHUR WOODWARD

WESTERNLORE PRESS . . . 1986 . . . TUCSON, ARIZONA 85740

Library of Congress Catalog No. 58-8718
ISBN: 0-87026-016-2

PRINTED IN THE UNITED STATES OF AMERICA BY WESTERNLORE PRESS

FOREWORD

DURING the 1870s and 1880s many army officers supplemented their meager pay by selling articles, and their journals of life in the field, to various national magazines. Today, many of those items, tucked away in periodicals now long since defunct or forgotten, have become valuable sources of frontier history.

In submitting his journal for publication, Lieutenant John Bigelow, Jr., was but following a trend. As indicated in his diary, he wrote with the deliberate intent of seeing it in print. Bigelow was at this time a first lieutenant, having graduated from the United States Military Academy at West Point in June 1877 as a second lieutenant. He was assigned to the 10th United States Cavalry, a Negro regiment, which had been organized July 28, 1866 at Fort Leavenworth, Kansas. The young officer was promoted to first lieutenant September 24, 1883 but had to wait ten years longer before he obtained his captaincy, April 1893. He was assigned to K Company of the 10th. The regiment was, by this time, a crack outfit, and had been first blooded in Indian warfare on the Plains on August 2, 1867. During the next few years the 10th was actively engaged in the Indian campaigns, and received its sobriquet "The Buffalo Soldiers" about 1871. Today, the regimental crest consists of, on a wreath of colors (brown and gold), a buffalo proper statant *gardant:* motto, READY AND FORWARD.

Lieutenant Bigelow's account of his experiences in southern Arizona and Mexico, as a result perhaps, of his intent to publish the journal, contains much more than a simple, daily routine mention of troop activities such as might be found in the dry, military reports of field patrols. In his observations on the terrain covered, the mines, the ranches, and the inhabitants of the Territory, as well as his firsthand relation of places and events, Lieutenant Bigelow approaches the level of good reporting as well as the drama, comedy and intelligent observations reached in the works of Captain John G. Bourke, whose two classics of life in the southwest, written and published during this same period, are now acknowledged as among the best pen pictures of border life in Arizona and New Mexico during the 1870s and 1880s as any that have been written. These volumes are: *On the Border with Crook,* first published by Charles Scribner's Sons, New York, 1891, and a scarcer and lesser known little item, *An Apache Campaign in the Sierra Madre.* The latter book first appeared, serially, in *Outing Magazine,* in 1885, in which periodical Lieutenant Bigelow's journal was also published serially, in fourteen parts beginning in March 1886 and terminating in in the April issue, 1887, under the title *After Geronimo.*

The editor of *Outing* at this time was Poultney Bigelow, well known in the annals of American journalism. His magazine carried many interesting and important articles on frontier life which were illustrated with black-and-white pen sketches and wash drawings by many noted illustrators of the day as well as talented beginners.

Captain Bourke's book, *An Apache Campaign in the Sierra Madre,* for example, was illustrated by a soldier-artist, a man from the ranks, yet a firm friend of both Captain Bourke and General Crook, Alexander Francis Harmer, who had joined the army in the early 1870s for the purpose of furthering his chosen profession as an artist by making sketches of the Apache Indians in the field. Harmer thus antedated Frederic Remington as an illustrator of the Southwest by nearly ten years.

Remington, however, after his graduation from Yale, had gone west, and was vitally interested in the portrayal of the Indians and the military.

In 1885 Remington was a struggling young artist seeking a foothold in the illustrating world. He had accumulated a portfolio of crude but spirited sketches of army life which he had submitted to the art editors of most of the large magazines in New York. One day he carried his portfolio into the office of Poultney Bigelow and discovered to his delight that the editor was an old classmate from Yale and with whom he had worked on the university organ, the *Yale Courant*. After the first boisterous reunion was over they got down to business. Poultney in his biography, *Seventy Summers,* described that meeting, and in telling of the event and of Remington's first sketches, said: "Genius was in the rough drawings and I loved them for their roughness."

As a result Poultney bought all of Remington's sketches in the portfolio, and what was more important, gave the artist his first commission to illustrate a serial of army life which he had recently accepted, parts of which had already appeared in print.

Thus it was that Frederic Remington, virtually unknown at the time, first appeared in *Outing* with a series of black and white pen sketches which illustrated the work of Lieutenant John Bigelow, *After Geronimo.*

It was a fortunate combination. Bigelow the young lieutenant who was breaking into print for the first time, and Remington, who was likewise doing his first important commission as an illustrator.

I might add that Bigelow in his journal, aside from his pertinent observations on frontier life, also made a sincere attempt to evaluate army life of the day, as seen through the eyes of a junior officer. His comments on the current trends of thought relative to the changing attitudes on the part of both the military and civilian officials toward the enlisted man at that time, the drift toward better schooling, better accommodations in barracks, a better regulated diet, reflects somewhat the undertone of a national awakening in this respect. The close of the Civil War saw a number of real or potential changes concerning the welfare of the man in the ranks, particularly with regard to punishments, clothing and general treatment. The reason was that the bulk of the Union army consisted of civilian volunteers and when these men returned home they turned to politics and were more conscious of the treatment of the enlisted men in the army than ever before in the history of the United States. True, some improvements were slow in becoming realities, but by the 1880s there was a definite movement along this line. The status of the common soldier was beginning to take on more national dignity.

It was such men as Captain Bourke and Lieutenant Bigelow who consciously or unconsciously spearheaded these changes by presenting to the public in printed form something of the hardships of army life on the frontier.

Likewise it was by the gifted pens and brushes of such men as J. R. Chapin and Edwin Forbes, artists of the Civil War, and their successors, A. F. Harmer and Frederic Remington, that the public saw the conditions under which the army moved and lived.

It was felt that Lt. Bigelow's delineation of his frontier experiences, illustrated by the veteran artists Chapin, Hooper, McDougall and others, and by the crude yet powerful sketches of Remington's first efforts at depicting army life, deserved to be reprinted. Hence this present volume.

ARTHUR WOODWARD.

INTRODUCTION

THE TERMINATION of the 1885-1886 campaign against the Apache brought to a close approximately half a century of bloody frontier warfare in the Southwest. During those fifty years hundreds of men, women and children lost their lives. The casualties were heavy on both sides. For nearly three centuries the Apache had been warring with the Spanish and Mexicans. In the early 1830s the Americans entered the conflict, siding with the Mexicans in an attempt to exterminate the Apache. Those were bitter, dark days when white men armed with rifles, pistols, and even cannon, hunted Apache men, women and children for blood money paid by the officials of Chihuahua for Apache scalps. No wonder then that the *Diné,* as the Apache called themselves, turned against the Americans. The Indians found themselves between two strong forces, and they fought savagely to outwit both groups of enemies. And they had to combat internecine troubles as well.

During the Civil War, after the regular troops had been withdrawn from Arizona and New Mexico, to be replaced soon thereafter by volunteers from California, Colorado and New Mexico, the Apache deemed the time ripe to crush their adversaries. It was during this time that some of the many military posts in Arizona and New Mexico were built and in the two decades that followed, more forts were established at strategic spots throughout the Territories. Regular companies of cavalry and infantry again moved into the desert lands and took up the monotonous task of patrolling the vast expanses of desert, mountain and cañon terrain—the homeland of the Apache.

The discovery of gold and silver in the Prescott region during the early 1860s brought hundreds of prospectors and miners into that section, and there was the inevitable conflict between the Indians and the white interlopers. As usual, the white men held the firm conviction that the tribesmen had no rights as human beings. Indians, particularly the Apache, were only animals in human form and as such were hunted and slain like animals. The newspapers of the 1860s-1870s carried items advising travelers as to the best methods of killing Indians. One editor suggested that prospectors or ranchers carry brown sugar, mixed with strychnine in quarter pound cakes, wrapped up with crackers in a roll, on the cantle of the saddle and when pursued by Indians, the advice was to cut loose the poisoned sugar and crackers, and then return in an hour or so to collect a crop of hair. A newspaper in Tucson noted:

> ON EXHIBITION: The Scalp of the Indian killed by Col. Barnard upon whom was found Col. Stone's gold bar, is on exhibition at Charley Brown's saloon. The hair is glossy and beautiful and the ears are decorated by pendant brass buttons.—*Weekly Arizonan,* Feb. 12, 1870.

The same issue carried a comment by the editor upon the success of the Mexican forces in Sonora under Col. Elias in exterminating the Apache:

> The inducements offered him by his government viz; $200 for every Apache scalp will be most certain to ensure his success. If our government were half so liberal the militia force of Arizona cooperating with that of Mexico would soon find a solution to the Indian problem.

Again the humane editor of the *Arizonan,* commenting further upon the action of the Sonora government in offering bounties for scalps, in his columns of December 31, 1870, mentioned the proposal of a Yankee genius from down east who had organized a "joint stock company . . . object of which is to exterminate the Apache Indians without the use of lead, steel, poison, fire, cholera or small pox. The *modus operandi* is as yet unkown outside the company; but should the scheme prove successful, Arizona will do her utmost to immortalize the name of the successful genius."

Sixteen years later the editor of the *Arizona Sentinel*, June 25, 1887, endorsed the method proposed by another white humanitarian, which was much along the same line as that proposed seventeen years earlier:

C. W. Culver of Pinal has inaugurated a movement that ought to be received with favor by the people of every county in the Territory. He is circulating for signatures an agreement by which the signers pledge themselves to pay one dollar each for each hostile Apache Indian killed by either soldier or civilian, the limit to be one hundred such assessments. It is believed that from one hundred to two hundred signatures can be obtained in Pinal county, and enough more in other counties to swell the bounty upon each scalp to $500 or possibly $1000. This method will bring in the scalps and no impertinent questions will be asked as to how they are obtained. It promises some little compensation for the risk of hunting down savages and if it succeeds in making a larger number of good Indians than are supposed to be raiding the country, no particular harm will be done.

With such hatred of the Apache engendered by the public press one need not wonder that the Indians retaliated in kind whenever the opportunity presented itself. Lonely ranches were attacked and the occupants slain or carried off into captivity. Prospectors and miners died under Apache bullets, lances and arrows or suffered slower deaths by torture. Wagon trains and stage coaches were ambushed and burned. During those fearful years it was almost impossible for would-be stock men to maintain their herds in Apache country. Only the hardiest survived. Pete Kitchen was one who defied every effort of the Indians to run him out of the country. There were others who tried, and failed. Mines were raided and the personnel killed.

Gradually, however, the military began to get the upper hand. Using the age-old strategy of divide and conquer, the experienced leaders of the soldiery, utilized the enmity of one tribal group for another to a good advantage. Indian scouts were enrolled and took the field against their red brethren. Without such aid the army could not have whipped the hostiles.

General Crook broke the back of the main Apache resistance in 1872-1873 by two major actions. The most devastating of these was the attack upon a large cave in Salt River Cañon, located high upon the sides of a cliff. Here the Apache had sought refuge with the women and children and here, early in the dawn of December 28, 1872, detachments of the Fifth Cavalry, aided by Apache and Pima scouts, attacked the cave. The Indians fought hard but there was no escape. They took refuge behind huge boulders and slabs of rocks in the cavern, which was very shallow, but the soldiers firing from vantage points above and below the cave mouth, aimed their bullets at the roof of the cave and at the slanting rocks in such a manner as to ricochet the slugs into every part of the shelter. Thus they died, warriors, old men, women and babies. When the smoke cleared away only the dead and wounded were left. The Apache mourned the seventy-six persons killed in that place for many years afterward. The wounded women and children were taken to old Camp Grant. This action in Salt River Cañon and the attack upon a supposedly impregnable Apache stronghold on the summit of Turret Butte by the combined forces of cavalry and infantry early in 1873 resulted in total defeat of the hostile band, the warriors of which, finding their escape cut off, leaped to their deaths from the top of the Butte.

General Crook believed that the Apache, if treated well, and made self-sustaining on reservations, would in time become good citizens. He put them to work digging irrigation ditches, planting crops, raising stock, and always he told them the truth. Accordingly the Apache were settled at Camp Verde, Fort Apache, and old Camp Grant at the mouth of the San Carlos. There were, however malcontents, who slipped away from the agencies and stirred up trouble. Likewise there were white men whose greed for a few extra dollars obtained by short changing the captive Indians on their rations, clothing, tools and forage, led to serious difficulties.

It was to the advantage of the latter class of men, some of whom were long time residents of Arizona, others were newly appointed political underlings sent out from Washington, to see that the Indians were underfed and otherwise mistreated. Quiet, peaceful Indians were not profitable to such men. They were also backed by the citizens in the various communities springing up throughout Arizona. Once the Apache menace subsided, the need for large bodies of troops passed and when the troops left the area, the merchants, freighters, ranchers and others who had been lining their pockets at the expense of the Indians and Uncle Sam had to look elsewhere for an honest dollar.

Thus, under the petty tyranny of newly appointed Indian agents, and the friction developed between the military and the civilian employees over the management of Indian affairs at the agencies, the Indians were again caught between the upper and nether burr stones of a new life, and trouble began. The younger Apache, fired by tales of the war trail, and made dangerous by the illicit rotgut whiskey sold them by "white vultures," as Capt. John G. Bourke called them, began slipping away on raids. The Chiricahua band was one group that had been specially exempted from General Crook's jurisdiction. Their main stronghold in the Dragoon Mountains was under the direct command of Cochise, a tall, finely built Indian. Part of the Chiricahuas had been sent to San Carlos and these were derided by their other brethren for doing "squaw" work. All of these factors, the cheating methods of the "Indian ring," *i.e.*, white men who wanted to profit at the Indian's expense regardless of human suffering and the malcontents among the Apache, both on and off the reservation, eventually culminated in more bloodshed.

General Crook was in the good graces of the civilian populace at large in March 1875, at which time he was transferred from the Department of Arizona and sent to another hot spot of aboriginal troubles, the Department of the Platte. For the time being at least the Apache were quiet, except for the occasional raids of the trouble-makers. This condition did not last long, and before the summer of 1882, Indian affairs in Arizona were again at low ebb. The Apache were once more upon the warpath, the vicious practices of the "Indian ring" and the bungling of the military left in command in Arizona had undone all of Crook's previous efforts. All of the young men had jumped the reservations and were skirmishing with the cavalry. The older men, women and children left at the agencies were in the depths of despair. These people had tried desperately to follow the new road laid out for them. They had planted crops, and had begun to raise cattle, but the cheap politicians and the "boys" of the "Tucson ring" who found their easy graft slipping through their fingers, harassed the Indians by defrauding them out of their cattle, their farms and their government rations. A grand jury investigation at Tucson, of the conditions at the agency of San Carlos in October 1882, established the fact that, to quote Bourke: "Fraud, peculation, conspiracy, plots and counterplots seem to be the rule of action upon this reservation. The Grand Jury little thought when they began this investigation that they were about to open a Pandora's box of iniquities seldom surpassed in the annals of crime. With the immense power wielded by the Indian agent almost any crime is possible. There seems to be no check upon his conduct."

The grand jury indictment then went on to enumerate many of the vicious practices of the agent, his underlings and the Government contractors. The foreman of the jury summed up the situation thus: "This was the united testimony of the Grand Jury, corroborated by white witnesses, and to these and kindred causes may be attributed the desolation and bloodshed which have dotted our plains with the graves of murdered victims."

It was into this mess of corruption that the army plunged its head trouble-shooter, General Crook, when he was once more recalled to duty as commander of the Department of Arizona in the fall of 1882.

In General Orders No. 43, issued at headquarters at Fort Whipple, October 5, 1882, Crook observed:

The commanding general, after making a thorough and exhaustive examination among the Indians of the eastern and southern part of this Territory, regrets to say that he finds among them a general feeling of distrust and want of confidence in the whites, especially the soldiery; and also that much dissatisfaction, dangerous to the peace of the country exists among them. Officers and soldiers serving in this department are reminded that one of the fundamental principles of the military character is justice to all—Indians as well as white men—and that a disregard of this principle is likely to bring about hostilities, and cause the death of the very persons they are sent to protect. In all their dealings with the Indians, officers must be careful not only to observe the strictest fidelity, but to make no promises not in their power to carry out; all grievances arising within their jurisdiction should be redressed, so that an accumulation of them may not cause an outbreak . . .

General Crook believed implicitly in the truth of his orders. He felt that his course of conduct with the Indians, absolute honesty and a firm but gentle hand, would win out. He reckoned without the manipulations of the powers of the Indian ring, the tentacles of which reached into offices of high officials in Washington. Then too, in his absence other factors had entered into the picture. New mines had been discovered and developed on lands set aside for the Apache. Unauthorized squatters in the guise of Mormon settlers or as friends of the crooked agents had usurped Apache farm lands and had destroyed Apache crops and stolen their cattle. Crook promptly evicted these intruders from the Apache reservations and opposed the curtailment of the reservation lands for the benefit of the white ranchers and miners. He also insisted that the Apache be given all the work which could be provided for them without the use of middlemen or contractors, and that the Indians receive the same wages as other men doing similar tasks, without wage deductions going to the white grafters.

Naturally the opposition did not submit tamely to all of these measures. The friends of the ousted ranchers, miners and Indian agents, as well as some newspaper editors, began a campaign of vilification against Crook and all others who dared to intimate that the Indians had the rights of human beings. In spite of this,

General Crook pursued his policy of dealing fairly with the Apaches who believed in him.

Governor Tritle of Arizona said: "The Indians know General Crook and his methods, and respect both." However, in spite of all that he could do, General Crook could not control all the tribesmen, especially those belonging to the Chiricahua who had slipped the leash and had gone to their hideouts in the Sierra Madre in Mexico.

In 1883 the military launched a campaign against the Chiricahua. In March of that year a band of twenty-six warriors under an intelligent and daring young leader, Chato, struck hard at the southern frontier of Arizona Territory. They killed, burned and raided, swiftly and mercilessly. General Crook swung into action. He visited Sonora and Chihuahua and held conferences with the Mexican authorities, both civilian and military, and arranged for their cooperation in running down the hostiles. A small force of one hundred and ninety-three Apache scouts was enlisted to aid detachments of the Third and Sixth Cavalry. Two of Crook's right-hand men were Captain Emmet Crawford of the Third Cavalry and Lieutenant Charles Gatewood of the Sixth. Other officers in the campaign were Captain John G. Bourke, Third Cavalry; Lieutenant Frank West, Lieutenant W. Forsyth, Lieutenant G. J. Febiger of the Engineers Corps and Major Chaffee. Archie McIntosh and Al Sieber acted as chiefs of scouts while Mickey Free, Severiano and Sam Bowman went along as interpreters. "Peaches" or Panayotishn, a White Mountain Apache, married to a Chiricahua woman, who had surrendered after a fight in the Whetstone Mountains, was one of the principal guides. Other native guides were To-klanni, Alchise and more friendly Apache.

After a long chase into Mexico, which took the U.S. troops two hundred miles into Mexican territory, the Chiricahua were defeated in one of their mountain strongholds, and absent warriors and the women were captured singly and in small groups as soon as they straggled back into their isolated camp from raids upon the Mexican villages. In turn these Indians were taken back to San Carlos Agency and put to work. All of the runaways had the same story to tell of the misery enforced upon them by the agent and his men.

In the meantime the storm of vilification against Crook increased in strength. The returned prisoners, as well as other Indians upon the reservations, were accused of every crime in the book, and many rumors of attacks, murders, and raids were spread deliberately by white men in order to rouse feeling against the Apache and the policies of General Crook. Among the lowest elements of pioneer society were those whom Captain Bourke characterized as "rum-poisoned bummers of the San Pedro Valley," and others who lived in the nearby towns. A quasi-military organization known as the "Tombstone Toughs" was composed of the "bummers," and all their fighting was done with big words in the saloons. They did fire upon one old decrepit Indian, a member of Eskiminzin's band, the members of which had been living at peace with their white neighbors in the lower San Pedro, raising stock and farming. After firing on the old Apache the "Toughs" ran away and were ridiculed by a Tucson editor as "senseless cowards, who sought to kill a few peaceable Indians, and thereby gain a little cheap notoriety, which cannot result otherwise than disastrously to the settlers in that vicinity."

Yes, there were a few white men who were fair-minded and knew that there were other means of settling the frontier problems without the rifle.

Two years passed and the Apache remained at peace, working hard on their small ranches at Camp Apache. They raised millions of pounds of corn, beans, wheat, pumpkins, potatoes, barley, musk and water melons as well as smaller amounts of cabbages, onions, cucumbers, etc. They sold their produce to the Quartermaster Department, to freighters and the traders at the agency. But always on the outskirts of the Apache lands were dealers in illicit liquor and as usual there was the friction between the Indian agent and the military as well as the Indians under agency control. The Apache saw and heard the bickerings between the civilian and the military, and when their friend and ally, Captain Crawford, who had been helping them at San Carlos, lost out in his arguments with the agent, they became restless and suspicious. The old, free method of living was remembered, and acted as a strong lure.

Then it happened. On May 17, 1885, one hundred and twenty-four Chiricahua of all ages and sexes, headed by Geronimo and Nachez, both of whom were strong leaders and who had worked hard at their farm work, jumped the reservation and headed south into Mexico. There seemed to be no definite factor which caused the break. The many petty irritations snow-balled, and a prolonged *tizwin* (Apache home brew) binge just before the Indians decamped, may have triggered the decision to leave the agency. At least three-fourths of the Apache refused to joined Geronimo. The friendly ones were headed by Chato, who was unfriendly to Geronimo.

However much General Crook hated to do it, as a soldier he could not do otherwise than once more take his troops to the field. Crook, and other officers who had worked with the Indians in peace and who had fought them in lonely canyons and on rocky heights, respected the Apache. A telegraph message sent to Crook by Lieutenant Britton Davis, under whose control the rebellious Indians had been working, reached the general too late for him to act.

General Crook maintained that: "It should not be expected that an Indian who has lived as a barbarian all his life will become an angel the moment he comes on a reservation and promises to behave himself . . . they are children in ignorance, not in innocence. I do not wish to be understood as in the least palliating their crimes, but I wish to say a word to stem the torrent of invective and abuse which has almost universally been indulged in against the whole Apache race.

"This, is not strange on the frontier from a certain class of vampires who prey on the misfortunes of their fellow-men, and who live best and easiest in time of Indian troubles. With them peace kills the goose that lays the golden egg. Greed and avarice on the part of the whites—in other words, the almighty dollar—is at the bottom of nine-tenths of all our Indian troubles."

So, once more the troops turned out from Camp Apache, Camp Bowie, Fort Grant and other scattered posts in Arizona. Among these troopers were those of the 10th United States Cavalry, the "buffalo soldiers," whose kinky hair had won them the nickname from the Plains Indians. The detachment under Lieutenant John Bigelow was not destined to take the long, hard trail into Mexico, but their work guarding the mountain passes leading out of Mexico into Arizona was a most important one. No one knew exactly where Geronimo and his band would strike. During this campaign of 1885-1886 the wily Apache leader hit savagely at isolated ranches and mines. Thirty-nine white people were slain in New Mexico and thirty-four died in Arizona. Nor were the whites the only sufferers. Friendly Apache who had remained quietly at home were attacked, and in November 1885, twelve friendlies were killed in their wickiups near Camp Apache, and six women and children carried off into captivity by the hostiles.

In the game of deadly hide-and-seek carried on in the hills and canyons of Sonora between the soldiers, the Mexican troops, and Geronimo's band, some of the latter were slain and the women and children taken captive. At last the grueling tempo of the chase began to tell upon the hostiles. Everywhere they turned they encountered enemies. The Sierra Madre hideouts were no longer sanctuaries because of the fact that the scouts with the troops knew the mountain trails, water holes and camps as well as did the renegades.

Then with the tide against him, Geronimo and his right hand man, Nachez, sent in word they would surrender to General Crook. The spot chosen was Cañon de los Embudos in the northeast corner of Sonora, and to this place came Geronimo and his head-men to meet General Crook and his troops.

That historic meeting is well known, and there is no point in repeating the occurrence here. Crook rode roughshod over Geronimo because he didn't trust him, and told him so. He also told

Geronimo that he could make up his mind then and there whether to surrender unconditionally or to stay out on the warpath. If he chose the latter course, said Crook, "I'll keep after you and kill the last one if it takes fifty years . . . I have said all I have to say; you had better think it over to-night and let me know in the morning."

On the next morning (March 27) Geronimo, Chihuahua, Nachita and Kutli again met with Crook, and surrendered, and agreed to return to the reservation. General Crook had told them that if they came in they would be sent away from their country for two years, and then they could return—provided they had behaved themselves.

Unfortunately General Crook, once the matter of surrender had been arranged, set out at once for Camp Bowie, leaving the Indians to come in under soldier escort. The night of the 27th, a white man, Tribollet by name, sold the Apache in Geronimo's band, including the chief himself, enough mescal and rotgut whiskey to make the whole outfit drunk. Once in their cups, old suspicions against the white men were revived. Tribolett and his men filled the drunken Indians with lies about the fate awaiting them when they returned to the reservation, and in the night Geronimo and Nachez, with part of their band, once more took to the hills.

As soon as he reached a telegraph office General Crook immediately informed General Sheridan of all that had taken place. He stated the terms which he had offered Geronimo and in reply was told that "The President cannot assent to the surrender of the hostiles on the terms of their imprisonment East for two years, with the understanding of their return to the reservation. He instructs you to enter again into negotiations on the terms of their unconditional surrender, only sparing their lives."

The upshot of this and other instructions to Crook from Washington was that the general, unable to reconcile his word of honor with the deceit and treachery implied in headquarters' instructions to capture or kill the hostiles, saw only one way out of the dilemma. He requested a transfer from the Department of Arizona. This was granted immediately, and General Nelson A. Miles was sent to replace Crook. The result is only too well known. Once more troops set out, and General Miles engineered Geronimo's ultimate surrender . . . but it wasn't Miles who went in personally to treat with the Apache chief. Although he never fully received the recognition due him for his services, the man who made the final contact and accepted Geronimo's surrender was Lieutenant Charles Gatewood. Read his personal letter sent to his wife on this memorable occasion. This letter is now among the personal papers of Colonel C. B. Gatewood, son of Lieutenant Gatewood, in the collection of the Arizona Pioneers Historical Society Museum, in Tucson, Arizona, through whose courtesy I am enabled to present this historic document. The letter was written on sheets of graph paper, evidently torn from a field note book. It is dated August 26, '86:

My Dear Wife:

I am now in camp on the Bavispe river about 30 miles south of the San Bernadina [*sic*]. Well, I've had a talk with Geronimo in person. It took all day yesterday and made me very tired. He and I are grown to be great friends. He laid his arms down and gave me a hearty shake of the hand. My escort was near and so was his. In a short time we all sat down unarmed. About 20 bucks all around, but my escort stayed to one side under arms. So you see I ran no risk. This morning Ger. came to this camp. Capt. L. and I went out to meet him, and he walked right into camp leaving his arms and horse outside. He told me he would go with me anywhere, as I never harmed him, but always helped him along when he was at Apache.

He wanted to meet Capt. L—— so they had a hugging match before the whole command. Yesterday I delivered General Miles' message to them, but they do not want to go to Florida. They would agree to go back to the White Mts. the same as before. He begged me to see Gen. M. in person and lay the case before him. They are tired of fighting and want to be united to their families once more. They were all cheerful, feeling sure that since Gen. M. sent me all the way from Stanton, to meet them, he must have a good heart, and they believe that I would do my best in talking to them to get their families together.

Every one of them showed great pleasure at meeting me and they would remind me every few minutes of my promise to talk to Gen. Miles.

They cracked lots of jokes and smoked lots of tobacco and were in a jolly good humor generally, except Natchez. He was very blue. All he would say was that he wanted to meet his children. I really felt sorry for him, for I know how it is to yearn after one's family.

It made me home sicker than usual to look at him. I want to see my wife and little ones too. Will they *all* be there by the time I get back? I hope so.

I intended to hurry into Bowie but after rejoining Lawton, found that a courier could reach the Gen. at Huachuca in two days, where it would take 3 days travel to get to Bowie and might have to come back. In a few days I expect the Gen. will be back in San B. on the line and peace will be made whereby I may be allowed to hug you a few at Stanton.

You have not heard from me for some days. It is because I have not had a chance to send you a letter. I have been going ahead of Lawton, and leaving him to join the other command and so that even the few couriers sent were not near me at all, and gave me no show. But when you get this I hope it will serve to partly make up for no news from me until I can get home and make it up entirely. Eh? At any rate, my mission will be ended when Geronimo and Miles meet and I shall be done with Mexico.

If the war continues, I may not get home so soon as I like, but my gadding about down here will end. I do so much want to be with you. But I feel rather light hearted today. If there is no bad break made, the hostiles will surrender and the war will end. I get so happy that I have to sit on myself to keep me down, thro' fear of disappointment.

Geronimo dislikes Davis, Chatto and Micky Free. He said to me, "You can come to our camp anywhere. You are no more responsible for this war than I. I know you. If Gen. Miles won't make peace; you come and tell us. Never fear harm. If I want to talk I will come to your camp anywhere and feel safe. I will go with you now, alone to Capt. L's camp if you desire it. That's the way I feel towards you." He sent a man ahead this morning to tell me to meet him just outside. I did so. He laid down his gun, took me by the hand and said, "I'll go with you."

He is now loafing around the camp, having his talk with Capt. L. They really want to surrender, but they want their families with them. Can any one blame a man for wanting to see his wife and children?

Wouldn't *I* prance around lively if they moved you off to Florida? Ger. wants to go to Washington to talk to the Great Father. I will write you again the soonest possible. The courier leaves directly and I have yet a full report to make to Gen. M. Hoping to embrace my *whole* family soon, I am still your loving Hub.

The letter was addressed to Mrs. C. B. Gatewood, Fort Stanton, New Mexico.

Such was the beginning of the end for Geronimo and his hostiles, as well as all other friendly Chiricahuas who had remained
peacefully on their farms when the soldiers were out hunting
the Apache who had left the reservation. Lieutenant Britton
Davis, another cavalry officer who served through the last big
Apache campaign, made a severe indictment of the United States
officials who engineered the final treacherous moves in the dark
tragedy. General Miles, in a conversation with Brigadier General James Parker, is quoted by Parker (See Davis, Britton, *The
Truth About Geronimo,* Yale Univ. Press, 1929, pp. 236-237)
thus:

Early in June, 1886 General Miles arrived at Fort Huachuca. To
get an idea of the country he and I (Gen'l. Parker) climbed to the summit of El Moro mountain near the post. I have never been slow at suggestions and I took this opportunity to ask General Miles if I could
make one.

"I have recently come from Fort Apache where the Chiricahuas not
with Geronimo are located," I said. "Whenever there is news of a raid,
the Chiricahuas, in order not to become involved in the fighting, go into
the post, and are quartered in the quartermaster corral.

"I would suggest a false report of a raid be spread and when the Indians are in the corral, they be surrounded by troops, disarmed, taken to
the railroad and shipped east as prisoners of war. Geronimo's band in
the field will then be isolated, will no longer receive aid and comfort, as
heretofore, and will surrender."

"Why that would be treachery," said the General, "I could never do
that . . ."

But nevertheless it was only a few weeks later when the Chiricahuas
at Fort Apache being assembled to receive rations, were surrounded by
troops, disarmed and sent by railroad to Florida. This was in August. In
September, Miles, in his negotiations with Geronimo used this fact to
bring about the surrender.

Davis's parting shot at the treachery employed in dealing with
both Apache hostiles and Apache allies, was "IN HOC SIGNO
VINCES: which, is this instance might be freely translated, BY
THESE MEANS WE CONQUERED THEM."

I

BAILEY'S WELLS,[1] May 19.—Yesterday forenoon, while in attendance at target practice, in charge of the troop to which I belong, I was told by the second lieutenant that the Chiricahua Indians had left their reservation, and that troops from Fort Apache were out in pursuit of them. Having come into the territory less than three weeks before, we knew little about Arizona's Indian affairs. We were not competent, therefore, to judge of the significance of the reported event. We set at once to conjecturing, however, whether, if an actuality, it would give us something to do in the field.

In the course of the forenoon we learned that the number of bucks, or male Indians, in the party was thirty-four, and that of the squaws and children about ninety. Upon going into the Post from the target range, I saw that the reported Indian trouble was a matter of general interest. It seemed to be the prevalent belief of the garrison, based upon a knowledge of the character and methods of our commanding officer, that it would not be long before some of us would be out.

At this time the commanding officer was at Willcox, the nearest station on the Southern Pacific Railroad. He was expected back in the evening, and it was thought that a conference of some of the older heads might be held upon his arrival and something decided upon.

Before going to bed, I made my preparation for taking the field. I rolled up together a good quilt and a pair of blankets, a change of underclothing, a few toilet articles, an overcoat, and a light rubber coat. I also laid my rifle out, with the intention of taking it with me on my horse. But no steps in the matter of military operations were taken, it seems, by the commanding officer last night. Reveille, this morning found me sleepier, I thought, than usual. Upon looking out on the parade ground, shortly afterwards, I saw officers and non-commissioned officers going to and from the adjutant's office, and observed a wakefulness about the Post that did not usually pertain to it until several hours later. It was plain to me that something was up, and I soon concluded that the garrison was preparing a contingent for the war path; was I to be in it?

I wanted to be. I had come off a long march from Fort Davis, Texas, less than three weeks before, but that had been uneventful, and in point of distinction, of course unprofitable. It was seven months since I had returned to my regiment from the East, and in that time, with the exception of the march from Texas, I had not been outside of the Post on duty. I had rejoined my regiment with the expectation of gaining in efficiency from experience in the field, and I realized the fact that the opportunities for doing so in our army were becoming fewer and harder to seize every year. I also realized that laurels were scarce along Indian trails, and that they grew in difficult places. It was principally for the practice of looking and reaching for them, with the hope that the skillfulness thus acquired might some day serve me under more favorable conditions, that I aspired to getting on the trail of these Chiricahuas. My mind was gratified early in the day with the prospect of doing so. While I was eating my breakfast, I was notified that my company commander wished to see me. Wondering whether I was to copy a muster-roll or make out a target report, or take some roll-call, or receive a command of a detachment for field service, I reported to him at once, and was notified that the troop was ordered to take the field, with the other four troops of the Post, at nine o'clock or in the course of about an hour; also that the officers were not allowed any baggage except what they could carry on their horses. The latter item of information caused my roll of bedding and underclothing to dwindle in my mind to diminutive proportions.

I gave up the idea of taking my rifle, and determined also upon not taking my saddle-bags. My new kit consisted of one blanket, in which was rolled up a heavy woolen overcoat, a light rubber coat, a small toilet case, and a Spanish Grammar. I never take the field without something to read.

Before describing our march, I must say something in regard to our point of departure, Fort Grant.[2] This beautifully-surrounded spot is on the west side of the Sierra Bonita, or as named by Americans, Graham Mountain, a rugged sierra, rising from gentle foot-slopes to a height of 6,500 feet above the plain, and of about 10,500 above the level of the sea. The fort is on the border-line, between the foot-slopes and the mountain proper, 4,600 feet above the sea. I say the fort; that is military parlance. There is really no fort here, and never has been. Most of our military posts bear that name, though but a small proportion deserve it. Some western posts that are not forts were such at one time, while others, like Fort Grant, never were. Those that are not are merely posts, which term includes, besides the position held and occupied the quarters and other buildings. Of those posts that are not named forts some are named barracks; Jefferson Barracks, etc., some, camp; Camp Rice, Camp Rio, etc.; while others are named simply after their locality, San Antonio, Governor's Island, Willett's Point, West Point, etc. Among the latter are some of the most deserving of the name of fort. At about ten o'clock the command of five troops of cavalry, numbering about thirty men to a troop, set out from the Post in a south-easterly direction to cross the Graham range.

We made our first halt at a creek about three miles out, where the horses are ordinarily watered on their way to herd. From there we continued our course obliquely across the range. About three miles further, we passed a ranch, whose occupants, among whom I saw only women and children, did not seem alarmed about the Indians. Their proximity to the Post gives them, no doubt, a sense of security. I could not but think, however, of the terrible possibilities of their situation. Hardly do I see a woman on a ranch but some Indian atrocity springs up in my mind too horrible for description here.

The American public does not know the meaning of the phrase, Indian atrocity—not its true meaning. For their sakes I am glad they do not, but for the sake of the small but not insignificant number of Americans whose homes are darkened through their knowledge of it, I wish the American public did know it.

The whites on our frontier are suffering the tyranny of a democracy. The Indian question is a local question, and the treatment of it by representatives of the people at large is naturally careless and defective. The people of Arizona and New Mexico are not allowed to settle their Indian troubles themselves, and the national government will not settle them for them.

It was a mistake ever to remove westward the Indians that had settled on reservations east of the Mississippi. If they had remained there, we should now have samples of Indian life and character, and more or less interest in Indian legislation in every section of the country. The Indian question, if there still were such a question, would be national in fact as well as in name, and its final answer not far off. As it is, people in the East can not know the horrible particulars of Indian murder, torture, and outrage. There is no public organ to give them utterance. Their revolting indecency often excludes them from every respectable paper and the lowest publication of sensations and horrors would reject them on the very eminence of their qualification for admission; for the most morbidly-depraved imagination would be sickened by them.

I scarcely noticed, in my abstraction, the graceful turns and gentle murmur of this brook, or the restful shade of its verdant banks. I had been told, before leaving Grant, that we should find plenty of water wherever we went, and this fair stream augurs well for the truth of the assertion. It is now after one o'clock; the column having halted, we will sit down here to lunch. What a satisfaction this sureness as to water! How far could we follow Indians in Texas without a prospect of thirsting to death? Now the bugle sounds, and we are off. I am with the captain, at the head of the troop; the second lieutenant rides companionless at the rear.

On this the first day out, the officers kept closely to their places in the column, the restraint of garrison life being still upon them. As time goes by, and the effect of drills and parades and guard duty wears off, we shall depart in this respect from the regulations.

Having gone several miles out of our way, we did not reach our camping place until seven o'clock. It promises badly as to competency of our guide that he loses his way the first day out.

We camped at Bailey's Wells, about thirty miles from the Post. There is a ranch here which, like many other ranches in Arizona and New Mexico, was started on a dry flat, with no water within less than a day's march of it. An artesian well, being sunk, it has now all the water it wants, which the owner sells to parties passing it at the usual rate of 10 cents a day for every head of stock watered. This water is somewhat alkaline, so will not do well for irrigation.

We ate our supper after dark, our tablecloth, a piece of shelter tent, being laid on the ground by the cork fire. Our fierce appetites having finally succumbed to beans and bacon, we got up and shook and stretched ourselves, and then, with the hope of learning something as to the movements of the morrow, we started out for camp headquarters. We found there, besides the commanding officer and some three or four other officers a civilian visitor, from whom the officers were drawing rumors and reports concerning the Indians. The most important of their elicitations was that Indians had been seen on the Upper Gila River (pronounced Heela), traveling south. From our camp across to the river is about thirty-five miles. It was a question for the commanding officer to decide whether we should proceed there on the morrow, or strike southeastward for the railroad. Going to the river, we should have a surer thing of finding a trail; on the other hand, going to the railroad, we should stand a better chance of heading the Indians off from Old Mexico, or of closely following them there. Track walkers, working parties, and engine drivers, etc., are so many scouts from whom information can be obtained at short intervals by means of the telegraph. We could depend upon being notified by them if the Indians had crossed the track, and where. Furthermore, on the railroad we should be sure of forage and water, and we should be in telegraphic communication with the department commander and other military authorities.

SAN SIMON, MAY 20.—Whether the commanding officer came to any conclusion, last night, as to what we should do, I cannot say. He probably revolved the matter in his mind for some time after his visitors had left him, they repairing, careless of what his cogitations might bring forth, to their respective places of repose.

Before the sun was visible on the horizon, the sound of the assembly of trumpeters who did not assemble—trumpeting is tabooed in an Indian country—brought me to consciousness, and to a sort of gratitude to the solar system.

Our march was almost due southeast, being directed upon the railroad station of San Simon, about thirty miles from Bailey's Wells. It was a hot, dusty, and difficult march, the ground being broken and heavy with sand. The first dismounting for punishment took place to-day. A man was made to walk for having unfitted himself for duty by getting drunk.

His punishment was illegal, but sanctioned by the custom of the service. If our military law were strictly carried out, there would hardly be any punishing, and, therefore, any discipline in the field. Our method of imposing punishment by trial before a court martial is adapted only to a garrison in time of peace; the further removed therefrom the situation is short of actual war, the more difficult is the application of this method. On a march,

APACHE CHIEF GERONIMO

—◦{ 7 }◦—

as, for instance, in changing station, a trial by court martial, though often inconvenient, is not impracticable, but on a trail in pursuit of hostile or marauding Indians, it is simply impossible. "In time of war, a field officer may be detailed in every regiment to try soldiers thereof for offenses not capital, and"—as if to doubly insure to the service the benefit of this provision—"no soldier serving with his regiment shall be tried by a regimental or garrison court martial when a field officer of his regiment may be so detailed." [*80th Article of War.*] Chasing Indians does not constitute war as here understood. We need some such provision as this for time of peace both in the garrison and in the field; also the sanctioning of punishment without trial for commanders of forces in which trials are impracticable, for want of officers; or, what would amount to nearly the same thing, the investment of such commanders *ex officio* with the authority of a field officer's court. Such a measure would simply sanction what is constantly taking place.

San Simon will probably dwell in the memory of every officer who has camped there, as the worst camping ground he has ever rested on. It is located somewhat east of the center of the San Simon Flat, an expanse of sand and clay some sixty miles long and twenty broad, exceedingly dusty in dry weather, and boggy in wet. There is not a tree within sight, and the grass is generally poor and sparse. Having camped here on our way from Texas, our various discomforts have not even the palliation of novelty.

We expected, when we stopped here, to set out early in the morning, but as time wore on and our commanding officer telegraphed for instructions and no instructions came, we became alive to the probability of our having at least to open the morrow where we were.

The men and officers have not remained in the fiery furnace in which the command unsaddled. The men are mostly strewn along the railroad track, asleep in the shade of the freight cars; others are in the pump-house, through which water is brought up from an artesian well into the railroad tank; others are lounging on the platform of the station. The officers are in the warehouse. They are an *ennuyé*-looking set at this hour of 4 P.M.; one of them is sleeping on the hand-truck—I see some youngster taking hold of it to tip him up; another on a rickety old cot, which every now and then gives out a significant creak, and is going soon to let him down on the floor; two or three are sleeping or reclining on a retired waiting-room bench; another is ill-humoredly shifting himself about on a cluster of sacks of ore; another, having left his Spanish Grammar over in camp, is lying on the floor, with his blouse over his feet, in the hope of a blessed and speedy unconsciousness. About 5 P.M. took place the great excitement of the day—a passenger train came in from the West, and stopped about five minutes. A brisk sale ensued of newspapers and California fruit, in which a crushing railroad monopoly possessed itself of many a last cent. One officer paid 4 *bits* (50 cents) for four oranges.

After the train left, most of the officers, as well as the men, were occupied in the watering of the horses. This was a slow process, having to be done at the troughs in the cattle pens, provided for keeping cattle awaiting railroad embarkation. Not more than one-third of a troop could water at a time, and the water ran so slowly that the troughs could not be kept full for this many. At the end of this diversion, the sun being on the horizon, the officers betook themselves mostly to their towels and canteens, in preparation for dinner.

It was cool and pleasant by the time we settled down to our evening meals. Some of us, thinking we could do better than at our own mess, at any rate secure a change from camp fare, ate at the Travellers' Resort, the house of the flagman. Our meal consisted of one course; in the main, beef and potatoes. As we paid our 50 cents, the usual price for a Western railroad meal, most of us thought that we had hardly got our money's worth. However, we had partaken of two good anti-scorbutics, and we did not know how long we might have to travel on salt meat and canned vegetables. Indeed, some of the officers had no canned vegetables.[3] They fared, like the men, on bread and bacon and coffee, with an occasional mess of boiled beans. These were the few who followed to the letter the order given us by the post commander, to take nothing but what we could carry on our horses. Many must have thought of the times when, even had they struck a line of travel, they could not have fared as well as we did at this primitive inn.

Before the railroad, in the days of stage-coaching, the Western traveler subsisted principally on fried bacon and canned tomatoes. To my mind, this diet is not inferior, either in point of tastefulness or of hygiene, to beef and potatoes. It is a common belief that salt meat produces scurvy, and fresh meat guards against it; whereas in fact the one produces it as surely, if not as soon, as the other. Scurvy is more the effect of sameness than of saltness of diet. It is quite common among cow-boys, whose diet is almost exclusively fresh beef; and troops coming upon a cattle camp have no difficulty, as a rule, in exchanging all the bacon they wish for an equal quantity of fresh meat.

SAN SIMON, May 21.—Upon rising from breakfast, we made our preparations to start.

We had our bedding rolled, and the men packed their saddles and the mule-panniers. We were confident that if marching orders had not come during the night, they would come in the course of the morning. The morning wore tediously on; the west-bound train came and went, telegraph messages passed east and west, and still no bugle roused us. We gradually lapsed into a worse state of depression than the day before. We had not only the prospect of a prolongation of our weariness, but also the certainty of our stock's running down from want of nourishment. Not having thoroughly recovered from the effects of their march from Texas, our horses were not in the best condition when they started out, and two hard marches without forage, followed by fasting in camp, was telling on them. Forage had been telegraphed for the day before, immediately upon our arrival, but none had come.

Our endeavors to kill time assumed very much the same form as the day before, and yielded about the same satisfaction. As we wended our way over to camp, at the end of another day, we felt as if we had lived in a warehouse for—I will not say how long, for fear of exaggerating. The information reached us, to-day, that on the morrow we should be joined by a detachment of the Fourth Cavalry, from Doubtful Cañon, northeast of us.

STEIN'S PASS, MAY 22.—We did not go as far in packing this morning as we did yesterday, and most of us, as we repaired to our club room, took with us such resources in smoking, and the more fortunate ones in reading, as would last us, if need be, through the day.

About ten o'clock the dust of the Fourth Cavalry, emerging from the range of hills, on the horizon, was seen sluggishly rolling and reeling down the foot-slopes towards the station. We looked at it from time to time through the quivering atmosphere, and derived from it appreciation for the shelter we enjoyed. Little by little the men and horses came into view, and finally the command was seen halting and going into camp. The officers, being at leisure, were soon affording us that common yet ever fresh enjoyment of army life of meeting old friends. Among our new companions were two fellow-cadets of mine at the Point, one of them a classmate; also one of my former instructors there, and one of my pupils. We learned that their detachment had accomplished nothing, and that they were as completely in the dark as to their future movements and operations as we were.

I noticed as soon as I met these officers that they were armed with the sabre. This is the first time I have ever seen a U. S. officer carrying that weapon in the field. Our command has not a sabre[4] or pistol with it, being armed only with the carbine. It is, therefore, unprepared to fight mounted. The independence of post and regimental commanders, not to say troop commanders, in the matter of arming their commands is, or rather has been, a striking peculiarity of our army. I say, has been, because it looks as if the present General of the Army had put an end to it. If it is advisable to have some variety of armament among the different regiments, the nature and extent of that variety should be determined by orders from the headquarters of the army.

CAPTAIN WOOD'S TROOP, FOURTH CAVALRY

II

WILLCOX, ARIZONA, July 26, 1885.—Arrived here this evening at ten o'clock, having left Fort Grant about three. I had
heard a rumor in the post the day before yesterday that the troops
were ordered to be in readiness for field service, and that a party
of Indians was reported in the Whetstone mountains. I was
therefore prepared for marching orders. About noon, as I was
sitting with my wife on our front porch, waiting rather impa-
tiently for lunch, I observed an unusual animation about the
garrison, considering it was Sunday. I saw the commissary store-
room open,—at this time it is regularly closed for the sergeant
to go to lunch,—and the adjutant and acting commissary of subsistence standing outside, as if on business. I saw orderlies moving about, and, what was particularly significant, a soldier walking rapidly to the commanding-officer's quarters with a frying-
pan in his hand.

Commenting upon all this with the remark that something
was up, that somebody was "going out," my wife prevailed upon
me—woman-like—to test the justness of my conclusion by inquiry. Stepping over to my troop-commander, I obtained decisive
proof of it in his statement that the troop was to take the field as
soon as ready, and that he wanted to be off with it at one o'clock.
I ate a hasty lunch and proceeded to pack. The captain telling
me I could take two blankets, I took a blanket and a quilt, having but one blanket suitable for the field. Being allowed to do
so, I also took a set of underclothing. A still further excess over
my last outfit was a regulation carbine, which I carry strapped to
the cantle of my saddle, the barrel slanting down and to the

front, under my right leg. In the matter of arming themselves for field service our officers differ greatly. Some never take any arm or weapon but a pistol, which they carry as much for protection against citizens as for use against Indians. They argue that an officer's function in action is to control and direct, not to fight; that, therefore, officers have no need of arms, and cannot use them without detriment to their efficiency; others, agreeing with them, carry, besides the pistol, the sabre, for what they claim as its moral effect upon their men from a disciplinary point of view, that is, as a badge of authority; some may carry the sabre alone; others again, recognizing the importance of undivided attention on the controlling and directing of an action, take into account the contingency of an officer's remaining in action after control and direction have ceased to be of primary importance, when men are fighting only for their lives, or for a sudden death, which case in regular warfare would be prevented by surrender; also that an Indian not only gives no quarter, but, in further violation of the usages of war, murders and assassinates; that an officer straying away from his camp or his column, hunting, or studying the country, may have occasion to make desperate use of his arms,—these officers carry a rifle or a carbine.

RILEY'S RANCH,[5] July 27.—Arrived here at Riley's ranch at about ten o'clock at night after a hard and tedious march in the rain. The cause of our dispatch from Willcox was a report made by a citizen, Mr. Campbell, to the effect that an Indian trail, numbering some twenty-five head of stock, had been seen that forenoon crossing the railroad about ten miles west of us. Upon communication with General Crook the following dispatches were received by our commanding-officer:—

BOWIE, July 27, 1885.

MAJOR VAN VLIET, WILLCOX,—General Crook directs that you send out immediately to investigate fully Campbell's report and to send frequent dispatches.

Telegraph everything you learn. Even the minutest information may be of greatest value. If information indicates Indians are going to reservation direct that nothing be spared to get earliest information here.

ROBERTS, *A.D.C.*

GENERAL CROOK

Major Van Vliet, Willcox,—General Crook directs that you send a company immediately to intercept the Indians with all dispatch, and report whether Indians were mounted, or whether they had families with them, or were all bucks. Give all attainable information at once. Send information also to Forsyth. Roberts.

Accordingly, quarter before two o'clock troop K, with fifteen days' rations on pack-mules, was sallying out. We were to ascertain whether there were any Indians north-west of Willcox making for the reservation, and to catch or intercept them if we could. Two companies were ordered south, one to Dragoon Spring, one to Canisteo. The other two companies of the battalion remained at the disposal of the battalion commander at Willcox. Just before we mounted it began to rain, and before we made our first halt it was pouring. I had no heavy overcoat with me, relying for protection upon a light rubber overcoat, bought at Fort Davis, Texas, that reached down below the tops of my boots, almost to my feet. I had carried this garment hundreds of miles without having serious occasion to use it, but ever hoping for that form of compensation for my trouble. The over-abundance with which this was dealt out to me by a north-east wind this afternoon militated against my enjoyment of it; and as I felt it creeping down my weather leg, so to speak, into my boot, I lost faith heavily in rubber overcoats and in post traders.

Our objective to-day was a point called Box Spring, distant about twenty-five miles, which we hoped to reach before dark. Our only guide was a corporal from another troop, who had once been there. We arrived about an hour after dark within a mile or two of the spring, but not knowing how to get to it, turned back to a ranch that we had left on our right, arriving there and going into our present camp, as already stated, at about ten o'clock.

When we determined to turn back the corporal had gone so far ahead of the column that he could not be recalled. We hallooed, and fired a number of shots, but to no effect.

We did not set out this morning until twenty minutes past ten o'clock, thus allowing the horses time to graze. They have no grain or hay. In the course of an hour and a half we arrived at Box Spring, a deliciously cool spot overhung with bright-green trees, at the head of a narrow ravine or "box" cañon.

From here we continued our course across the hills that we had skirted yesterday, our plan being to reach a high range ahead of us, between which and ourselves the Indians presumably passed if making for the reservation. We were afraid that their trail had been made before yesterday's heavy rain, which would have well-nigh obliterated it; whereas, if made since the rain, it would have been and would still be a very plain one.

We camped to-night near an abandoned ranch. A man left in charge of it, Shotgun Smith, so called from his having once stood off a party of Indians with a shotgun, had moved to other parts upon seeing a party of from three to five Indians going down the valley. I think I have learned the origin and deep meaning of the expression "skipped the ranch." Our camp is charmingly located in the angle formed by two dry creek-beds lined with good-sized trees. We have an extensive view of the valley, including Fort Grant, opposite to us, about twenty-five miles off. The grass is excellent. Upon their being unsaddled, the horses were watered and turned out to graze. About sundown they were taken in as usual and groomed, and then picketed between the creek-beds.

BATTLE-GROUND, July 29.—To-day we struck across the Sulphur Spring valley to look for trails, going into the Gila valley, through the pass at Cedar Spring.[6] As the troop started on its march I was detached up the valley directly to the point of —— mountains about a mile and a half from our camp, to make sure that the Indians had not passed this side of it. About noon we came upon the oasis of Eureka Spring. A ranch here, owned by two brothers from Ohio, Messrs. Leitch, numbers from 600 to 700 acres, and is stocked with about 2,000 head of cattle. Neither of the owners being present, I obtained information in regard to it from a man I took to be in charge of it. He told me that if sold out today, it would bring from $25,000 to $30,000. Its water is excellent and abundant. There is a good, substantial adobe house on it, the front of which is graced and shaded by fine cotton-wood trees. The front yard is just beginning to grow Bermuda grass, and is surrounded by a neat white fence. The other principal improvement is a wire-fenced corral, more than large enough to contain the whole herd. One can double one's money, or get one's invested money back, ranching in this valley, in three years. In estimating the cost of stocking a ranch one should calculate on the following prices:—

American beef cow	$25 to $30
" milk cow and calf . . .	30 " 40
Mexican yearling cow, or steer . . .	8 " 12
" 2-year old heifer	16
" " steer	13
" cow and calf	25

The nearest railroad station is Willcox, distant thirty-five miles. I could not but reflect, as I sat in a comfortable wicker rocking-chair on the front porch, fanned by a breeze from the trim well-sodded court-yard in rear of the house, upon the singular variance from its environment exhibited by this genteel abode, the home of women and children as well as men. Only a few weeks ago painted Indians passed horribly close to it. Thanks to the railway, we are getting a new class of pioneers!

From Eureka Spring we took a straight course to the Battle-ground, so the point is called from an engagement having taken place there about three years ago between a party of Indians and United States troops. The distance is not over seven miles, but the marching was very difficult. We found the Battle-ground occupied by three Americans and one Mexican. On it these men are building a plain, substantial stone house, and supporting a goodly bunch of cattle.

CEDAR SPRING, July 30.—Marched seven miles to-day to Cedar Spring. Until within two years ago this was Williams station, on the stage line. Situated at the entrance of a pass connecting the

Sulphur Spring valley with that of the Gila river, the nearest pass, with a good road north of Fort Grant, it is still a stopping-place for travelers between Fort Grant and Fort Thomas.

Our reconnaissance was completed; we have ascertained that the party of Indians reported to have crossed the Southern Pacific Railroad ten miles west of Willcox is not making for the reservation, at least not by the shortest route. Two important items of news imparted to us at the Battle-ground, which however we had not fully credited (we had traveled too much in this country for that), are not only not confirmed here but are thought to be false. One is that a couple of deserters, a white and a colored soldier, had been killed by Indians on the other side of the valley; the other, that chief Geronimo is captured and held in irons at Fort Thomas.

FORT GRANT, July 31.—I learned the history of the engagement at the Battle-ground. About three years ago a party of Chiricahua Indians on a raid went through Cedar Spring pass and killed six men, teamsters of a train that they captured near there laden with flour and other supplies for the reservation. They killed besides the six teamsters, four soldiers working on the telegraph line, and a mail-carrier on his way to Fort Grant. From their camp, on the spot now known as the Battle-ground, only about three hundred yards off the regular stage-road, they fired into a detachment of cavalry convoying a number of Indian prisoners. After an unsuccessful attempt to dislodge them the troops withdrew, leaving the Indians in possession of their plunder as well as of the field.

APACHE BOYS, TONTOS

III

TEMPEST MINE, August 12.—One of the men who was sent to McCullough's ranch to-day to get some provisions for the mess brought back information that, night before last, a signal fire was seen in the Mowry Pass, about five miles below our camp, and that men from the ranch had gone there and found four moccasin and two unshod pony tracks. The captain has decided, upon going out in the morning, to investigate the matter.[7]

Finished "The House on the Marsh." Of the few novels I have read, this is one of the most interesting and best written. But I miss the fragments of thought and reflection characteristic of standard fiction, and resent the hit at our government of fetching up in our House of Representatives the greatest rogue in the story. The style is *spirituel*.

The wet season, which was late in coming this year, is now full upon us. It rains almost every day, and the country is beautifully green, quite unlike what I am accustomed to in the Southwest. It makes me think of the spring on the Hudson. I only hope that the wetness of the weather will favor us on the trail, that the rain will soften the ground for the renegades, and not efface their tracks behind them. Two of our Indian scouts went out hunting to-day, accompanied by two soldiers, but brought back nothing.

Their failure compensated me for its disappointment of my gastronomic desire by a sort of comfort it afforded my self-esteem as a hunter, which was wounded by my recent failure.

Not only are these Indians expert hunters, but they have the incentive of a want of fresh meat such as I probably have never experienced, for they had not had any for a number of days, and, savage like, they fare badly without it.

TEMPEST MINE, August 13.—Last night, between ten and eleven o'clock, I was waked up by the sentinel coming to tell the captain that there was a signal fire visible from his lookout. He located it about where we saw the first fire over in Mexico, four days ago. He had watched it for an hour, more or less, before it went out and had seen it go down and come up again a half dozen times. Shortly after breakfast the captain set out with ten of our men and three Indian scouts to ascertain what truth there was in the different reports in regard to signal fires, especially those in the Mowry Pass. He found nothing at the Pass, but he learned from Miss McCullough that she herself had seen the fires—for there were several—but she was not sure that they were not camp-fires. As to the tracks, it appeared from the man who reported them, who was with the captain, that they were not at the Pass, but below on the river. (He had given both the captain and myself to understand that they were at the Pass.) The captain found no traces of them. It appeared that they had been reported to the McCulloughs by a Mexican, and that this was the only ground on which they had been reported to us. We had understood from our man that the McCulloughs had seen the tracks. We are too suspicious of *canards* to give credence to the report of a stranger, especially a Mexican. The intelligence of our enlisted men, especially the colored, and more especially the colored cavalry, is not up to the military requirements of our age. Work is required of them, both in peace and in war, which they must either fail to do or do very imperfectly. What is more important, especially in a cavalryman, than ability to render a clear and correct account of what he sees? How is marksmanship to be mastered without the modicum of intelligence underlying this ability? How is all the writing to be done pertaining to a troop, company or battery, and such organization to be at the same time properly disciplined and instructed (admitting the presence with it of its full complement of officers) without a certain proportion of rank and file that can read and write?

The War Department has shown itself alive to this evil in the establishment of post schools; I am looking for it to show itself alive to the fact that these schools are a failure. As long as attendance is voluntary the evil will continue to be; and I doubt whether compulsory attendance can make them a success. If the object of these schools were only to teach soldiers their letters and how to put them together into words and sentences, and how to use figures in simple sum in arithmetic—in other words, if merely to teach the three R's they might, through compulsory attendance, attain their object, and incidentally do some good to the mother wit; but as to their opening out and adequately developing a mind confirmed in dullness through twenty years, more or less (maybe twenty generations) of illiteracy, they cannot do it. It is a pity that we do not recruit the army altogether from our literate population, and sad it were if we could not do it. For the present the schools should concentrate their efforts, as I believe they generally do, upon teaching the men that which they need to know in the performance of their routine duties. They should know, for instance, how to read a muster-roll, and clothing-roll, and how to sign them; some should know how to make out these and other papers; they should all know how to keep their target records. The school instruction necessary to this end should be regarded as the soldier's mental setting-up, equally important with his physical. As to the development of his faculties beyond the incidence of such instruction, it can be done better outside of the school-room than in it, for the reason that his interest and attention can be better secured and retained. It should therefore be left to his commanding officer, and should be required of him. The objection to the enforcement of school attendance in the army as an abuse of military authority indicates a failure either to appreciate the state of advancement of the military art or to comprehend the nature of military authority. Our prejudice against the spelling-book is the analogue to the late prejudice of

European troops (not yet wholly overcome) against the spade. May we not have to wait for war to give us the former as it did the latter? Now that marked improvements are taking place in the soldier's physical well-being, let us hope for a commensurate improvement in his mental. In this country of free schools and free reading-rooms, what business has a pate unpenetrated by the A, B, C resting upon a pillow in a white pillow case, or a form with such a head-piece lying between white sheets on a wire mattress?

About two o'clock this afternoon a couple of six-mule teams arrived with forage for the animals and some commissaries for our mess. One of them upset and had to be righted and reloaded, about 300 yards from camp. There was a sharp turn in the road, on the outside of which a gentle slope, and on the inside, where the road had been cut, a rocky ledge, about three feet high. Having seen the first wagon tip nearly over, I cautioned the driver before he started around, and again after he started; but— whether from inexperience or from a long association with mules—he did just as I cautioned him not to do. Thinking it useless to contend against such perversity, I watched with complacent interest the operation of the law of stability. I saw the inside wheel go up a number of times, and come down again, each time seeming to return a little slower than before; I watched it tremble for an instant, balanced with the wagon body on the outer wheel, and then start on its decisive aberration; and I finally saw—as the crash of the wagon-bows caused the driver to turn around in his saddle—the wagon inverted, its four wheels in the air, with the sacks of grain neatly piled underneath, where they could hardly be perceived. Having made certain reflections upon the driving I had witnessed, I walked off toward the other wagon, and, as I did so, heard the words behind me: "No other wagon was ever upset; nobody else ever met with an accident;" and certain unintelligible retorts, all of which I delicately affected not to hear. I had some trouble getting this forage-train around the shaft, which stands right in the road.

As the second wagon came crashing down a steep hill, over fragments of rock too large to be called stones, the head of it seeming to bump against the wheel-mules, I forgot the headlessness of the driver in my appreciation of his recklessness. The wagons were kept from going over sidewise by ropes thrown around them and held on the safe side.

TEMPEST MINE, August 14.—Spent nearly the whole day in my tent. I felt like bracing myself up with a walk, but refrained out of consideration for the state of one of my ankles, hurt on my last deer-hunt. I thought it prudent to do nothing that tended to disable me as a pedestrian. Having nothing left of my own to read, I fell back upon the "Life of Frank James," brother of the distinguished bandit, Jesse James, which I had borrowed from my Swedish friend at the mine.

About dark, just as the men finished grooming, a party of three men came into camp, who turned out to be Doctor Wood,[8] of the army, and escort. The doctor is making the rounds of the line of camps to do what he can for such sick as he may find. He left Mescal Spring this morning, and was told by the officer in command that our camp was only eighteen miles from the Spring, whereas it is about forty-five. We took him into our tent, and while he waited for the cheer we were able to give him, and partook of it, we plied him with questions in regard to the campaign, and other matters. He gave us the important information that he had seen a trail of eighteen horses, all unshod, striking south on the east side of the Patagonia Mountains. He said that their crossing of the railroad was in open order, in bunches of three, at a gallop. Before we turned in, the Captain told me, much to my satisfaction, that he would send me out with a detachment in the morning.

LOCHIEL,[9] August 15.—At 7:35 this morning, I set out with twenty of our men, two Indian scouts, and the Doctor. I had but two days' rations, all that the Captain could give me. My instructions being to look for trails, especially the trail reported by Dr. Wood, and to see the Doctor safely to the next camp, my plan was to strike south along the Patagonia Mountains, and, crossing them at the San Antonio Pass, to make for the camp of Captain Hatfield, the nearest to us, where I hoped to be able to ration up. In traveling over this course, I should probably cut the trail of the Doctor's Indians.

The Mowry and the San Antonio are the only two passes I know of in the Patagonia Mountains. My two Mohaves, mounted, took up the regular trail to the Mowry Pass, and, after following it for about two miles, led us towards it by a more direct course. I wanted to go well into the Pass, and let the Indians thoroughly look for signs before going on to the San Antonio.

The cutting across country was hard marching, requiring a good deal of dismounting, but we had work before us that was to make that appear easy. Having gotten well into the Pass, and traveled it some distance in the hope of finding water and of making my way out through a sort of branch I supposed to be on the other side of a hill in my right front as I went in, I came upon what I rightly took to be the Mowry trail. Judging that the traveling out in the direction in which I wanted to go would at best be difficult, and, from what the Doctor said in regard to the location of Captain Hatfield's camp, that the San Antonio Pass was considerably out of my way, together with the shortness of my ration supply, and the uncertainty of my adding to it, I determined upon crossing the mountains by the Mowry Pass, and leaving the passing through the San Antonio to my return. Here, therefore, I changed my course. The term pass is liable to give one a wrong idea of this route across the mountain. The trail does not lead up the bottom of the so-called pass, nor does it follow a parallel course along a side, but goes zig-zagging up a buttress-like spur. We had to lead our horses the whole way, stopping often to close up and get breath. We of Troop K have been so inactive during the last week or two that we are in poor condition for such work. I enjoyed studying the view from our resting-places. The Sonoita and Santa Cruz Rivers, the one from the north and the other from the east, marked by the timber along their banks, joined each other directly in our front. Slightly timbered spurs and foot-slopes ran out from us in the directions of both streams, beyond which were fragments, and, behind these, the masses of the Santa Ritas and Pajaritas, or Small-bird Mountains. Finally, we reached the top of the Patagonias, and got on our horses. We had not gone more than a few hundred yards when we came upon an abandoned house or hut, a little off the main trail.

Thinking I might water my horses there, I sent the Indians over to look for water. They found none, but indicated the discovery of two pony tracks going divergently down the mountain side. Neither of my Indians can speak English, but managing to make me understand from their words and gestures that the plainer of the two trails was going the way we were, I told them to follow that one. About five miles from there we came to the last that we could see of it, at the Mowry Mine.[10] We found a house near by, where I made inquiry as to Indians, but got no news.

I was told to my surprise that the point I was aiming at, Lochiel, was only seven miles from there. Refreshed by a lunch and rest, and stimulated more or less by a curiosity to see what was beyond, we resumed our march at about one o'clock, on the stage-road to Lochiel. A mile or two from the house, the Doctor pointed out to me the place where the stage-driver was shot about three weeks ago, and the spot where the Chiricahua assassin was ambushed, about ten feet from the road. A little farther on, as we came back to this road, after straying a short distance from it, I had especial occasion to observe the ease and security with which such a crime is committed. An open wagon—I believe it was the stage—or the mail wagon, came rattling along and passed immediately in front and within easy hailing distance of us. The two men in it looked neither to the right nor to the left, but kept their eyes fixed, it seemed, upon the place of the late ambush. I thought of calling to them and asking them what

Indian news they had, but, loth to startle them, I hesitated, and then waited for them to see us—which I thought they would surely do—until it was too late. We were coming with our fourteen horses and three pack-mules obliquely towards them down a slightly-wooded slope. If a body of cavalry can, in broad daylight, march unperceived up to within fifty yards of a person on the look-out for danger, how easy must it be for a dark-skinned Apache, aided by the uncertainty of twilight or moonlight, his long black hair hiding his neck, and giving him the outline of a stump, to conceal himself behind a bush or shrub or tree, or in the grass, within effective range of an unsuspecting victim.

Entering the loose collection of adobes constituting the Post Office town of Lochiel, I stopped at the first store I came to and asked for Indian news, but obtained none; I was asked then if I wanted to buy forage, to which I replied in the negative, not without a certain satisfaction at the disappointment of the questioner. I cannot help enjoying the discomfiture of would-be speculators on Indian outrages. Going to the only other store in town, I got my mail—two letters from my wife. Upon the information and advice there given me, I determined upon camping at Lochiel over night. I was told that there was to be a *baile,* and that among the people coming to it from the country around were those who could give me all the latest reliable Indian news. "What training does not a cavalry officer require? When is his education complete?" I said to myself, seeing the unexpected turn that my reconnoissance was taking. My informants advisers were Mr. Sydow and Colonel Green. The former has succeeded in taking most of the trade from the other store, as a natural consequence of which its proprietor is not on cordial terms with him. Indeed the rival merchant would not attend this *baile,* given by Mr. Sydow in commemoration of his birthday, and ugly rumors were afloat of his having caused others than himself to stay away. The principal business of both stores, I am told, is to furnish smugglers with goods to be sold in the interior of Sonora. It would seem to be a lively business. The

Mexican line runs through Lochiel, so that part of the town is in the United States and part in Mexico. Colonel Green has fought Frenchmen, Indians, and Mexicans in the Mexican army.

The Doctor, a "youngster" from Boston, Mass., recently joined from Harvard College, had never been at a Mexican ball, or *baile;* so it was with certain feelings of a chaperone that I went with him, after our dinner, in search of the music and dancers. Besides his freshness for the occasion, my *débutant* possessed an advantage over me in his light Saxon hair and complexion. Blonds are great successes among the dark-complexioned daughters of Montezuma. In our perambulation we ran upon Mr. Sydow and Colonel Green, who brought us at once to our desired destination. The entertainment had not yet commenced, not more than half a dozen people having arrived. The ball-room was the interior of a plain, barn-like building, the floor of which was sprinkled with water and chips of wax. On one side was a bench for the *señoritas* and their chaperones, and on the other were shelves for the gentlemen's hats, pistols, coats, etc. The decorations consisted of greens and variously-colored strips of tissue paper, these being mostly suspended from the rafters after the manner of sky scenery on the stage.

As soon as the company began to increase, I drifted into its lighter element, to whose active principle I contributed with short intervals of rest until about one o'clock. I then thought it best, in view of my contemplated early start, to go and compose myself for sleep.

A feature of this entertainment that I had never seen in a *baile* before was singing. It was brought about by my wishing to hear a Mexican song—Mr. Sydow having told me that singing was customary, or not unusual at a Mexican ball—and my going through the formality of asking for it. To do this I had to bring up a chair and guitar in front of my chosen performer and, after sitting down on the chair, present her with the instrument. Having done this and heard a pleasing song, in which I understood the recurring word *Corazon** and very little else, I was told that

*Heart.

I had to ask every lady in the room under pain of giving offense. I was surprised, but on the whole, rather pleased with this instance of Mexican *punctilio*, and complying with, evoked several other pretty songs; but, what was my consternation upon being told, as I was removing my chair and guitar, that a song was expected from me, and that it was *de rigueur*. I soon saw that my inability to sing would not be credited, and that my *only proper* course was to demonstrate it; so, reflecting that there was nobody present that I should be likely to meet again, except perhaps the Doctor, who would not be unkind to me, and encouraging myself with the thought that I had enjoyed listening to some pretty poor singing myself, I sat down in front of a young lady who consented to accompany me, and having first hummed the air to her, made my little endeavor.

This was a high-toned *baile*. I saw but one gentleman uncoated, and he wore a very becoming white flannel shirt. There was no smoking on the part of the women. In regard to the dresses, I can only say that they seemed well fitted and substantially made, and that a prevalent material among them was a sort of red plaid; I remember two plain black dresses, but no white, and no low necks.

There were the usual round dances—played fast, I thought, even for Mexican dancing—and the Mexican square dances; there was also the Virginia reel—played slow. The women were less disinclined to talk than I had usually found them, and I doubt not that, had I commanded their language, I should have conversed with them much to my edification. They strengthened my already strong desire to penetrate into their country.

COPPER CAÑON, August 15.—At half-past six this morning we were filing out of camp in the direction of the Huachuca Mountains. The Doctor and I had not slept more than three hours, but we felt perfectly refreshed. A tonic not in the pharmacopœia, a night's excitement, had more than compensated for our loss of sleep. After a march of twenty-eight miles, almost wholly off the road, and at least one-third of which was made on foot, leading our horses up and down stony places, we found ourselves at the mouth of Copper Cañon, in the camp of Captain Hatfield's Troop, of the Fourth Cavalry. During the whole march, the Stony Point or Peñasco marking our destination was in sight—most of the time directly in our front. This made the march seem first shorter than it was, and then longer. When we at last reached the base of this landmark and began circling around it—the ravines being close together, and steeper and rockier than before—it seemed almost as if it were turning with us and was not to be rounded. But, "In the bright lexicon of youth, etc."—so on we went, up and down, up and down, until, in the crossing of ridges and ravines, the necessary sliding and scrambling, and slipping, and stumbling is done, and the Doctor, pointing to the road, remarks to me, "You have just room enough to straighten out in, to come into camp in style." When my stragglers have come up, I give the always welcome command, *"Prepare to mount—mount,"* and as I thereupon move forward, attended by my staff and scouts and body servant, at the head of my column, my eight combatants in their most imposing formation at proper distance behind me, and my nimble supply train bringing up the rear, I jerk my wearing apparel into shape and place, and endeavor to look unconscious.

Having reported myself and command to Captain Hatfield, whom I found reclining in a chair in company with his Lieutenant, in front of his tent, I was shown a suitable place to camp. Having unsaddled, I made inquiry of the Captain as to his means of rationing me. (I had rations only to include breakfast in the morning.) He gave me a satisfactory answer and proceeded then, at my request, to supply me. I took from him five days' rations.

Resolving to rest here one day, I took also two days' forage, which would allow me a half a day's to carry with me. As he led me back from the store tent to his private tent, the Captain showed me with just pride the plan and structure of his little post. The men's tents—in a row facing south, or in the direction of Mexico—were shaded and concealed by an arbor, affording room between the tents and a vertical screen in their front for a lounge or stroll. In rear of the tents was the picket line, and in rear of this were two A tents for the Indian scouts, and two wall tents for the officers. In rear of all this, as the hidden source of its life, was the shallow, smoke-stained, kettle-and-pan-encircled hole in the ground breathed into by the Captain's cook in the creek running past the camp.

Resting on an embankment of stone, at about the level of a horse's chest, was a wooden trough, brimming full of clear, cool, running water. It was carried from the stream into the trough in a wooden gutter, and ran out over a sort of lip, making a cascade, under which the Captain takes his daily douche. The whole structure was put up by the Captain's men from material found at hand or borrowed from Mr. Pump, a ranchman on whose land the camp is situated. Immediately back of the picket line, on a line with the forage and the tents of the Indians and the officers, is the corral in which he keeps his goats. He has lost a number of fine angoras through the depredations of Mexican lions. I bade goodbye with much regret to Dr. Wood, who was going off with the Captain's Lieutenant to a camp nearer Fort Huachuca, whence he intended to go into the post in the morning. I gave him a note to Colonel Forsyth accounting to him for my presence with Captain Hatfield and of my failure to find any Indian signs. In the evening the Captain and I betook ourselves to the Indians' tents, where there was singing and other merriment going on. The former consisted mainly of monotonous vowel ejaculation, and seemed to be songs without words. At any rate its language was not that of Indian prose. The songs frequently ended in laughs and giggles.

COPPER CAÑON, August 17.—Spent the day in rest and recreation. Having lounged and talked a little after breakfast, I took a short climb with the Captain, back of the camp. As we sat looking at the view, it was decided that we should make an attempt after lunch to improve our appreciation of it by climbing to the top of the mountain, and observing it from there. A decision of far greater moment to me,—likewise, perhaps, an inspiration of our picturesque enviroment—was that of the Captain, to furnish me with sketches for the illustration of my journal. He had told me of his having notes and sketches, which he thought would grow in interest as they grew in age, disclaiming at the same time, the thought of ever becoming "d—d fool enough to publish a journal or anything of that sort." Hating hypocrisy, I owned up to the purpose he so forcibly reprehended, and requested him, though he should not justify it to himself to confirm me in my justification of it by the promise of his cooperation with the pencil.

I observe in this camp the same idleness on the part of the men as in our own. They seem to have no regular duties, but groom and feed the horses and to mount guard. I have been in a number of cavalry camps, but I have never yet seen the advantages they offer for instruction and discipline turned to account. This goes to show that in order to carry on the proper training of our cavalry something is required besides the curtailment of guard and fatigue duty and extra and daily duty; for in camp, these are certainly at a minimum.

At half-past one o'clock, armed with our six shooters and government No. 8's,[11] we started on our second and decisive assault, the Huachucas. We attempted no turning or other manœuvring, but went straight for the key of the position, stopping every hundred yards or so under such cover as we could find, from the plunging fire of heaven, to rest and breathe. Having triumphantly cleared the summit, and settled down to its occupation, we had the most interesting and impressive view before us, or rather about us, that I have seen. The White Mountains from Mount Washington are a greater but hardly a grander prospect. They are to this as the abstract is to the concrete, more comprehensive, but less expressive. I was soon satisfied with the view from the Summit House and retained little from it beside my first surprise at the indistinctness of a wonderful multiplicity of details, but from that south point of the Huachuca Mountains, long and intently as I looked, I could not look my fill. Across the wooded line of the San Pedro River, far down in the province of Sonora, I took up my field of vision's border-line of mountains, and following it eastward, thread the hazy tops of the Sierra Madres, and thence northward over the plainer Chiricahuas and along the still plainer Dragoons Mountains and Galinros to opposite Fort Grant. Passing around by the west, I scanned the jagged Santa Barbaras, the Sierra Azul or Blue Mountain, the Pajaritas, and the familiar Santa Rita Mountains. Within the circle of these Sierras were numerous minor mountains: the Patagonias, the Cobre, the Cananeas, the San José, the Mule Mountains, etc., intervening among which were plains and flats, joined to them by gracefully-curving slopes. I learned more about the topography of Southern Arizona and Sonora in ten minutes' observation on this mountain top than I should have learned in ten weeks of scouting. A glance, too, showed me the relative moisture of the two sides of the Huachucas. On the west, the long ravine-furrowed foot-slopes, were green with fresh grass and evergreen oaks; on the east, a parched and treeless plain extended with short conjoining curvature, up to the base of the mountain. Here, as well as wherever else I have seen adjoining sections of Mexico and the United States, I was struck by the contrast between the two countries in point of civilization. On the American side of the line could be seen roads and houses and settlements—not many, but enough to suggest a prosperous and growing population; on the Mexican side, not a road was to be seen, and the only visible signs of man were the custom house, and a few miles from it, an unsealed distillery, from which a regular contraband business is carried on with the United States. Beyond these structures, both of which were immediately on the Mexican side of the line, the whole landscape was dreary and weird. Its most notable feature was a long, regular incline, as of a tilted plain, that stretched away, barren and desolate, towards the Sierras in the west. In its rents and flaws, impenetrable to my peering eye,

I was fain to fancy running water and the habitations of man.

Our climb and subsequent contemplations had made us extremely thirsty, so that, thinking of the spring below, we were aided in our descent by the attraction upon our minds as well as upon our bodies. But for the dense shrubbery through which we had to pass, we should have made better time going down than we did, though we might not have reached the bottom in a sound condition. When about a quarter of the way down, I became separated from the Captain, and, calling to him a number of times without being answered, became quite uneasy about him. He was a convalescent from a debilitating camp disease, and I feared that his exertion had prostrated him. I pushed on towards camp, thinking that if I should not find him there, I should get some Indians and soldiers to help me look for him. About half way down the mountain, I came upon a path or trail, in which I looked anxiously for my friend's tracks, but did not find them. I quickened my pace, and looked more eagerly for the indications of a spring. Already I had followed the rocky creek-bed through various stages of humidity, from the merest sediment of dried-up rain through the darker deposit, with well-defined water-marks, of standing water: then past dark earth and stringy mould-growing grass and water-flowers, and palm-like herbs and shrubs, before I finally came upon the picturesque bower and herbarium in which I found the spring. As I wound my way up to it, I was startled by a suppressed whoop, and, looking in the direction from which it came, I saw, through a grating of green shrubbery, my lost-and-found companion, smiling at me across the spring. If it had been the purest nectar, or—as perhaps more gratifying to our earthly tastes—genuine Golden Seal, instead of water, that sparkled before us, he could not have beamed more pleasure and conviviality. Having cooled off, and gloated meanwhile over our wholesome feast, we took off the edge of our appetite by a draught which, speaking for myself, would have been most imprudent in anything but the purest water. In less than a half a minute I took another draught, and shortly afterwards, another. In the course of a half an hour I must have drank a half-a-dozen times, thus averaging one drink every five minutes, and I felt no after-effects reproaching me for imprudence or intemperance.

OUR TENT IN THE FIELD
(From a sketch by Captain Hatfield, Fourth Cavalry, U.S.A.)

IV

COPPER CAÑON, August 17, 1885.—We spent the evening partly with the Indians and partly in quiet converse, principally on army topics, under our own arbor. We agreed in that it is well for these Indians, as for scouts generally, to be mounted. It is assertedly one that one cannot trail well on horseback, that one must be near the ground in order to see well enough. While a man on a horse may not see the ground under him as well as he might on foot, he can see better what is beyond him; and, as a general thing, he is compensated through length of range for indistinctness of observation at short range: when he is not, he simply dismounts. The practical question, therefore, is not whether trailing is better done mounted or dismounted, but whether it is better done being at all times dismounted or being at times mounted and at times dismounted. Scouts, if they are mounted at all, and are not to retard the march, must be well mounted. For they, of course, take the lead—especially Indian scouts, whose nature it is not to see anything if there is any one ahead of them.

I heard the story from the captain of the "jumping" of Captain Lawton's supply camp in the Guadalupe Cañon in the early part of the campaign. There were eight men in it, and the attacking party numbered ten bucks. Is was a bold deed for skulking Chiricahuas, especially as it was done in broad daylight. The man on watch, it seems, came down from his post to ask the sergeant in charge if it was not time for him to be relieved. "No," said the sergeant, "it is now a quarter of twelve, and you are not to be relieved until twelve; but now that you are here, you may as well stay and get your dinner." That relaxation of discipline cost the lives of three men and all the supplies in the camp. While this man was eating his dinner, a shot resounded through the little camp, and, looking up, some of his shocked companions uttered the exclamation, "Why, Niehaus has shot himself," and before they could collect themselves, the shot was followed by a volley. The men now started for shelter and were even compelled, by the murderous threats of the sergeant, who was wounded himself, to go for their carbines. These they succeeded in getting, despite the continuous fire from their concealed enemy. After an unsuccessful attempt at holding the wagons they withdrew at a run up a steep hill back of the camp, stopping every now and then to fire back and being each time forced from their position by a flanking or reverse fire, accompanied by loud laughs and hoots and yells. They were not pursued beyond the top of the hill, whence they made their way with no little hardship to some neighboring settlements.

It is hardly a matter of surprise that one or two of them seized this opportunity to desert. After driving them off, the Indians returned to the camp and looted it. This affair is evidence of the lack of training among our soldiers. It bears testimony, too, to the shrewdness of the shrewdest band of the shrewdest tribe of American Indians. Instead of opening the action with a volley, which they knew would stampede the camp, they began by making sure of one man, anticipating the paralyzation of the others long enough to aim and fire a volley. It is said that only one Indian was seen, so that the soldiers had nothing to aim at but puffs of smoke.

The affair testifies, moreover, to the poor marksmanship of Indians in action. The first shot, which killed the derelict vedette, with a piece of bacon in his mouth and his coffee cup in his hand, was fired from within twenty-five yards of him, presumably from a rest. The range of the volley that followed was about fifty yards, and its only effect was to wound the sergeant. A gallant comrade tried to save his life by carrying him off, and had got with him to the top of the hill—he was just going to clear it and go down safely on the other side—when the sergeant was shot dead in his arms. The name of this brave private has escaped my memory. I should like to know that he was rewarded, but not, as our officers and soldiers commonly are, by promotion out of their field of distinction and especial usefulness, into a non-combatant branch of the service. The third and last man killed was shot while trying to get his horse. So much for tactics; viewed from the stand-point of the strategist, the operation of these Indians was the rare one of the seizure and complete destruction of an enemy's base. They burned up the wagon that they plundered, the other one having been set on fire by the blaze of the men's guns.

TEMPEST MINE, August 18.—At quarter of eight this morning I bade a sad farewell to the captain and set out for Lochiel.

I noticed shortly after starting that one of my Indians had nothing on or around his head, and it was not long before I saw him wearing a substitute for his missing head-gear, in the form of a wreath of green sprigs. The Indian's hair is his hat, and the band he commonly wears is no mere ornament. Without it he would be more or less uncovered with every rapid motion and every puff of wind. The hair-band, or crown of primitive man is no doubt the origin of the emblem of royalty, as well as that of the hat-band.

If our hair were exposed as much as the Indian's, to the sun, and wind, and rain, it would be as thick and as long as his, but we must cover ours up, first from vanity, and then from necessity. The hat should seem to be but a substitute for hair; in other words, false hair; and therefore, hat-wearers, at least the present generation, are greater wearers of false hair than bonnet-wearers. But who ever thinks, as he stops in front of his glass and poises his shining Dunlap, that he is fixing his false hair without hairpins; or, as he takes it off to a lady across the street, that he is in the act of raising his hair without scalping-knife.

About five miles from Lochiel I was accosted by a ranchman whom I had met at the *baile,* and told to "look out," that there were lots of Indians in the country; that some thirty had lately given fight to some Mexicans on the other side of the line; and that wagons had gone out from Lochiel to bring in the wounded. I asked him if he had seen the trail of these Indians; he said he had not, but that his partner had seen persons who had. He suggested my notifying Captain Hatfield, but I was too old a campaigner for such hastiness. I did not tell him how little faith I put in what he said, but hastened on to Lochiel, hoping that I might find some truth in it. I was satisfied that I could communicate with Captain Hatfield in time to bring him to the Mexican line by morning.

At Lochiel the report was substantially corroborated, the number of Indians however, being stated at from ten to twenty, instead of thirty. It appeared that there were two Mexicans wounded; no one had seen the trail, but the general impression seemed to be that the Indians were making west or northwest.

This report making it advisable, in my judgment, to communicate with the troop as soon as possible, I decided to return by the Washington Pass, as the shortest route across the Patagonias. Another reason for not taking the San Antonio was the fact, which I ascertained at Lochiel, that it lies for the greater part in Mexico, and our troops are allowed to cross the line only on a fresh trail. Before leaving Lochiel I got the most explicit directions I could as to the way through the Washington Pass.

I was told that I could not miss it, but having been falsely assured in those same words before, I gave little weight to them. The gentleman who last enlightened me on the subject was moved by the sight of my two Indians to impart to me his distrust of Indian allies, observing, "If Uncle Sam would only enlist some of our American mountaineers!" I thought I should as lief trust to friendly Indians in a tight place as to his "American mountaineers." The citizen soldiery of Arizona have not as yet distinguished themselves above the Government mercenaries.

I had to pass several branchings of the road and, though following the instructions I received as I understood and remembered them, I did get out of my course. A miner going home from the Washington mine put me back on it.

At the Washington mine I saw the only attempt at concentration that I have seen in the Patagonias. It is a wet process, by which the mineral of four tons of ore is gotten into one. Ore worth $25 a ton, not enough to pay for smelting, is profitably reduced by it to a "concentrate" worth $100. Guided by the forementioned miner, I footed it along a trail to what is known as the Washington Camp, as distinguished from the mine. When I arrived there it was about six o'clock but I pushed on across the mountain, intending to march as long as I could find my way, and then camp wherever I might. The night was so clear and light, however, that my Indians managed to keep the trail that I was traveling, and so I went on, without stopping even to cook dinner, to K troop camp, where we arrived at eleven o'clock. The trail down the mountain was not as long or as steep as the Mowry, which we had ascended two days before. But its indistinctness in the starlight partly neutralized these advantages; beside which, the lower end of it was somewhat further from our camp than that of the Mowry.

Our hardest work was getting across the foot-hills. I estimated the distance we marched to-day at forty-five miles. We were challenged with vigor and received with formality by the challenger. The body of the guard, scattered over a mound back of the sentinel, straggled toward us at our answer, "body of armed men," and stood watching us, as we advanced and filed by, their forms showing like silhouettes against the silvery sky. The captain was rather surprised at our arrival. No Indian rumors or reports had reached him, and he gave little credit to those I brought, not enough to think of going out. While our cook was getting me something to eat I looked over my private and the Captain's official mail. Among the latter was the following grateful reading:

--◆{ 41 }◆--

OLD NANA, THE FAMOUS APACHE CHIEF

FORT BOWIE, A. T., Aug. 17, 1885.

To General Forsyth, Fort Huachuca, Arizona:

Captain Davis, Fourth Cavalry, reports on the 10th that Lieutenant Day with his scouts struck Geronimo's camp, northeast of Nakasonia, August 17, and killed Nana, and two other bucks, one squaw, and Geronimo's son, aged thirteen years, captured fifteen women and children, among them the wives and five children of Geronimo, and Uno, the wife of Mangas; also, on the 29 ult., his scouts ambushed a party of four Chiricahuas and killed two bucks, and captured all the horses and plunder of the party. In the fight of the 9th Geronimo was wounded, and was followed some distance by his blood. Only two other bucks and one squaw escaped, and everything in the camp was captured. The Indians are evidently split up, and it is possible that some of them may try to work back through our lines. Inform Mrs. Davis.

(Signed)   ROBERTS,
                 A.A.D.C.

Official copy respectfully furnished the commanding officer, Troop D, Tenth Cavalry, who, after reading this dispatch, will forward it at once by special courier to the commanding officer, Troop K, Tenth Cavalry, at Tempest Mine. A strict lookout will be kept by troop commanders.

By order Lieut.-Col. Forsyth,

J. S. RICHARDS, JR.,
First Lieutenant and Adjutant Fourth Cavalry.

This is the first good news of importance we have yet received from the front. It gives me pleasure to see my friend and classmate Lieutenant Day so honorably mentioned. I only hope that he is not lost to the line of the army.

The following is another official communication of some interest that came in my absence:

HEADQUARTERS DEPARTMENT OF ARIZONA, IN THE FIELD,
August 14, 1885.

Second Lieutenant W. E. Shipp, Tenth Cavalry, Commanding Indian Scouts.

SIR:—The Department Commander directs me to furnish you the following additional instructions for your guidance in the management of Indian scouts:

The first principle is to show them that we trust them. We have to depend upon their fidelity, and they are quick to note any lack of confidence. They appreciate the situation, and understand thoroughly what is expected of them, and know best how to do their work. They understand this business better than we do, and to attempt to direct them in details will merely disgust them and make them "time-servers." They will work in your presence, and when away from you loaf. The only directions that can be given them, with any probability of good results, is to explain to them what you expect of them, and let them do their work in their own way, holding them responsible that it is done. It must be understood that the scouts must not be required to stand post, either as sentinels or pickets. They are for scouting purposes to keep watch. They know better how to obtain the information which is needed—namely the presence of the renegades—than we do, and should be allowed to use their own methods in getting it. Much caution must be exercised lest the life and ambition of the scouts be taken out of them by unnecessary labor. We cannot expect them to act automatically as drilled soldiers do. Their best quality is their individuality, and as soon as this is destroyed or impaired their efficiency goes with it. It is understood that officers in command of scouts and of the different stations along the line feel great responsibility, and that they are all eager and anxious to carry out the instructions received, and necessarily would be much mortified were any of the renegades to pass the line in their vicinity without being discovered. These facts are known and appreciated. The question is how to get the most valuable service, and hence the caution sought to be conveyed in this letter, which is based on long experience in the use of Indians as scouts and auxiliaries.

By order of Brig.-General Crook.

C. S. ROBERTS,
Captain Seventeenth Infantry A.A.D.C.

I do not know whether the policy of utilizing natives to fight natives was an original conception with General Crook, or an adoption from the British; however that may be, the general's method of carrying out that policy is, from all I can learn, quite different from that of the British. The latter drill and discipline their native auxiliaries, and officer them with a view to leading and directing them in action. General Crook simply turns his natives loose in stronger numbers than the enemy, and with an unfailing supply of provisions and ammunition, relying upon those two advantages for their success. He does not attempt to force upon them our discipline or our tactics. General Crook

GARGONIO, MEDICINE MAN OF MESCALERO APACHES

makes of his Indian auxiliaries, not soldiers, but more formidable Indians.

TEMPEST MINE, August 19.—I see from my last *Army and Navy Journal* that the Secretary of War has ordered the limitation of the detail as staff officer to three years. He seems to be engaged in a reformation in the military service corresponding to that going on in the civil. I expect to see him revoke the order excluding cavalry officers from details at so-called military colleges. That a troop of cavalry numbering, say sixty men—an uncommonly large number—cannot be managed by two officers when three is all that the law allows for the management of a hundred, is remarkable idea to be entertained by the War Department. It is as much as two officers can do to find wholesome employment in the management of the worst single troop of sixty men in the service, and is more than three can undertake to do without being in one another's way. I am now in the field with a troop of twenty-nine men present, under the command of the captain. I have to climb and hunt to keep my body in healthy exercise. If the second lieutenant were with us, we should not have ten men—not a corporal's command—to an officer. Now, if the cavalry were enabled and required to be thoroughly trained, three officers would not be too many for a troop, even on a peace footing; but a similar remark would apply to the artillery. I say that, taking things as they are, the cavalry can spare one officer to a troop for self-improvement on detached service just as well as the artillery can spare three to every two batteries. If the artillery can spare, and has been sparing 3-8 of its battery officers, as against 3-9 of the troop officers that the cavalry can spare, is not the present importance to the cavalry of its due of detached service to the importance to the artillery of its due, as 3-8 is to 3-9, or, as 27 to 24? There is nothing in the consideration that cavalry is more likely to be in active service in the field than the artillery. Two officers are enough for the average troop in the field, as well as in the post.

CRITTENDEN,[12] August 27.—Since my return from the Huachucas I have been continuously in camp, sitting or lying down most of the time on my blankets, reading or writing, and I am glad at a day or two's change. I came to-day to Crittenden to purchase writing-materials with which to make out the muster-rolls. At the thought of this object of my journey, I cannot help feeling like the boy cutting his own switch.

TEMPEST MINE, August 29.—Spent most of the day writing out muster-rolls. The making of duplicates, triplicates, and quadruplicates of official returns should not devolve upon a commissioned officer. It is true, the average commissioned officer has little enough to do, beside to afford the time for such scribbling; that is the saddest thing about it.

TEMPEST MINE, August 30.—Finished my clerical work for the troop. As a test and discipline to the attention, the muster-roll follows close upon the pure mathematics.

The captain made out the monthly return for the regimental adjutant, and the rolls of the Indian scouts; so we are now ready for tomorrow's bi-monthly muster and inspection.

The following are the names of our five Indians, taken from their muster-rolls:

1. Yaos-te-he.
2. Mad-des-at.
3. A-gnow-gita.
4. Hat-o-ena.
5. The-ho-auna.

I do not recognize any of them in this list. One whom I call John is the only one that has a name to me. Him and the corporal I can tell at sight. These two came to me the other evening, when the captain was away, to inform me that they had eaten nothing since noon and were very hungry. Upon inquiry I learned that they had consumed their five days' rations in three days and a half. I had the sergeant give them a half a day's supply, to last them one day and a-half. Indians should receive their rations at short intervals. A good practice is to issue their meals to them as to the men, issuing them uncooked if they so prefer them. They ordinarily like to cook for themselves.

Mr. Manning arrived here to-day and took dinner with the captain and myself. We had a good camp-spread, bean soup and boiled beans, venison, onions, coffee, and slapjacks. After the cloth—or rather, rubber*—was removed, and cigars had been served, I walked our guest around.

TEMPEST MINE, September 1.—The captain came back to camp this afternoon, having gone yesterday to Crittenden to mail his returns. He brought with him a letter from Fort Grant intimating that he or I might be ordered in to the post to attend to some business there connected with the troop, and he offered to let me go in first. I spent part of the afternoon examining an abandoned mine in front of our tent. It must be over a hundred years since it was worked. All that we could see of it was the dump, and what we took to be the site of the filled-in shaft. Picking over the "waste," we found some good low-grade ore. A curiosity of this old work is a palm-tree, some ten feet high, growing out of the dump. It is probably the only tree of its kind in the territory, whence the name, Lone Palm, given, not to this mine, but to the first claim established near it, the one in which Lindberg is working. The tree must have been transplanted generations ago by the pioneer miners of this region, Jesuit *padres*, delving for the enrichment of their mission and their church.

TEMPEST MINE, September 3.—Went hunting this morning with John, the Indian. He took breakfast with me, and we started immediately afterwards. We had not gone far before we were joined by another Indian, a particular friend of John's. We went slowly along the base of the mountains about a mile, and then up a ravine to the top. The Indians then took to the valley beyond, and followed it northward, while I worked my way near the top, along the side. They had the better ground for deer,

*We usually dine off a poncho. This article of wearing apparel, issued to soldiers in lieu of rubber overcoats, consists of a piece of rubber almost five feet square, with a slit in the middle for the head to protrude through.

and I was in hopes that they would start one up towards me. Having come to a low saddle in the mountain. I stopped to rest and give the Indians time to cross back to the side of our camp; and, as they did so, circling around me over this saddle, I lost sight of them. I made my way back to camp alone without much difficulty, as I had got my bearings before coming down the mountain.

I did not see a deer or anything else that a sportsman would fire at, unless it were a cotton-tail rabbit. Most sportsmen disdain such game, and few can hit it—that is, with a bullet. I saw a number of deer-tracks and what I took to be bear-tracks. There was a bear killed back of our camp, in the mountains, a week or two ago, by a miner. He could have got ten dollars reward for its head, but did not know it.

As I neared camp the fresh tracks of a wagon confirmed me in the belief that one had arrived. I saw one from near the top of the mountain which I thought was bound for the Tempest. Upon my arrival in camp, I found that the wagon had brought out some more boots for the men, who are now pretty well shod again. Some of them were the new Leavenworth knee-boot. I do not like it for our cavalry in this country. It is too heavy for the dismounted work we have to do. A shoe and gaiter would be the best thing for Arizona. Some of the Indians, it seems, are badly off for foot protection. When I started out of camp this morning both my Indians were barefooted. They carried their moccasins in their hands or in their belts, to save them. John did not put his on until we had crossed the top of the mountain. I had not supposed that, Indian though he was, he would willingly barefoot it over the broken rocks and stones of the Patagonias.

I received a letter from Captain Hatfield, in which he says that the trail reported to us by Doctor Wood when he was last in our camp was truly an Indian trail, and that the party that made it was the party that fought the Mexicans in Sonora, as reported to me at Lochiel. I wonder if the captain is satisfied as to the reality of the signal fire I tried to make him see from his camp the evening before I left? The doctor is with us again for a day; he is on his second tour of the camps.

The two miners at the Lone Palm, Henry and his partner John, came around after dinner to make their farewell call. In the course of the evening we were joined by Mr. Manning, who is going, I believe, to open the Tempest. He told us that the report is abroad that Geronimo is dead. If it is true, the troops will soon be going back to their posts.

MOWRY MINE, September 6.—Arrived here this evening from the Tempest, after a march of over thirty miles, which should have been but twenty-five. We made the Sonoita Creek from our camp by the road. Having watered there, and rested awhile in the shade of fine, tall trees, we followed the road up the stream to the stage road, and branched off on the latter around the north point of the Patagonias. The hills were green along the whole way. Keeping in the bottom, we had no climbing to do until after we passed Harshaw, the only settlement we saw. Like most primitive American towns, it consists of one street, lined with box-like frame houses, largely eating and drinking places; in front of these we saw an assortment of Harshaw's men of leisure, whose facial expressions conveyed a seeming determination not to be the first to say good-day.

MOWRY MINE, September 7.—Came in about half an hour ago from a tramp in search of deer. I cannot call it a hunt, having seen nothing worthy of a shot. I started out earlier and more hopeful than usual, having been told by a Mexican yesterday evening that deer abounded hereabouts; also bear, which, he said, were *"muy bravo."* I had Cropper with me for company and assistance. We made our way through the wet grass and bushes, and over stones and rocks along the top of the mountain, looking now on the shady, now on the sunny side, down and across arroyos and ravines as we successively crossed them. Upon reaching the trail across the mountain from Washington Camp, we followed it to the camp, where we rested about half an hour. The mines there were not working, principally, I understood, on account of an after-Sunday indisposition on the part of the work-men. This is Monday. We came back by the beaten trail, having gotten over, altogether, about eight miles of ground. I gathered from what I heard at Washington Camp that its mines are as poor as to working capital as those we have just left; and more-over, that the mines at Harshaw are not much better off. The mining in every part of the Patagonias, I take it, is done princi-pally by prospectors in partnerships. There is, however, some "chloriding" done—that is, working for a share of the profits.

I stopped outside of our camp at an attractive pool in the rocky bed of the creek, and let Cropper go in and get me my clean raiment while I cooled off for a bath. Upon his return I gave a delicious climax to my morning's exhilaration.

Since night before last, when we had a violent wind in our old camp, more particularly since we have moved to the top of the mountain, the weather has been decidedly autumnal. As I hear the west wind rustling through heavy branches, and see shaking grass and butter-cups, and waving golden-rods, and stiffly nodding scrub-oaks, all green and hardly dry from last night's rain, I am oblivious to fiery Arizona, and fancy myself among the Catskills.

I have, moreover, an artificial reminder of the East in the ruins of the Mowry Smelter. The central figure, so to speak, of this interesting relic is a chimney, about a hundred feet high, of genuine furnace-baked brick, the first that I have seen in Ari-zona. This structure is pretty well preserved. One can read the words on a white band around the top: "Mowry Silver Mine, T. Scheuner fecit, 1862." Near it is another slighter chimney, also of red brick. Around these are the remains of adobe walls and furnaces. The whole property, mine and smelter, are now owned by two gentlemen of Tucson, who value it, I am told, at about $100,000. Mr. Mowry, who gave it its name, was a captain in the regular army. Being a secessionist, he resigned at the open-ing of the war, but instead of joining the Confederacy, he went to making money off this mine. The fortune that he made may

MANGAS, CHIRICAHUA CHIEF

be judged from the scale that his enterprise assumed and his mode of living while engaged in it. He gave employment to 300 men, including 100 guards and herdsmen. The machinery of his smelter was shipped from the East to Guaymas, in Mexico, whence it was transported here on ore wagons. Many a man was killed by Indians in the escorting of it, and many a one, too, in working about the mine. Captain Mowry thought seriously at one time of procuring a few pieces of artillery for the defense of his industry. His bricks (adobe and other) he had made here himself.

This industrial baron knew how to endear himself to his Mexican menials, by whom he is reverently remembered and spoken of to this day. Every Saturday at noon the shafts and furnaces were closed, and a round of feasting and dancing commenced that lasted until midnight Sunday—company coming from far and near. Among the roomy ruins of his mansion, I identified, to my own satisfaction, the ballroom and the wine-cellar. Through ragged edged openings, once occupied by doors and windows, I looked out upon loop-holed walls, behind which the revelers may oft-times have gathered at a signal shot or an Apache yell.

The fall of the house of Mowry was as sudden as its rise. Towards the close of the war its lord and master was arrested and confined in Fort Yuma under charge of selling lead to the Confederates, and held there for two years. The charge, however, was never legally substantiated. Upon his release he sued the government for damages, and recovered a share of what the abandonment of his works had cost him. He then went to England, broken in health, if not in spirit, and there died. Having lain idle ever since their founder was arrested, the Mowry works have been crumbling away now for nearly a quarter of a century. The adobe houses occupied by the workers are still to be seen, however, scattered about between the shafts and the smelter. One of them is occupied by the present keeper of the estate, a venerable German, who came to this country from Bonn, on the Rhine, in 1824.

I see from the *Army and Navy Journal* that an order is likely to be issued from the War Department restricting the appointments to the ordnance to graduates from the Military Academy, recommended for that corps by the Academic Board. I hope it will not be done. It would be a mistake to exclude from the ordnance all non-graduates from West Point, and all graduates not deemed especially qualified for it at graduation. It is, moreover, unjust to a graduate to have his record at the academy follow him with a species of disqualification for a period of five years, more or less, after graduation. To determine order of choice of service among classmates at graduation is all the influence of West Point standing that should be awarded to it by order or regulation. The fact that appointments to the ordnance are not made immediately and directly from the academy testifies that the recommendations of the Academic Board are mere conjectures as to future qualifications.

The aspirants to the ordnance go into the line to attain that qualification to complete their preparation. Who will say that such complement may not more than compensate for antecedent imperfection or inferiority? The recommending to the ordnance by the Academic Board—a relic of the time when appointments were made directly from the academy—had better be discontinued altogether. If, however, it continues, and the appointments are based thereon, the service in the line of the officers recommended should be made subservient to its all important purpose. Instead of being restricted to the artillery, it should be made to extend into the infantry and the cavalry. No system of appointment to the ordnance should seem judicious that does not exact prior service in the three branches of the line.

V

CAMP CRITTENDEN, ARIZONA, September 8, 1885.—Wishing to look at some mines, I assumed charge, this morning, of a party of three of our men going with a pack-mule to Harshaw, five miles from camp, to purchase provisions for the officers' mess. The captain charged me with ascertaining at what price he might sell the bacon savings of the troop.

A short distance out of camp I met our blacksmith and another man, with a pack-mule, on their way back from Fort Huachuca, where they had been sent to fit some horse-shoes. From a package of mail they brought with them, I took my letters.

Upon arriving at Harshaw,[13] I went first to the general provision store, one of the two owners of which is Mr. Sydow, by whom the doctor and I were entertained at Lochiel.

His partner, with whom I dealt, told me that they would buy bacon from us at 15 cents a pound. I asked him to notify a certain Chinaman, who furnishes the store with fruit and vegetables, to make a visit with a stock of fruit to our camp. Mr. Sydow sells potatoes at 4 cents a pound, lard at 15 cents, onions at 5 cents.

Having declined an invitation to take a morning dram, I was conducted from the general provision store to the butcher store by the butcher, who, seeing me come into town, called upon me with true Yankee tact to find out what he could do for me.

I bought from him 5 pounds of beef at the rate of 15 cents a pound, a high price for this country, and ascertained that he would exchange beef with the captain for his bacon at the rate of three pounds of beef for two of bacon. The captain expects to get two pounds of beef for one of bacon.

Having allowed my men time to spend their little money, and learned that there were no mines working nearer to Harshaw than those we passed, I started back to camp. The mines in the immediate vicinity of Harshaw are failing, it seems, in consequence of the usual mistake of Western mining, extravagant and incompetent management. Upon arriving at the mines referred to, nearer camp, I directed my men, with the exception of one whom I kept to hold my horse, to go on with the provisions and tell the captain that I would be back in about an hour. I then struck up the steep road branching off to the shafts. After proceeding about 200 yards, I dismounted to make my way over steeper ground a few yards further to where I could see the dumps, over which I soon made my way to the sorting shed outside of the entrance to the *Blue Nose,* or old *Home Again* mine. This is one of the richest mines in Arizona. The ore is easily sorted, being almost free from rock, and it has the advantage of an admixture of lead in a proportion very favorable to smelting. The *Blue Nose* is owned by five men, who, along its glittering ledge, are steadily working themselves from laborers into capitalists.

"When we began here," said one of them, who showed me around, "we had not money enough to buy beans; that we hadn't." They now employ thirty workmen, paying them four dollars a day, the highest mining wages paid in the territory.

With one exception—the half owner—the owners do daily work as regularly as their employees, eight hours at night, nine in the day time. A shot having just been fired in each shaft, I could not go below, but I went into a tunnel far enough to perceive the affluence of the "mother lead." I am afraid to say, with any positiveness, how broad it was; I estimate about fifty yards. On my way across it I passed shafts and chambers and side galleries. As I stopped and looked into one of these chambers, I was greeted by a grimy six-footer, whom, in the uncertain light of shifting candles, I recognized as a late fellow-guest of mine at Lochiel, the mirthful stentorian who distinguished himself calling out the square dances. The *Blue Nose* has the only hoisting engine I have seen in the Patagonias, and it is soon to have a concentrator. Its principal ore is *copper silver glance* (the stromeyerite of mineralogists). The mother rock is a magnesian limestone.

Declining an invitation to stop to dinner, and promising to come again when I might go down into the shafts, I took leave of my guide and rode off. Upon arriving in camp, I found the paymaster paying off. The captain informed me that I was authorized to go into Fort Grant, to be gone ten days. I inquired of the paymaster if he could take me into Huachuca in his ambulance. I thought I might see that post, and take the railroad to Huachuca Station. But he had not room for me. Having then to take the less interesting but quicker route over Crittenden Station, I resolved upon enhancing its one advantage by taking it as soon as possible. The captain ordered dinner at once, and lent me money for my journey. I set out shortly after dinner, having with me Cropper and two other men, besides a sergeant, and a pack-mule to carry my bedding. I took only a light lunch to do me for supper, as I would breakfast next morning at the Crittenden Hotel. The sergeant was a prudential after-thought on the part of the captain, prompted by the recent payment of the men.

At the first saloon we came to, the one at the *Home Again* camp, I cast my head around to see how the detachment was coming on. I saw two of my men halted in front of the saloon, and the sergeant just leaving them, and closing up at a trot, looking a little sheepish. One of the men that had halted struck out after the mule. Immediately thereupon Cropper came out of the saloon, and was going to mount his horse, held by the other man, when I called him to me, and asked him if he had permission to dismount. With an innocent look, he said he had not; that he had only gone into the store to get some matches, of which he showed me a bunch. Doubting very much whether that was all that he dismounted for, I told him not to dismount without my permission, and let him mount. I was near making him walk, but thought he might, as well as my "striker,"* have been unconscious of doing wrong in leaving the column to procure the means of starting a fire for me. Some officers would have thought nothing of it. The sergeant's deportment was more reprehensible than that of the private's, and would have been more vexatious had I not been prepared for it. As it was, I hardly gave it a thought, and said nothing to him about it. The great difficulty in the government of colored troops is the securing of efficient non-commissioned officers. I find, as a general thing, not more than two or three efficient ones to a troop. It is only up to a certain point, and that not a high one, that colored troops are more easily disciplined than white. To attain high or even proper discipline they require more training than white men.

Arriving at Harshaw, the sergeant asked my permission for the packer to fall out to buy him a cigar, which I did not grant. Besides being disinclined to favor him, I was impatient to reach Crittenden. It was then a quarter of six, and I had still ten miles to go. Part of this distance being on a road unknown to me, I was anxious to get over the road before dark. As, however, I wound my way out from among the foot-hills of the Patagonias into the Sonoita Valley, about half way between Harshaw and Crittenden, it was deep twilight, and I saw that I should not make the railroad and the familiar wagon road beyond it until after dark.

Coming sharply around a bend in the road, which brought me suddenly facing a conical hill about five hundred yards from me, I started at the sight of what appeared to be an Indian standing on the summit. Having often before been deceived in such a sight—as most people have who have traveled by twilight or moonlight in a Spanish-bayonet country—I would not believe in the reality of this one. I expected to recognize, as I drew nearer, the dead *bayonets* drooping in the form of a skirt around the stalk as around a pair of legs; and to distinguish above the wilted body of my spectral Indian the round, bristling head of a Span-

*Body Servant.

ish-bayonet plant. But I received no such comforting assurance of hallucination. The road did not lead to him, but took me past him, at a distance of about a hundred yards. More than once I thought I saw him stir, as if to raise a gun; and looking around, as I crossed his front, I fancied he was lowering himself slowly on one knee. It was not until I had put more than rifle range between us that I dismissed him wholly from my mind.

Arriving at Crittenden at eight o'clock, I telegraphed, as soon as I found the telegraph operator, to the commanding officer at Fort Grant, requesting him to send an ambulance to meet me at Willcox. I spent most of the evening in the ticket and telegraph office, in company with the operator. Here I met the stage driver, who succeeded the one that was killed near the Mowry Mine. He carries mail and passengers between Crittenden and Lochiel, and has engaged to leave our mail for us at our camp. An old soldier in the Fifth Cavalry, he talked with pride and satisfaction of the service that he did in Arizona, before the days of railroad and telegraph. The mail was then carried from post to post by well-mounted couriers, who set out shortly after retreat, and had to make their destination, sometimes forty or fifty miles off, before daylight.

FORT GRANT, ARIZONA, September 9.—Slept, last night, on the platform of the railroad station. The men, with the exception of Cropper, who kept me company, slept by the horses, in the *corral* back of the store. This arrangement obviated the necessity of a guard. I was up at five o'clock, having spent a rather restless night. A bell mule, or bell horse, or bell cow—I could not make out the animal—strolled around the station until a late hour, deluding me, in its moments of special intentness on nibbling, into thinking that it had settled down to rest; and at irregular intervals through the night, a number of loud-mouthed watch dogs in the Mexican quarter asserted themselves in a concert of discordances.

I learned from Mr. Manning that the Denver mining expert had reported favorably in regard to the quality of the ore about

Crittenden, and that the firm he represented was likely, upon the return of one of the members from Washington, to decide upon the establishment of the smelting works.

At about six o'clock I breakfasted at the hotel, which, standing close to the track, about 150 yards from the station, competes as a traveler's resort with a German restaurant in the main row of houses opposite the station. At seven o'clock I was off in the train, with a ticket to Benson, the northern terminus of the Sonora Railway. My ticket cost me five dollars and a half, or eleven cents per mile. From past experience as a south-western traveler, I thought it imprudent to let my baggage, which was not under lock and key, go into the baggage car; I therefore took my bedding, with its dingy shelter tent wrapping and its clothes line fastening, with me into the passenger car. I had intended to send it back to camp with my escort, but upon reflection decided to take it along, not knowing when and where I might next be sent out into the field. It is a good general principle not to separate oneself from one's baggage. The car that I went into, though marked *Iera Clase*, was severely simple in its appointments, and very dirty. However, the wicker covered spring seats were softer than the grassiest ground, and the foreign faces—there were several evidently well-to-do Mexicans in the car—the engine's shrieking and ringing, the rapid and tremulous motion of the car, even the conductor's and the newsboy's troublesome visitations, contributed to revive in me a pleasant association of ideas. From Huachuca station to Willcox I had the company of Major and Mrs. Beaumont and Miss Beaumont. Having been under the weather, the Major had gone for a change of air to Fort Huachuca, taking his family with him, and was now on his way back to his post, Fort Bowie. I enjoyed hearing him talk about our army and the armies that he had visited abroad. He regards the British cavalry as the best, as far as it goes, in Europe.

Shortly after we had started from Huachuca he was presented by a Mexican gentleman, a polite stranger, with a couple of pomegranates, fresh, cool, and ripe, one of which we immediately discussed. The pomegranate is the perfection of summer fruit, being juicy, crisp and tart.

At Benson, we had to change cars. Having an hour to wait, I walked up and down the town a number of times, and looked into some of the stores in the hope of finding something characteristic of the place or the region to take home with me, but I was disappointed. In one store, I picked up a sort of grass or reed basket, thinking it the work of Mexicans or Indians; and was pleased to learn that it cost but—I forget how much, not more than half a dollar. Upon asking where it was made, I was told, "In the East." Repressing the evil thought of palming it off on my wife for the simple art of untutored minds, I laid it down with regret, and bought a pound of California pears.

At Dragoon Station, we were joined by Lieutenant Elliot, of the Major's regiment, the Fourth Cavalry. I was surprised to hear from him that Geronimo was on this side of the line, with nine or ten warriors, including Chief Nana, reported, several weeks ago, to have been killed. Geronimo is thought to be making for the San Mateo Mountains, the Indian stronghold in New Mexico. I expect soon to hear of a movement of troops from the border towards the interior.

At about two o'clock, I got out at Willcox. There being no ambulance waiting for me, I was thrown upon the kindness of Major Coxe, the paymaster, who held an ambulance for himself and his clerk, whereby I secured comfortable transportation and good company. Included in the latter was Captain Kelly, of my regiment, just in from his camp in the Chiricahuas. The oaken, iron-bound traveling safe was placed under the front seat, where it was secured by the Major's watchful eye and the presence on the seat of the clerk and myself; while behind the ambulance, close enough to catch its dust, rattled the escort wagon with its force of *Long Toms*. We chatted away most of the three and a half hours taken by our six mule team in making the twenty-six miles to the post. The questions of the day, notably promotion and detached service, were discussed. One of us implied the belief that the policy of the Secretary of War concerning staff appointments would be discarded by his successor.

FORT GRANT, September 12.—Went on, this morning, as officer of the day. A wretch in the guard-house, by the name of Bill Smith, sentenced to five years' hard labor for desertion, has been filing his shackles through and trying to escape. He is now confined in a cell, his shackles and handcuffs being connected by an iron rod, so that he cannot reach his feet with his hands.

How many of our military prisoners are the victims of idleness and *ennui* and bitter disappointment, whose troubles might have been prevented by proper military training.

FORT GRANT, September 13.—Private ——, absent from retreat and tattoo. Explanation—been drinking. I confined him in the guard-house, regretting having to thrust him into companionship with hardened offenders.

FORT GRANT, September 14.—Assisted at the trial of Private ——; the court fined him one dollar; not much I thought, for two absences.

FORT GRANT, September 15.—Officer of the day again. I have not much time to attend to my own affairs. Had a new pair of trousers made by the tailor of H Troop, to replace those used up in the field. Paid one dollar for the making of them. The tailor tells me, and appears much concerned in the matter, that the non-commissioned officers are having the same stripes put on their trousers as the commissioned officers. I think, with the tailor, that officers should protect the distinctiveness of their uniform.

A colored woman, an officer's cook, was buried in the post cemetery this afternoon. Her husband a prisoner in the guard-house, has been on parole for several days to visit her. After the funeral he returned to confinement and hard labor.

FORT GRANT, September 16.—Telegraphed to Captain Lebo* that I would be at Crittenden on the 19th, ten days after my departure.

*Captain Thomas C. Lebo, 10th Cavalry.

FORT GRANT, September 17.—The post commander notified me to-day that I should not leave the post until I heard from him; that he would telegraph General Crook for authority to retain me here. There are more men of our troop in the post than there are in the field. I do not see why they are not all out.

FORT GRANT, September 18.—Officer of the day. The colonel commanding heard to-day from General Crook to the effect that he could retain me here until further orders.

FORT GRANT, September 19.—Lieutenant Davis, on duty with Indian scouts, came in, yesterday evening, from the field. He thinks that Geronimo is dead, but is not hopeful as to the early termination of the campaign. Superintended the target practice, this morning, of the band and non-commissioned staff.

I am satisfied, from what I see of rifle and carbine practice, that our men are not sufficiently drilled preparatory to going on the range. Several men wanted, at 500 yards to fire kneeling. The manual prescribes the position of lying down. It seems to me that if a man can fire better kneeling than lying down, there should be no objection to his taking that position.

FORT GRANT, September 20.—Bought a horse from Lieutenant Grierson[14] for $150, a larger and somewhat older horse than the one I have in the field. He is an excellent walker, and well adapted, I think, in other respects, to the cavalry service. I shall never again buy a small horse, no matter how tough or otherwise excellent he may be: for such a horse must be a slow walker, and I dislike marching at a jog-trot.

FORT GRANT, September 21.—Officer of the day. Acted as member and recorder of a board of survey. We condemned 1,100 pounds, or more, of maggoty bacon, which must have been badly cured when received. In this dry, hot climate, bacon loses 5, and sugar 6, per cent. of its weight, through natural wastage. All that the government allows for, in each case, is 3 per cent. There is a post, I am told, in Arizona, Fort Mohave, where the temperature has been 112° at midnight.

Fort Grant, September 22.—Am detailed, for to-morrow, as officer of the day. Had I not much to do besides of a private and official nature I should not mind the so frequent recurrence of this duty, there being nothing irksome about it except the inspecting of the guard and prisons after midnight.

Fort Grant, September 27.—Patterson's trimmings not properly cleaned at inspection. Ordered him to report to me upon coming off guard to-morrow morning. Spent most of the day writing up court martial proceedings. Prosecuted five cases yesterday.

Fort Grant, September 28.—Required Patterson to clean up his trimmings, including his sabre, which he was not required to wear at inspection. As I had spoken to him about this matter once before, I had a mind to put him in the guard-house, but I could not be so hard on a soldier whose life consists almost wholly of guard duty, inspection and fatigue. It would seem that every pleasant and attractive feature of a soldier's life had been purposely effaced and excluded from that of the American soldier, and nothing left but irksomeness and drudgery on the one hand, and idleness and dissipation on the other; and yet the question is asked in our army, "Why all this desertion?" and long-winded reports are devoted to the answering of it.

Fort Grant, September 29.—At about half-past two o'clock, while I was eating my dinner, an orderly notified me that the commanding officer wished to see me. Upon my reporting to him, I was directed to get ready in half an hour or so, to take the field. The horses being herded a long way out of the post, it was about two hours before they could be gotten in.

Having to allow for their feeding and for the rationing of the men and the issuing to them of 100 rounds of ammunition, which had first to be drawn from the ordnance sergeant; and having to wait for the verification by the Post Adjutant of the detail constituting my detachment, it was one-quarter of six before I finally marched out. I had in my saddle pocket the following letter of instruction:

FORT GRANT, A. T., September 29, 1885.
LIEUT. JOHN BIGELOW, JR.,

SIR: The Commanding Officer directs that you proceed at once to Solomonville, and thence to Ash Spring, in Stein's Peak Range, should you not obtain definite information as to the whereabouts of Indians before reaching that point. From Ash Spring, or that vicinity, you will use every effort possible to successfully carry out the instructions of the Department Commander as contained in inclosed telegram. Should you find it necessary to employ a guide you are hereby authorized to do so.

Very respectfully,
Your obedient servant,
THOMAS H. BARRY,
1st Lt. and R. O. M. 1st Infantry.
Post Adjutant.

Telegram.

FORT BOWIE, A. T., April 29, 1885.

TO COMMANDING OFFICER, FORT GRANT: Information just received states that a party of about twenty-five bucks passed Guadalupe Cañon, going north, yesterday morning, moving rapidly. Department Commander directs that you send at once a party to Mire Hilda [*sic*], in Stockton Pass, with orders to allow no one to leave the house, and also to kill or capture any Indians approaching, as it is supposed that the Indians may come in there for information. The party must conceal themselves carefully. In addition to this, General Crook desires you to send out such a party as you can spare to endeavor to intercept the Indians, who are moving north through Stein's Peak Range. Warn all citizens to guard and secure their stock, and, if possible, kill some of the Indians.

(Signed) ROBERTS, *A.A., D.C.*

My command consists of twenty-six enlisted men from the two troops K and L, whose remnants in the post I have been commanding. They are armed with the carbine, and provided with 100 rounds of ammunition, having neither sabre nor pistol, nothing to use in a charge but their lungs and their horses' hoofs. They carry four days' rations in their saddle pockets. I have no pack-mules. About three or four miles from the post I got off the road and had some hard scrambling in the dark, crossing gullies to get back to it. Soon after succeeding in this, I came upon Lieutenant Hunt's detachment, which left the post shortly before I did, ordered to Mire Hild's [Merejilda]. This is an old Mexican who was captured by the Apaches as a child, and kept by them ten years, more or less. He was for a number of years a government guide, but was discharged, about four years ago, under suspicion of bad faith. We went together nearly through Stockton Pass, separating at Gillespie's Ranch. Before we arrived there, a courier had overtaken us, bringing me the following dispatch:

FORT BOWIE.

COMMANDING OFFICER, FORT GRANT:—Fort Thomas has sent troops to Ash Springs.

GEORGE CROOK,
Brig.-General Commanding.

This was endorsed by the commanding officer of Fort Grant, as follows:

FORT GRANT, September 29.

Within just received. You had best strike right across from mouth of Stockton's Pass to a point in Stein's Peak Range, near the R. R., say on the old telegraph road to Bayard.

Accordingly I directed my march from Gillespie's as straight as I could upon Bailey's Wells. After following the road for about two miles around an intervening hill, I traveled by my pocket compass due east ten miles, which brought me directly upon the house at the Wells. It was three o'clock when I halted there, and went into camp.

WHITLOCK'S CIENEGA, September 30.—Picketed to bare ground, the horses had neither grass, hay, nor grain during the night. I fed them barley, this morning, furnished by Mr. Bailey on receipt. I could not procure a guide. Broke camp at 6:45, directing my march upon this point, Whitlock's Cienega. About an hour after starting, I was joined by a man, from Bailey's Wells, who thought he would go with me to learn what Indian news he could. I was glad of his company and his guidance. He informed me that the fall *round-up* was soon to take place. The cattle are rounded up, or driven together twice a year for counting and branding. They are shipped, as a rule, but once a year, in the fall

KA-E-TE-NAY OR GAIT-EN-EH, HEAD CHIEF WARM SPRING APACHES

or winter. The main object of rounding up bi-yearly is to catch the unbranded calves running with their mothers, in order to brand them before they become yearlings.

I traveled seventeen miles on a good road in preference to twelve on a rough trail. About a mile short of my destination I met Mr. Smythe, the owner of the water and the ranch. Whitlock is the name of a former captain in the regular army, who had a fight with Indians here, killing some forty or fifty. Cienega is the Spanish for marsh. A few hundred yards from the house Mr. Smythe left me to warn his wife of our arrival, that she should not be alarmed by our dust. Having watered the horses at the water-hole, or pond, I halted at the house, at about eleven o'clock, and there being no grass thereabouts, gave the horses a small feed of hay. While they were consuming it, and the men cooking their dinners, went into one of the several little huts and tents constituting Mr. Smythe's habitation, and took lunch with him and Mrs. Smythe; after which, reflecting upon what I had learned from conversation, and from my maps, I determined upon stopping here over night. The men having unsaddled, the horses were put up in a corral near the house. Shortly after lunch I repaired to a species of under-ground apartment called a "dug-out," the thatched or mud-cemented roof of which rests on the surface of the ground, and slept soundly on a cot until near sunset. Dined with the Smythes and their *boys,* in eastern parlance, their workmen or farm hands. The conversation turning on the affairs of the ranch, I learned that Mr. Smythe was apprehensive that the Indians would prevent his getting in his hay. He is having it cut with a mowing machine, an uncommon method, I take it, in this wild country. There was some discussion as to what had best be done for her security with Mrs. Smythe. Like a true frontiersman's wife, she was for going out to the hay camp with the men. It was decided that she should go to some point on the railroad. Dinner over, I sat with my kind host and hostess in their parlor, and bed-room, tent, and listened, for the first time with pleasure, to a woman singing to her own accompaniment on the harp. The only music associated in my memory with this instrument was that of Italian street singers and Mexican dance players. Fortunately for me, Mrs. Smythe was a beginner, and her simple performance all within my comprehension. I especially enjoyed her "Annie Laurie." After I had retired to the "dug-out" for the night, a man arrived from Bowie Station with a note from Mr. Wickersham, the storekeeper there, to Mr. Smythe, informing him that the hostile Indians were reported all back in the Chiricahua Mountains, heading northward. Having framed a note, to forward in the morning to General Crook, I laid myself down on my cot, and was soon as soundly asleep as if I had not slept since morning.

WHITLOCK'S CIENEGA, ARIZONA, October 1, 1885.—I sent my note this morning to General Crook, thereby informing him that I was about to start for a spring twelve miles east of Whitlock's; that my twenty-six men were rationed for three days; and that I was destitute of pack animals. The horses being fed and groomed at day-break, at half-past six, I started out, guided by Mr. Smythe, for the spring. Passing around the north point of an elevation back of the house or houses, we came upon a dry lake, on one side of which was the cienega or marsh. The lake looked as if it could never have been more than two inches deep, so even is its dry, hard surface. The so-called marsh is nothing but a patch of soft sod. All about it are Indian relics in stone and pottery, indicating that it was once the center of a permanent Indian camp or village. As we filed past it across the lake, I tried to reproduce its ancient scene of Indian life. I fancied the lake full from a recent rain, the ducks and deer taking themselves away from it. Startled by the movements in the awakening camp, the curls of smoke ascending from the newly-lighted fires, and the brightly attired figures—their heads enveloped in loose black hair—grouped, standing and crouching, about them.

Leaving the cienega, we entered a shallow cañon, narrowing and deepening as we advanced into it. About five or six miles from its entrance we reached a point from which we could see the small adobe house, among green cotton-wood trees, marking the spring that we were looking for. Leaving the horses behind, I approached it cautiously with a few men, and perceiving nothing human, brought up my command and examined the surroundings with a view to going into camp. I found good water in a well—barely sufficient for my horses, but running in at a good rate. The trails and other signs showed that the place had been abandoned by its owners, or regular occupants, within a day or two. There being no grass within sight, I gave up the idea of camping here, and after dispatching a telegraphic message by courier to General Crook, *via* San Simon, I started back by a new course to Smythe's Ranch. After going a little further up the cañon, I crossed the ridge separating me from the San Simon Flat, and proceeding along the northern edge of the latter to a convenient point, struck across a range of hills for the Smythe Homestead. Many of the hills across and among which I had traveled, were thickly strewn with a dark, honeycombed, volcanic rock from which they get the Mexican name of Peloncillo, brown sugar. Going and coming, I had a view of the Chiricahua Mountains across the San Simon Flat. Chiricahua is the Apache word for Turkey. The mountains owe their name to the large number of turkeys originally found in them, and the Apache band of Chiricahuas are named after the mountains on account of their having long inhabited them. I recognized Fort Bowie's landmark, Helen's Dome. It is said that from this peak a soldier's wife threw herself to her death, heart-broken at the loss of her husband, killed in a fight with Indians. According to an equally sad though less romantic legend, the peak is named after a soldier's betrothed who was accidentally killed, falling from it. What was left of the afternoon, after returning to camp, I spent mostly in writing up my journal in Mr. Smythe's tent.

NEAR DUNCAN, October 7.—After breakfast, I had the command formed, mounted without packs, and having inspected the arms, put it through a lively drill, mounted and dismounted. Between eleven and twelve my couriers came back from San Simon, bringing me the following dispatch from Fort Bowie:

FORT BOWIE, via WILLCOX, October 1, 1885.

Lieutenant Bigelow, Whitlock's Cienega, via Courier from San Simon.
(Operator forward by courier who is waiting.)

Information received that hostiles have gone into Dragoon Mountains. Commander directs you return with your party to Grant.

ROBERTS.

My couriers communicated to me verbally that Indians were thick in and about the Stein's Peak Range; that a party was being followed by troops C and H of our regiment towards Doubtful Cañon; and that a large fresh trail ran northward between the cienega and our camp. A railroad engineer told them he had seen a party of Indians standing by the side of the track near Stein's Pass. Satisfied that I was ordered to Grant in ignorance of the substance of these reports, I determined, on my own responsibility, to suspend the execution of the order for the present.

After considering whether to remain where I was or proceed toward Doubtful Cañon, or some point farther north, I made up my mind to strike for Ash Spring, and accordingly, at some quarter past one o'clock, having eaten another good lunch with the Smythes, my men cooking and eating their dinners meanwhile, I saddled up and put my little force in motion. About three miles out I learned from Mr. Smythe, who overtook me to put me on my way, that in going to Ash Spring I should diverge from the trail that was reported to me and which I wanted to cut, upon which I changed my objective point to Duncan, on the Gila River. Having accompanied me about five miles farther, he bade me good-bye, and turned back towards his house, which, his men being out cutting hay, was unguarded and unprotected. Mrs. Smythe, however, had gone for security to Bowie Station. He was bent, moreover, on going to the cienega to investigate the matter of the reported trail, which we had not yet struck, and which he suspected was made by his own horses. It was hard for me to part with him; never in the course of my military traveling in Texas, Arizona, and New Mexico, have I met with hospitality so true and generous, and so pleasing, as that extended to me by this good ranchman and his wife.

About six o'clock, as the sun was disappearing below the hilly horizon, I stood on the top of the divide between the Gila River and the San Simon Flat, looking at a stretch of trees in the Gila Valley, seemingly ten or twelve miles off, which I took to be on the river. Looking about for a road, or a path or trail to guide me—the country was broken, and there was no moon—I saw, about a mile ahead of me a piece of road pointing, as I thought, towards the river. I got on this road and, having followed it about three miles, perceived that it was changing its general direction. I then struck straight for the fore-mentioned trees, and, remembering Mr. Smythe's instructions to trust to cow trails took up a plain fresh trail in the midst of several older ones.

I was soon prevented by the darkness from seeing the cheerful foliage of the river, but the stars gave me light enough to make out the plateaux; looming up like a row of giant mausoleums on the opposite side of the valley, and to pursue my crooked pathway. About an hour after dark I made out a fire among some trees ahead of me. Having proceeded to within a few hundred yards of it, I halted, dismounted the troop, and advanced with my ranking non-commissioned officer to determine what it was. The corporal put his ear to the ground and reported, "They are cowboys, sir; I hear the voices." So I mounted and pushed on. When about one hundred yards farther, we crossed a railroad and a hard level stretch beyond it, and came upon a stream about twenty feet across, which I took to be the Gila. I worked my way along it towards the fires on the opposite bank, hallooing for some one to come and show me where to cross. I was soon answered by a man standing close to the water's edge, who told me to do so where I stood, and asked me who I was. Upon telling him, I asked him, with lively curiosity, "Who are you?"

"I am Lieutenant Reade."

It turned out to be my friend and classmate, Lieutenant Reade, of my regiment, and my corporal's alleged cowboys were his men.

Having watered, I put my command in camp by the side of his, and in the cozy seclusion of his shelter tent, lighted by a Government candle—issued as part of the ration—was soon engaged in replenishing my vital fires with bacon and hard tack, and in discussing the military situation. The following telegram, by which he was guided and governed, showed Lieutenant Reade to be on the look-out for the same party of Indians that I was; it showed moreover, that General Crook was not, as I had assumed him to be, in ignorance of the existence of that party, or of its movements.

DUNCAN, A. T.

To Lieutenant Reade:—

Telegram received. Latest information is, that Indians were at Gayleville yesterday, probably crossed San Simon last night towards Doubtful Cañon. It is reported that thirteen bucks crossed railroad near *Cochise*, west of Dragoon Station, yesterday, going towards "Point of Mountain." You can get grain and rations at Clifton. Department Commander has no special intructions, but wishes you to act on such information as you receive. You should place your command at some point where it can be thoroughly hidden, and endeavor to see the Indians first.

ROBERTS, A.A., D.C.

CLIFTON, October 3.—At six o'clock this morning I set out with my trumpeter for the little town of Duncan, about four miles up the river, to communicate by telegraph with General Crook. I found the telegraph office closed, and learned that the operator was off hunting, and was expected back in about half an hour. While waiting for him to return I conversed with some Arizona militiamen who were about to set out on their ponies for Doubtful Cañon. They were banded cowboys, not even uniformed. After the lapse of more than half an hour, the operator not having returned, I was joined by Lieutenant Reade, who entered the telegraph office and set to operating himself; I envied him his useful accomplishment. There being a supply depot at Clifton, the northern terminus of the railroad, he first got up the operator there and inquired of Lieutenant Maus, 1st infantry, in charge of the depot, if he could forward us forage and rations by today's train, which was to leave Clifton at about 9:30 A.M. We learned from him that he could not have them weighed out in time, and that moreover he had not the authority to ship anything; that, however, he would apply therefor to General Crook. To make things sure—my rations and all our forage being out this evening—we decided to push on, to-day, to Clifton. I therefore sent a telegram to General Crook informing him of my recent and of my impending movement, and returned at once to camp. I gave the men time to cook and eat dinner, and then the command to saddle up. At 1:20, my detachment was in motion, proceeding down the river with a march before us of thirty-three miles. The glaring, dusty, alkali road soon confirmed me in my unfavorable preconceptions of the Gila basin. We passed a number of cattle ranches, the houses of which were, on an average, about four or five miles apart. They showed no cultivation or other sign of human life, except about the houses, where, beside the indispensable corral, were usually to be seen, enveloped in quivering, colorless, unconsuming flames—a well, a chicken coop, and a horse shed. There were no trees except immediately along the river, and there was no grass. It is thought that many cattle will be lost along the Gila, if there is not a rain soon. What grass there is on the mesas, or table lands, is burned to a crisp; it is too dry altogether for hay. The population is largely Mexican of the commonest sort, the sort that sits on a mud floor in preference to sitting on a chair, and is used to the companionship of pigs and chickens.

Having followed the river about fifteen miles, I had to choose between two routes—the one continuing several miles farther along the Gila, the other taking directly across the mesas to the San Francisco. Being told that the latter was a plain road, I decided upon taking it, as probably the shorter and firmer. After traveling it for about two hours, I halted, at dark, for Lieutenant

Reade to overtake me. Having mules to pack, he was not ready to start when I was, and has been following me about a mile in rear. Lighted on our way by a heaven full of stars, we continued our march together; every now and then going down a steep hill into a gully, and up again on the mesa beyond. Finally, from the top of the divide, as it is called, we wound our way down a long, gradual slope into the valley of the San Francisco River, entering it under the archway, as it were, of the railroad trestle-bridge, which structure we had at first taken to be an aqueduct, or some such work connected with the mines. Fording the river where we entered the valley, we proceeded about a mile up stream, and found ourselves confronted with the lights of a town. Fording it again, I halted the column and went forward with Lieutenant Reade—crossing the river for the third time—to the upper end of the town, inquiring after Lieutenant Maus. Having found him, and been recommended to go into camp about where we found him, I had the column move up through the lighted street, and form line and unsaddle in the space—about fifty yards across—between the street and the river. While coming into the town, I had noticed a peculiar intermittent light on it, which I thought might come from an electric light; now I saw that it came from a smelting work across the river. It was produced by the fresh slag; the pigs—that is, I believe, what they call them—breaking open as they rolled down the side of the dump, exposing the incandescent mass inside. Having seen to the feeding and grooming of my horses, I started out with Lieutenant Reade in search of a dinner. We wandered down the street to near the end of the town, and entered the largest and brightest-lighted of the many resorts that we passed—a typical mining-town amusement hall. From a sort of large box I looked over a breast-high, counter-like partition into the main room upon a crowd of men and women of various ages and nationalities. At the middle of the side opposite the entrance was the bar. At the farthest end, from which came the sounds of lively music on the violin and other instruments, I could see figures bobbing and whirling through square and round dances.

About the middle of the room was a mixture of Mexicans and Americans, sprinkled with Germans, English, Irish and other nationalities. They were gathered, principally, about the fore-mentioned bar, with its two tenders behind it, one of whom appeared to be Mexican and the other American. Some of these people were playing at the billiard-tables, others were seated in the room opposite the bar, or standing about the floor engaged

THE MINING TOWN AMUSEMENT HALL

in more or less excited conversation. The women, coming up in their promenades between the dances for a change of scene and air—sometimes for refreshment at the bar—were fewer here than at the farther end of the room. As seated at one of the restaurant tables, I took in the animated scene, I questioned to myself the propriety of my being where I was, especially of my being seen there in uniform. Before I had answered this questioning to my entire satisfaction, a couple of well-dressed gentlemen came into our little room, and as they sat down at the table next to ours, one of them was designated to me as the Governor of the Territory. I had no further concern as to the propriety of my situation. Having eaten a good supper, I repaired, rather tired, to my saddle and blankets for the night.

CLIFTON, October 4.—Slept badly, on account of the cold. About five o'clock I was up, walking to get warm. I crossed the river, walked up the cañon past the smelting works, and then up the hill back of them. At the top of this rocky prominence was a wooden cross about six feet high, fixed in a pile of stone, and on the side of the town coated with tin, which gave it from below the appearance of being of metal. It is a common custom of Mexicans to make such symbolical invocation of divine favor upon their town or settlement. From near this cross, which I dared not quite go up to on account of its closeness to the precipitous edge of the cliff, I obtained a good view of the town and stream. In the rocky enclosure, from 100 to 200 feet high, I perceived the origin of the name *Clifton*.[15] The river, the San Francisco, is probably named after the saint on whose day it was christened, or discovered. Between the never-failing stream of saintly name, separating it from the wicked town in its front, and the spire-borne symbol of the Church, sparkling at its back, the bustling, fiery smelter suggested a busy purgatory devoted to the especial interests of Clifton.

Drew rations to-day to include the seventh, on which day I calculated being back at Grant. My plan is to make Sheldon (ten miles this side of Duncan) to-morrow; Solomonville next day, and Grant next. It is pretty close calculation; but I must calculate closely in order to avoid unnecessary *impedimenta*. After drawing rations, I went to the telegraph office for news. Learned that from latest information General Crook concludes that the Indians have returned to Sonora. Telegraphed to my wife that I would be back on the 7th.

After lunch Lieutenant Reade and myself went over the smelting works, ciceroned by Mr. C——, the assayer of the company. He took us to the top, where the ore comes in, shoved in hand-cars from the mines, and showed us the bins in which the different kinds and the different slag materials are kept; he then showed us the crushers, and the weighing and assaying arrangements; then the furnaces; and finally, the pigs of copper in the freight cars ready for transportation. The principal ores worked are the carbonates, oxides, sulphides and silicates. The three or four mines about twelve miles from Clifton that furnish the ore, employ about five hundred men; the smelting works, about one hundred. This labor is mostly Mexican. The pig produced brings nine cents a pound, the copper of Lake Superior bringing a little more. The Clifton pigs, which comprise 98 per cent. of copper, one of silver, and one of lead and other impurities, are shipped mostly to New York and there refined.

By way of giving my men employment, and satisfying myself as to their readiness for action, I had an evening inspection. I found the arms and clothing generally in good condition. One man, however, had lost his blouse. Having no horse-shoes or shoeing tools, I am more concerned about my horses than I am about my men. Fortunately, I have a zealous and capable farrier, who borrows the means of rough-shoeing wherever he can, and who, if pushed to it, will nail a shoe on with a stone. After inspection, I went with Reade to a stag dinner, to which we were invited by some of our newly-made acquaintances of Clifton, who run their own mess. Their Chinese cook gave us an excellent dinner, in which quail and duck constituted, together, the *piecé de résistance.*

CLIFTON, October 5.—Immediately upon my appearance at stables, this morning, my corporal informed me that seven loaves of bread, cooked for the men, had been stolen from near the cook-fire during the night, also that suspicion pointed to Curley Young, one of the cooks. Fitzgerald, the other cook, says he called to Young as he was walking away from the cook-fire, asking him where he was going, and received no answer; that half an hour before that, the loaves had been counted and found all present, and that an hour after his being called to, they were again counted, and the seven loaves missed. I relieved Young from duty as cook, and decided to take no steps against him until I had him in the post—first, because I did not know that the charge was well founded; secondly, because an arbitrary punishment of mine might be more than allowed for in the subsequent sentence of a court-martial, and thus his proper punishment be prevented; and thirdly, because a prisoner would be a trouble both to myself and to my men, requiring the detailing of at least one additional man for guard.

I would forever avoid involving innocent people in the suffering or discomfort incurred by the guilty. In the army, such injustice is too common. If something goes wrong, it is not thought sufficient to rectify the matter and reprimand or punish the offender, making an example of him; somebody must be burdened with the responsibility of preventing its recurrence, and the thing must thenceforth be done in a different way, a way entailing, perhaps, twice the amount of labor with which it was formerly done.

At about half-past eight, Lieutenant Reade and myself were on the march for Sheldon, where forage was to be sent us by rail. From the top of the divide we took a different route from the one by which we had approached the San Francisco, keeping close to the Gila. We had made about half a day's march when two men on ponies came galloping up to us, and reported that Indian fires had been seen about twelve miles from Clifton, in the mountains about the Medcalf mines, and that Lieutenant Maus had told them that they had better notify us. Asking them if any trails had been seen, I was told that the people at the mines were afraid to go out to look for them. From personal acquaintance with the couriers, I was satisfied that they were acting in good faith, and from their mission being suggested by Lieutenant Maus, that there was some good ground for it. At the same time, I doubted whether the fires were anything more than signals made by runners from the reservation, on the lookout for friends returning from Mexico, and whether, therefore, our return to Clifton would lead to any pursuit. Reflecting, on the other hand, that in war there is nothing so certain as the uncertain, I thought that things might be worse than represented. I imagined Lieutenant Reade sustaining a bloody and losing contest against superior numbers of Apaches, and I moving directly away from him. I thought of what would be said by the *Clifton Clarion,* the *Tombstone Epitaph,* the *Arizona Daily Star,* and other such censors of the army; also of the possible misconstruction of my action by my military superiors and brother officers, and of the length of time that might elapse before I should redeem myself, if, indeed, I should ever be able to do so. All this determined me to retrace my steps at once; and accordingly, at about half-past two this afternoon, I was making a second entry into Clifton. Learning here, as I had apprehended doing, that there were no trails visible, and probably none discoverable, also that the route to the place where they were reported was a difficult one, I let Lieutenant Reade, with his better equipped command, take charge of the whole investigation and operation; and, repairing with my own command to my camping-ground of the night before, I went into camp. Lieutenant Reade set out at once for the mines. Talking this evening with some of the citizens, I was told that the reported camp fires were probably a fabrication or imagination. One of them related to me how when he was a soldier in a northern department, the command dug its way through snow six feet deep to get to a ranch where Indians were reported, and found, upon reaching it, that no Indian had been near it, and that the report had been started merely to draw troops to whom to sell a stock of provisions. On account of the deep snow, the command had to remain at this place about three months.

SHELDON, October 6.—Before starting, I telegraphed to General Crook that I should proceed to-day to Sheldon, *en route* for Grant, and to the commanding officer at Grant that I should be back on the evening of the eighth. I set a man on foot for making his horse's back sore, and another for answering a non-commissioned officer disrespectfully. Marched by the road over the mesas, which I prefer to the one along the river.

Went into camp at about three o'clock, at Sheldon, twenty-five miles from Clifton. The place is marked by nothing but a stage-stand. A man lives in it who attends to what is to be done for the railroad company which consists principally, I suppose, in stopping the train for people who want to get on, and taking care, as he did of our forage, of anything thrown off. He was, years ago, connected in some way with the army, from which experience he evidently retains a kindly feeling towards soldiers. When I started to reprimand my men for taking some of his wood, he expostulated: "Now don't say anything to them about it. I know just how it is. I should have done the same thing myself." Referring to the growlers at Crook's methods, he said: "If they had seen General Crook as I've seen him, roughing it over this country in canvas clothes, as no soldier roughed it, they wouldn't have so much to say."[16]

Found to my disgust that the river is dry here, and was told that to water my stock I should have to go two miles below or four miles above, unless I should come upon a water hole before coming to the running stream. The river runs underground along here for a space of about six miles. I thought a little of not watering at all, it being but six miles to water on tomorrow's march. But that was represented to me as very uncertain, both in quality and in quantity; and beyond it were twenty-five miles without water. So about an hour before sundown, I had the men take their carbines, and mount their unsaddled horses, and putting myself at their head, I led them down the road in search of water. About a mile from camp, where we came to the river, I took along the dry bottom and, following it a quarter of a mile, found what I wanted in a hole under an overhanging bank. Going back to camp, I spared my horses some laboring through sand, by marching them on the railroad. Being ballasted up in the middle, even with the ties, it made good marching single file. The railroad affords the best pathway in the valley.

Immediately after dark I had a fire made on an elevation back of the camp, for the guidance of my two dismounted men. They came into camp about nine o'clock, having walked twenty miles on a hot and, in many places, heavy and dusty road.

SOLOMONVILLE,[17] October 7.—Broke camp at six o'clock, and started on an up-hill road toward the west. At eight o'clock we came upon Ash Spring, where we watered our horses in a hole fed from the spring. There were several head of cattle standing in it, as we approached, who made what seemed a spiteful stir and splash as they scampered out. The water being green-brown, from a mixture of mud and cow dung, the horses drank very little; some sniffed and tasted, and would not drink. I congratulated myself on not having camped here, as I had thought of doing. About half past ten we reached the top of the divide, and commenced going down into the San Simon Flat. Every now and then we caught a glimpse of our destination, but in its general features the scene before us never changed. The sky was unrelieved, as usual, by even a speck of cloud, and the low, stunted, shriveled-up vegetation was fixed and motionless, as if of stone or iron. Through the still hot air the thirsty horses descended the even slope at a good pace, as if impelled by instinct towards the water in the bottom.

About three o'clock we entered the town of Solomonville, so named from an influential Hebrew merchant who had an ear no doubt to the family name of *The Solomons of Solomonville*.

Mr. Solomon being a government forage agent, I went at once to his store, and having ordered hay and grain, went into camp near by. At the kind invitation of Mrs. Solomon, Mr. Solomon being away, I took supper with her and the members of her household.

FORT GRANT, October 8.—Was glad to get up at half-past four this morning and stand by a camp fire while the men were being roused. I was kept awake by the cold about half the night. Grooming being over, I ate a substantial breakfast—fried bacon and hot coffee—prepared from supplies in my saddle pocket, fried eggs from a purchase at the store, and flapjacks from the rations of my faithful servant. A shivering Mexican, who came up while I was waiting in a happy state of repletion for my men to finish their breakfast, accepted the remnant of my coffee, and entertained me with his experiences as a soldier in the Mexican army in the days of Maximilian. This man informed me, too, that the word *Gila* was a woman's name.[18] It must be the feminine of *Gill,* the Spanish for Giles. At half-past five my detachment was on march for Fort Grant. I started without watering, expecting to do so at the cienega about ten miles from camp. There being nobody to guide or direct me, I passed the watering-place before I knew it, and then had nine or ten miles to go to Gillespie's Ranch, the next water. About half way there we entered a dry, rocky, sandy and stony ravine leading up to it. We followed the numerous cow-paths as well as we could; they were often lost in the rocks and sand and brush. The three or four miles thus performed were the hardest of the whole trip. About five hundred yards from the head of the ravine, that is, from Gillespie's Ranch, we came upon water sufficient for the horses and men. Not knowing how near we were to the ranch, I halted here for an hour. I had the horses unsaddled and watered with caution, directing them to be drawn back when they raised their heads the first time. It was about noon, and they had not drank since the night before. At Gillespie's Ranch we got on the plain road to Grant. A few miles beyond it I took the wrong branch and went higher up the mountain than was necessary, which provoked me very much, as the day's march was a hard one enough at the best.

At Meek's Ranch, our last stopping-place, I saw a couple of army saddles, evidently in service on the ranch. In no other military department have I noticed so much army equipment among civilians as I have in this. It does not surprise me now to see a Springfield rifle or carbine anywhere. I am told that it is an officer's duty to take up army property such as clothing, arms, equipment and ammunition, wherever he sees it, no such property being ever legally disposed of to outsiders. I want to know to what extent force my be used in the performance of this duty, if it is a duty, before I engage in it. The seizing of arms is an especially delicate matter—I mean from a legal point of view—for the reason that they are sometimes regularly issued to civilians for use in self-defense. Several Springfield rifles have thus been loaned out from Fort Grant since the beginning of the campaign.

From Meek's Ranch we had an easy, down-hill march into the post, which was visible to us almost the whole way. As soon as the horses were fed and groomed, and the men marched to their barracks, Private Curley Young was confined in the guard-house by my order, on the charge brought against him at Clifton of stealing bread.

THE ARMY SUPPLY WAGON

VII

FORT GRANT, December 4, 1885.—Spent most of the day
making preparations to go out to the troop. When I came in
here, I expected to make a stay of about ten days, and have
stayed nearly three months, prosecuting twenty-four cases before
a General Court Martial, taking my regular turn as Officer of the
Day; and commanding the separate detachments of cavalry, the
fag-ends of troops in the field. It often seemed to me that I
should find camp life a pleasant, restful change.

CRITTENDEN, December 5, 1885.—Arrived here about 7
o'clock this evening, having left Fort Grant in an ambulance at 8
o'clock this cool and hazy morning. The Galiuro Mountains were
colored as I had never seen them before, a rich purplish pink. I
whiled away part of the journey to the railroad by practising myself driving a six-in-hand. The driver was an old acquaintance of
mine, Private Watkins of H troop. He was in Company B when
I first joined the regiment in that company, at Fort Duncan,
Texas in 1877, and served under me at Fort Stockton. I rode
from Willcox to Benson in the sleeper. There I had to change to
a wicker-seated coach on the New Mexico and Sonora railroad,
which does not run any sleepers. I made the acquaintance of a
Presbyterian minister, a graduate of Princeton College, who
is established at Benson. He was on his way from Willcox, where
he performed the funeral service yesterday over the boy who
was killed by Indians a few days ago, up the Sulphur Spring
Valley.

I put up at the hotel, procuring the one room on which its
title as hotel rests. This apartment, which surprised me by its

neatness, was simply but sufficiently furnished, containing a double bedstead, two chairs and a wash-stand.

MOWRY MINE, December 6, 1885.—After breakfast, I went over to see the captain of my troop, who, being on his way to the post, had some parting instructions to give me. Having taken leave of him on the train at seven o'clock, I had my escort, lately the captain's, water their animals, and saddle, and pack. A little before nine o'clock, I set out for the Mowry Mine. My roll of bedding was on the mule that my escort had brought with it from camp. My Gladstone bag I left behind to come by the buck-board that carries the mail. I arrived in camp at about one o'clock, and found it much improved. The men are now all in common tents, which are large enough for four men to sleep in comfortably. The captain has had two wall tents put up for the officers, one in front of the other, with a Sibley stove in the front one. The back tent is the bedroom, the front, the parlor and din-ing room. A Sibley stove consists of a hollow cone with an open-ing in the top connecting with the pipe, a door about half way down the side to put the fuel through, and a little opening at the bottom to admit the air. The draught is regulated by means of a stone or any other suitable object placed against this opening. To clean the ashes out, the stove is raised off the ground, pipe and all.

I accepted, this evening, an invitation tendered me by the In-dians to witness a dance.[19] After some waiting about the genial, crackling foot-light, the performance was commenced by the ap-pearance of an individual in a guise, which I undertake with dif-fidence to describe. His head was completely enveloped in a piece of blanket, fitting like a mask, and bandaged about his throat with a strip of red calico. Two beads about a quarter of an inch in diameter, stood out, evidently for eyes. There must have been holes in it to look through, but I could not see them. This head-gear was topped off by two vertical sticks, notched and carved, and ornamented with numerous little appendages, pre-sumably, bits of wood, which two horn-like protrusions were connected about a third of the way down by a cross-piece similar to the vertical pieces. The rest of this costume consisted of a slender fore and aft section of a breech cloth, a light sprinkling of flour and a cartridge belt.

In each hand, the performer held a stick or wand, and as he capered around the camp fire, would now and then strike an attitude as if going to fence with one stick or the other. At other times, he would take a few steps outward from the fire and, holding both wands up over his head, mumble a sort of incantation. Occasionally, he would retire to rest and to readjust his trappings.

These actions were regulated or accompanied by the music, if I may so call it, of a tom-tom formed by securing a piece of deer skin over the top of a tin pan. The implement by means of which the said music was evoked consisted of a twig bent at the end into a loop, as shown here. ————o The performance thus far was suggestive, not to say convincing of the superstitious nature of the Apache. One of the Indian musicians I noticed was more sparsely attired even than the dancer, and as I shivered in my overcoat, I wondered whether he was doing penance, or was as insensible to the cold as he appeared to be.

Presently the dancer was joined by one or two others. How long the performance was continued by these three I do not know, but it long outlasted my interest in it. I should not have waited as I did for its termination but for the calls I heard from the attendance, for the performers to bring out their guns, from which I inferred that something new and interesting was to come. These calls were answered by the Indian who seemed to be chief musician, with the vaguely implied promise, "By and by." At length, after a retirement to the green-room, they came before the impatient spectators with their "Long Toms,"[20] and gave them a war-dance. Two of the performers were all but naked, and the other had on a knit undershirt. The dusky face of each was whitened on one side with flour from the ear to the ridge of the nose. They circled around the fire with a high step, swaying the body from side to side, these combined calisthenics evincing an admirable suppleness and elasticity. They kept together in single file, holding their pieces in both hands in a position like our "ready," the muzzles pointing now outward from the fire, now inward towards it. After going around once or twice, a couple, or all three of them, would get down on one knee and fire, those behind pointing over the shoulders of those in front; they would then rise and resume their peculiar *pas gymnastique,* looking, as before, now to the right, now to the left, and shifting their guns accordingly. Every now and then, after firing, which was done only by representation, some of them would utter a broken whoop, effected by rapidly clapping the hand two or three times while emitting a whoop—which action I took to signify that one of the enemy had fallen.

MOWRY MINE, December 7, 1885.—I inspected the whole command this morning with the exception of four men, who are at Fort Huachuca, two of them procuring a supply of horse and mule shoes for the command, and two sick in the post hospital. I found a shortage of canteens, also of spurs and surcingles, and other pieces of horse equipment. These articles have been lost, partly through neglect, and partly through the cardinal vice of the negro, stealing. We should have a more honest and generally better class of colored men in the army if our colored regiments were recruited exclusively by officers of those regiments; for, as compared to the general run of officers they are better judges of colored people. How often does one hear a person say that to him or to her all negroes are alike. Under that condition of mind, an officer recruiting for a colored regiment takes anybody with kinky hair.

MOWRY MINE, December 8.—This morning I gave the troop a field exercise, a sort of maneuver drill, in which I used the horses to transfer the men rapidly to where I assumed I might take the enemy by surprise, or at a disadvantage. I mean to have this exercise three times a week, with the object of accustoming the non-commissioned officers to command and the men to intelligent and energetic subordination. I allow myself to make certain departures from the drill regulations, which I deem to be in the direction of improvement. To fight on foot, I give the command, "To fight on foot—dismount." At the first command the men prepare to dismount. This movement I endeavor to execute always from column or line of columns. As soon as the men have alighted they give their reins to No. 3, and form in line. Line being formed, I give the command: "No. 1 as skirmishers—march." No. 2 and 4 I use as reinforcements and reserves. A non-commissioned officer as chief of horses, sees that the horses of each platoon are kept in rear of their platoon, and at the proper distance from it. He is instructed to avoid wheeling by fours, but to maneuver in column, or line of columns.

MOWRY MINE, December 10.—I have two enlisted men in camp, whose terms of enlistment expired several days ago. They are working with the aid of other men of the troop, on one of the old Mowry buildings, fixing it up for a rum-shop, which they mean to run in partnership. It would give me great satisfaction to move camp about the time they are ready for business, or to provide against the payments coming here.

My five Indian scouts have also served out their time, and have asked me more than once whether "Indians no go home." These Apaches have strong domestic instincts. Even those scouts that were across the line had to be called in at the end of their six month's term of enlistment and discharged, and conducted to their reservations before they would re-enlist, and many of them did not re-enlist.

I had a call this afternoon from Colonel Green, whom I first met at Lochiel, last summer. I kept him to dinner. He told me that Captain Mowry, whom the colonel knew well, had indeed a line of military supplies running from Guaymas through this estate over El Paso, Texas, to the Confederates in that State, and that the officer who arrested him here was the captain's roommate at West Point. He had destroyed Fort Crittenden to prevent its being turned to account by the Confederates. After our civil war, Colonel Green commanded in Mexico what was known as the Legion of Honor, a regiment composed of ex-officers and soldiers of both the Union and Confederate army.

MOWRY MINE, December 11, 1885.—Doctor Terrill came into camp this afternoon from Captain Hatfield's camp in the Huachuca Mountains. I shall have a sick call in the morning. About sundown my two men came back from Fort Huachuca with the horse and mule shoes that I sent for. I have determined upon a detail of twenty-eight enlisted men out of the forty that I have in camp to take with me in case I have to go on the war path. These twenty-eight troopers, with the five Indians, the civilian packer and myself, will make a force of thirty-five men. I have selected four extra horses to "lead." These, with the mounted horses and six mules (five to pack and one to be ridden by the packer), will make a total of forty-four head of stock. On my five pack mules I purpose taking ten days' rations. Estimating the ration at three pounds, my rations for one day will weigh 35x3 or 105 pounds. Ten days' rations will weigh 1050 pounds, which will make 1050÷5, or 210 pounds to a mule, a light load.

MOWRY MINE, December 12, 1885.—I find that the men have not 100 rounds of ammunition apiece, and that the Indians are nearly out. I have written to Fort Huachuca for a supply. When I go after Chiricahuas I want to have at least 150 rounds per man. I find too, that the men have no pistols, and of course they have no sabres.

These arms are boxed up or stowed away in the ordnance room in the post; they might better be in the arsenal from which they were issued.

I see from recent orders that now, when our troops are not even taught the use of their arms, they are to be taught the waving of a signal torch and flag and disk, and what not, and monthly reports of this *wig-wag,* as the drill was called at West Point, are to be furnished the Chief Signal officer of the army, which means more scribbling for the lieutenants.

MOWRY MINE, December 14, 1885.—Received a load of hay from Mr. Sydow, the contractor. It is pretty poor stuff, but better than none, and the horses have had none since my return. Mr. Sydow informed me that there is to be a celebration of Christmas at Lahoria, Lochiel, a tree and a baile, and invited me to attend. I told him that I could not leave the camp, while the only officer in it, and that when the captain returned, if he should return before Christmas, I might have to go back to the post. I should like to spend the remainder of the campaign in the command of this troop, but there is little likelihood of that, as the captain wants to get back to it as soon as he has concluded his paper work in the post. It would suit me still better to command a troop of my own, or one that I had the assurance of retaining command of for an indefinite time. One cannot do oneself justice in a temporary command, owing to the difficulty of satisfying both oneself and the absent commander.

A detachment arrived from Mescal Spring, bringing me five Indians to relieve those I have. There are four Tontos and one Mojave. Every Indian on the reservation has, beside his name, a designation by letter and number which he bears on a brass tag,[21] attached usually to his belt. My new Indians, for instance, are designated as A, 13; C, 6; C, 10; F, 22; and D, 3. The first is a corporal, and his American name is Charlie; he is called Corporal Charlie, F, 22, is known among Americans as Tonto Jim. I had these Indians and the old ones in my tent yesterday evening, and transferred to the former the arms and accoutrements of the latter. Each one received a Springfield rifle, a cartridge belt, a canteen, a tin cup, and eight cartridges; in addition the corporal received for the detachment, a frying pan, a mess pan, a camp-kettle, and one shelter tent. The detachment brought two shelter tents with them. They were disgusted with the small number of cartridges given them. They want ammunition to hunt with, being dependent upon fresh meat for their healthy sustenance, and besides they have a feeling of insecurity when their cartridge belts are depleted, not only when they are out of camp, as, for instance, when hunting or on the lookout, but even when in camp. They cannot tell when a party of Chiricahuas may spring upon them. But being short of ammunition myself, I could not give them more. They would shoot it all away hunting, and I must be able to fill their belts for them if I put them on a trail.

The corporal prevailed upon me to try to get two common tents for his detachment from Fort Huachuca. I have made out a requisition, but doubt whether I shall get them. They would probably have been sent out for the Indians that have been here, if there had been any available or procurable for that purpose.

After issuing them their arms, ammunition, accoutrements and camp equippage, I proceeded to take down the wants of my Indians in the way of clothing, which struck me as rather capricious. Some wanted a hat, and some did not; the same was the case with boots. Those who took the latter all wanted the high Leavenworth boot. Every one took a pair of gauntlets and two pairs of woolen socks. In order to get at the sizes they needed, I had to let them try on my own boots and hat and gauntlets. Of the four pairs of boots wanted, two were eights and two sixes. One Indian amused us very much in his first attempt to utilize a boot-jack. The heel of his booted foot being lightly inserted in the aperture, he pulled with both hands at his knee, while with the other he gently rested his toe upon the rear edge of the machine. He had two or three men holding him, and more making suggestions.

MOWRY MINE, December 17, 1885.—Every morning after breakfast I make a visit to a neighboring Mexican—Señor Saturnin Rios—a *vaquero* or cow-man, of Mr. Colin Cameron's. I usually find the family, consisting of the old man and wife, and two little children, at their breakfast; or the other members waiting for it while the mother prepares it. I partook this morning of their coffee and *frijoles,* or Mexican beans. This dish was enriched with an admixture of Mexican cheese, resembling Swiss cheese. Their bread is usually the Mexican *tortilla*, a pan-cake the size of a large plate, about an eighth of an inch thick, unleavened. With their coffee and *tortillas* they eat for breakfast a beef hash strongly flavored with Mexican red pepper (*Chili Colorado*). This is not so strong as another kind of pepper which, they tell me, grows wild in the interior of Mexico, where it is much prized as a remedy for stomachic affections. I could hardly repress a smile as the old man remarked, in commendation of it, "*Es muy bravo, muy diablo.*"

The house of my *vaquero* is an adobe of two rooms, with thatched roof and mud floor. In one room there are two rude beds, the posts of which are stakes driven into the ground. This is where the family sleeps. The other room, in which I usually find them, is their dining-room and kitchen; it serves also as a bed-room to a middle-aged Mexican—Señor Sebastian Villanneva—who seems to be a permanent boarder with the family, and to any wayfarer who may stop over-night. This morning two Americans had breakfasted and gone on their way before I arrived; the people of the house had postponed their own breakfast on account of them. While we were at the table the fore-mentioned middle-aged man emerged from a roll of bedding which I had observed lying on the floor—a patch of coarse black hair protruding from one end of it.

Mowry Mine, December 18, 1885.—After my visit to the Mexican's I took the little girl, Blasita, over to my tent and gave her a half a dozen apples. She is as bright and amusing a child as I have ever seen. In preparation for her visit to camp, she had on a clean red and white calico dress and a sun-bonnet, though the air was cool and the sky heavily overcast, threatening every moment to rain or snow. Her mother, also, was dressed in calico, and wore a clean white Turkish towel about her head, the ends of which were tied under her chin. I was touched by the little girl's telling me, in her rattle of childish confidences: "Yo me acuesto temprano, porque tengo frio" (*I go to bed early because I am cold*).

MOWRY MINE, December 20, 1885.—I ran out of grain yesterday morning, and have received none since. The horses whinnied and neighed pitifully for it both yesterday evening and this morning. I am also out of hay, having given my last feed last evening. A cavalryman's horse is so much a part of himself that he is depressed when its proper nourishment fails it. The men of this troop show more than ordinary interest in their horses. Without special instructions, they pick and brush out the tail and mane, and most of them have a piece of blanket, or cloth of some kind, with which, after exhausting the efficacy of the regulation curry-comb and brush, they rub the horse to give it a good gloss. The first sergeant allows them plenty of time for doing it, and I sometimes suspect, as he reports to me upon saluting, "Sir, the horses are groomed," that he is repressing a smile at my impatience. The horses are kept over night in the corral, in which they are groomed and fed. The guard sleeps inside of the corral, close to the gate, and a sentinel walks around it on the outside. Until a few days ago the grain had been kept in one of the little adobe houses about the camp, but since it was reported to me by the acting quartermaster-sergeant that a sack or two had been stolen, I have had it kept inside the corral. The hay, also, which, until recently had been stacked against the outside of the corral, where stray horses and cattle could munch at it, is now kept inside. The following is a plan of Camp Mowry:

The store[22] is that of ex-Sergeant Haddox and Private Hall, lately discharged. They keep liquors and cigars and a small stock of clothing—the equivalent of a small sutler store. I am rather glad of their enterprise. I believe I have convinced them that it is more to their interest to keep good whisky, even charging high for it, than to keep poor; and hope that their establishment will withhold the men from worse places. Their house is one of the old adobes of the Mowry, which they have rented for a dollar a month. The cook-house is a similar building. The Indians' tent is made of pieces of shelter tent, and is equal in capacity to about three such tents. It is almost surrounded by a sort of hurdle, constructed partly, I presume, to break the wind and partly to keep people from approaching without being seen or heard. Their fire is made within an enclosure formed of the ruined walls of an adobe. In the men's cook-house is but one serviceable room, of which the door is marked on the plan. In there the rations are sheltered and secured, and the head cook is comfortably quartered. The latter turns out and commences work at about four o'clock in the morning, being waked by the sentinel, whose post extends from around the corral to the packer's tent,

A DIFFERENCE OF OPINION

VIII

MOWRY MINE, ARIZONA, December 21, 1885.—Doctor Terrill arrived this afternoon from Captain Hatfield's camp, escorted by one private. I was especially glad to see him, as Blacksmith Giles had complained to me early in the day of a pain in the stomach, for which I had no remedy. Among the doctor's visitors at sick call, which was sounded a half an hour after his arrival, was Private B——, who had his head cut with a bottle, and his finger badly bitten by Private——, the waiter and domestic of the officers' mess. These men were at the store of Hall & Haddox, last night, after taps, and got into a quarrel and then into a fight over a game of cards. They are now both under charge of the guard. I thought seriously of sending them to Fort Huachuca for trial, but concluded afterwards that the offenses would hardly warrant it. They did not seem to think it a breach of discipline to be out of camp after taps, at which I was not surprised, as they were not taught to respect that call in the post. It appears from the investigation that I have made that they were playing what is called *Rush Ruben*. B—— played on P——'s hand, and put a bean down, which rolled into P——'s pile, whereupon P—— called B—— the worst of names, B—— retaliating in kind. P—— then took up a bottle that was serving as candlestick, and struck at B—— with it, but missed him. Both men then clinched and tussled. P—— got B——'s head in a barrel, and B——'s thumb in his mouth, but he could not make him holloa "Enough!" The two men being separated, P—— threw a bottle at his antagonist, but missed him, whereupon he threw another, which struck and dazed him. Thereupon B——

went out and lay for P—— by the side of the door with a pole; and P——, getting wind of it came out by a window, and creeping up behind B——, threw two bottles at him again, the second of which struck him in the head, inflicting the fore-mentioned wound. The doctor said that the man's thumb was bitten through to the bone. When he was brought over to the guard tent last night by the corporal of the guard, his head was bleeding badly, the blood running down over his shoulder. I had gotten up on hearing him asking to see me. I thought then I should have to send him into the post for surgical treatment. I was not a little surprised, therefore, to see him at stables this morning without a bandage or a plaster on his head, grooming with the rest of the men.

The Indians had a war dance this evening, very much like the one I have already described. The step was mincing as compared with that of the latter, and the dancers were in their ordinary dress. Every now and then the corporal, who was the principal performer, would stop short, and, standing on one leg, work the other convulsively up and down, suggesting Galvani's experiment with the frog; at the same time holding his gun up at his shoulder, taking aim. The musicians marked time with the tom-tom and their throats, their bodies bobbing in unison with it. I could not but wonder what their throats were lined with.

Such pastime as this furnishes our aborigines the excitement, and some of the intoxication, derived by their civilized guardians and custodians from balls and dinners and champagne suppers.

MOWRY MINE, December 23, 1885.—Brevet General Forsyth,[23] of the Fourth Cavalry, commanding this part of the Arizona line, arrived in camp this afternoon on a tour of inspection. He had with him Captain Hatfield, of the Fourth Cavalry, and Colonel Green, whom he probably picked up at the Washington Mine. After a short talk, during which we in turn performed our ablutions, I took the party around the Mowry estate, showing them first the new store. The stock-in-trade was sampled by Colonel Green and Captain Hatfield. After dinner, the general walked around the corral, looking at the stock, which he remarked was looking very well. I think the horses have improved in appearance, in consequence of the mounted drills. They have lost some flesh, but their coats are smoother and brighter.

Having seen active service during the war, and since, and traveled abroad, the general's conversation was most interesting and instructive. I remember especially two pieces of advice he gave me for active service. 1. Endeavor to put into practice each day what you have learned by experience the day before. 2. Always be a little ahead of time and of the enemy. "That," he said, "is a great point. If you are ordered to attack at four o'clock, attack at 3:59."

MOWRY MINE, December 25, 1885.—This being Christmas day, I had no drill, and no duty but the necessary guard and fatigue duty. The horses, not being put on herd, were watered at nine o'clock instead of eight, the usual hour. At ten o'clock began a series of physical contests among the men, which I had arranged and prepared with no little trouble. I told first sergeant, the day before yesterday, that I wanted to have something of the kind on Christmas day, in lieu of drill, and told him to have some five or six men come to me as a committee. No one came. I asked the sergeant about it the next day, and was told that the men were great growlers, that very few seemed to care anything about my scheme; that Private —— had seemed at first to take some interest in the matter, but finding himself detailed for guard on Christmas day, had seemed to lose it all. "Some of these men, sir," said the sergeant, "if they go in for anything of that kind, will expect to be excused from duty for a week afterwards." Finding out from him that Cropper and Hazard were still interested, I sent for them, and with their aid drew up a programme of exercises. I then told them to get what men they could as competitors, and to let me know how many they got. About one o'clock, having then a small number, they informed me that some of the men wanted to know, before entering, whether there would be prizes, and that others said that they had enough exercise drilling (they have one drill a day); they did not want any running and jumping. I told my committee to go ahead and make the necessary preparations, and gave the corporal of fatigue orders to assist them.

Yesterday evening I drew up the final programme, as follows:

	Prize
One-fourth of a mile run	$1.00
200 yard dash	1.00
One mile walk	1.00
Sraight running jump	1.00
Straight standing jump	.50
Hop, skip, and jump	.50
Running high jump	1.00
Three single jump	1.00
Tug-of-war	

The quarter of a mile run fell through; all the other contests, however, came off, many participating who had before shown no interest in them.

The athletics being put through, the next thing that claimed my attention was the roast pig for dinner. There being no one in camp who knew how to make a barbecue, I had got the packer, who had had some experience, he said, in cooking beef's heads, to undertake the cooking of my piece of pork. He had a hole dug in the ground about eighteen inches deep, and a layer of bright embers put in the bottom. On this he put a layer of gunny sacks, and on this the meat. He then covered the meat with gunny sacks and the sacks with embers and ashes and earth. This was accomplished about "taps" last night. At 1:15 to-day, when the cut was taken out by mean of cords passed under it—the operation suggesting the reversal of a burial—it was done to a turn, and exhaled a delicious aroma. A piece presented to me for dinner proved the most savory pork viand that I have ever tasted.

I was visited this afternoon by my Mexican neighbors, man, woman, and two children. I took them to see the pig unearthed and treated them in my tent to cigarettes and canned peaches. The latter were enjoyed especially by the children. The little boy having eaten all I gave him, which was more, I thought, than was good for him, helped his sister finish hers.

Like myself, these good people spent their Christmas eve at home. It was a more cheerless evening than the ordinary one to me, a howling wind flapping my loose canvas, and making my candles flicker, so that I could hardly read. The illumination of my tent consists of two stearine candles stuck through a hole in the top of an yeast powder can filled with sand to give it stability.

MOWRY MINE, December 26, 1885.—The Indians had another war dance last night with the usual accompaniment of song and tom-tom. They went around the camp-fire with their rifles as if on a trail, symbolizing now a rapid, now a slow and cautious advance, and now a retreat. I wish that my men had the predilection for the use of their arms that these Indians have. Fondness for a soldier's weapon and for military exercise is an excellent criterion of military spirit, which, applied to the Indians and the soldiers in this camp, is as favorable to the former as it is unfavorable to the latter. Our men hardly ever touch a gun unless they have to. They rarely even go hunting—sometimes not a man out for weeks and months. Rarely, on the other hand, does a week go by that there is not a party of Indians out.

Below is the schedule of calls established by the captain:

Reveille, sunrise; stables, immediately after; breakfast, 15 minutes after stables; water and fatigue, immediately after breakfast; drill call, Monday, Wednesday and Friday, 10 A.M.; recall from drill, 11 A.M.; recall from fatigue, 12 P.M.; dinner call, 12:30 P.M.; guard mounting, 3:45 P.M.; supper, 4 P.M.; tattoo (roll call), 8:30 P.M.; taps (lights out), 9 P.M.; Sunday morning inspection, 9 A.M.

The above drills are dismounted. I have interpolated a mounted drill on Tuesday, Thursday and Saturday. The horses are watered at nine o'clock. Upon coming in from drill they are allowed time to cool off, and then watered and put out on herd. It is my rule to have Sunday morning inspection mounted. Without any first sergeant's call, the first sergeant reports to me every morning after the troop comes back from water to receive such orders or instructions as I may have to give him for the day. I endeavor never to send for him, noting down for the occasion of his reporting to me anything that I have to communicate to him. I know from experience the annoyance of being repeatedly sent for.

As taps went off last night I noticed that it was very badly sounded, and upon inquiring the cause of it this morning of the trumpeter, I learned that he had allowed Corporal ——— to sound it for him, the corporal having repeatedly asked him, he said, to let him do it. In consequence of his amiability the trumpeter is now at hard labor under charge of the guard; as for the corporal, I only told him that I was disgusted with his want of self-respect as a non-commissioned officer, and that I supposed his having gotten a man into trouble—he whose duty it was to keep men out of trouble by keeping them from doing wrong—was sufficient punishment for him.

MOWRY MINE, December 27, 1885.—It has been raining off and on all day, beginning at about eleven o'clock. This is the first good rain I have seen here. After inspection I had the troop formed a short distance in front of my tent (every man present except the sentinel over the spring), and read the articles of war; or rather those that I think of special importance to enlisted men, namely, the 2d, 16th, 17th, 19th, to 28th incl., 30th to 40th incl., 42d to 48th incl., 50th, 51st, 55th to 58th incl., 60th, 62d, 64th, and 66th. My idea was to read only those that impose obligatious upon enlisted men, hence the omission of all those relating to courts-martial, to commissioned officers, and to civil employees. It was not two hours after I finished reading the articles of war that I had to put two privates under charge of the guard for violating them. Private ———, in charge of the prisoner, allowed himself to be relieved by Private B—— without the presence or the authority of the corporal of the guard or anybody else; and between them they allowed a horse to get out of the corral.

I am afraid we are not going to receive any more hay for some time, Mr. Sydow, the contractor, having lost his mowing machine. He sent it across the line to cut some hay, without paying duty, and it was confiscated by the Mexican custom officials. It is held as security for the payment of a fine, the amount of which is not yet determined.

MOWRY MINE, December 28, 1885.—Looking out of my tent, as I crawled from between my blankets this morning, I saw the ground covered with snow. It is the first I have seen in Arizona, that is to walk on. I have often seen it from Fort Grant, on the top of Graham Mountain. It has snowed off and on all day. I had to send out an extra strong detail to bring in wood, it having to be hauled as usual by the men in our escort wagon. Chopping and gathering wood, and pushing and pulling it is pretty hard work in a driving snow storm. I was amused this morning observing a party coming into camp with an immense log, which they were carrying after the manner of pall bearers, whistling and keeping time to Chopin's funeral march.

I had a long visit today from four of my Indians. I feel for the poor fellows, with nothing to sleep under but a long shelter tent. Two of them are barefooted. They asked when their boots were coming, but I could not tell them. It seems wrong that they should have to suffer as they do. While there may be some excuse for our inability to capture or kill the hostile Chiricahuas, owing to their peculiar advantages of training, instincts, knowledge of country, etc., I see none for our inability to keep our little force along the line properly supplied.

This is the second time in the three weeks that I have been in command here that we have been out of grain. We issued our last sack this morning, and we are not to have any more the rest of the month. My horses are in an open corral, exposed to driving snow; they cannot go out and graze, the grass being all under snow and ice.

The quartermaster at Fort Huachuca says in his last letter: "I can get no more grain until new contract goes into effect, January 1, so the chief quartermaster says. I have made an equal division among the troops."

MOWRY MINE, December 29, 1885.—For some reason or other, the buckboard driver, who usually brings us our mail, did not bring it yesterday; nor would he take our mail to Crittenden, having, he said, no place to put it in. I suppose it being cold and wet, he did not want the bother of taking and securing it. I wanted especially to send a letter by him over Crittenden to Fort Huachuca, ordering provisions for the officers' mess, which will be out on the first of January. I sent it this morning directly to the post by courier. I also sent a party to Crittenden to bring back the captain, if he is there, and wants to come. My horses made a sorry sight this morning, standing in the cold, wet wind, whinnying in vain for something to eat. I sent them out after breakfast to herd on the sunny side of a hill east of camp, where the snow is largely melted or driven off. I have taken the responsibility of requesting Mr. Sydow to furnish me, on receipt, with grain to last me till the end of the month.

The men have had no target practice since the 18th of last May, the day before the battalion set out from Fort Grant after the renegades from Fort Apache. It is thought imprudent, on account of the notice it might give to hostile parties of our whereabouts, to have target practice in the camps on the line. I think that the hostiles are more advantaged by the unskillfulness of our men consequent upon the neglect of this exercise, than they would be by any information they might gain through it. In the forty men now under my command, there are six who have not fired a shot at a target since they joined the troop, and one who went to target practice just once by mistake. So there are seven men who may be said to know nothing about shooting. And in the whole troop there is not one marksman, let alone sharpshooter.

The School of Application at Fort Leavenworth has not yet made itself generally felt through the line of the army. It is to be hoped that it will do so ere long, and, together with the projected cavalry school at Fort Riley, bring about the thorough instruction and discipline of our cavalry. It cannot do so, however, without a new system of drill regulations. A number of our officers have done what they could towards providing one, but the War Department has not seen fit to adopt any yet presented to it. The question of the instruction of our cavalry is an especially unsettled one; the relative merits of the sabre and the pistol, and of the carbine and the rifle, not being officially settled; and it being, moreover, a matter of mere conjecture whether our cavalry is going to have principally to do with Indians, mobs, or troops—regular, militia, or partisan. It should be qualified to meet any of these classes of enemies, through thorough training as cavalry proper, and as dragoons. In the five years of an enlistment, if not in less, a man worthy of being an American soldier would become an expert cavalryman in both capacities. The drill regulations necessary for such training can hardly be the work of one man. Cavalry officers should work together to produce jointly by contribution to their several specialties, the material for a complete system of drill regulations, one that shall fit the dismounted soldier for stealthily advancing in his own way upon an Indian village, or obediently springing forward and firing, and springing forward again, upon a line of troops; and the mounted soldier, for dashing in open order through the woods and thickets and over broken ground, rapidly to dismount and fire, and as rapidly remount and dart off, to dismount elsewhere; or to charge in serried ranks over open ground, with sabre or pistol in hand, up to and through the opposing formation. In order that the method of instruction to be employed shall have the unity of a system, the contributions for its composition must undergo a certain revision and rearrangement, and the whole be finally arranged by a single person. Being trained in such a system in time of peace, our regular cavalry would be ready in time of war to fight according to the method that should then appear to be the best, and to instruct our volunteer cavalry in it.

December 30, 1885.—We heard to-day from the mail-carrier that a party of troops crossed the railroad at Elgin Station, west of Huachuca Siding, yesterday evening in pursuit of Indians, heading for the Santa Ritas. We knew nothing as to the number or other particulars. The captain gave the driver one man as escort to Lochiel and back. Our Indians are ordered to keep a sharp lookout over the San Raphael Valley. As the buckboard passed our tent this evening on its return trip, we asked the driver and his one passenger into our tent and treated them to a drink of first-class mescal from a quart bottle presented to me by an American coming from Mexico. The driver strongly advised me to "take in" the *baile* to be given by the La Noria Goose Club to-morrow night, to which I am invited.

MOWRY MINE, December 31, 1885.—Having made up my mind to go to La Noria, I got Trumpeter Hayne to shave me shortly after breakfast, and a little before noon took a bath and had my boots blacked and fixed myself up generally. I had hardly finished my bath, however, when I was called to by Colonel Green and informed that Indian fires were seen last night from Washington camp on Washington Peak. The captain first thought of sending me alone with a small party to see what foundation there was to this report, but afterwards determined to go himself with a detachment, taking me with him. I did not yet give up all expectation of going to the ball. While the horses were coming in and the mules being packed, etc., we had lunch and discussed the probabilities of a chase. At about two o'clock we moved out of camp with twenty-one men and three Indian scouts. Arriving at the Washington camp, about four miles from the Mowry, without seeing any Indian signs, we interviewed some of the people whose statements had started Colonel Green for our camp. The man who had seen moccasin tracks and was prepared to show them to us was soon convinced that those tracks were made by our own scouts. One of the men who stated that he had seen the signals, described them to us as a succession of four bright lights, each being raised as if on a pole, once, and then lowered and put out. The very spot, between two bushes in a notch near the top of the peak where they appeared, was pointed out to us. We marched on up the mountain to within about a quarter of a mile of this spot and dismounted. Colonel Green, the captain, and myself proceeded thence on foot, taking three Indians with us and leaving the men behind. As we scrambled on our way, we looked closely and diligently for signs of a fire or of a moccasin, but saw not the slightest. Circumstances were most favorable, too, to our seeing them: the earth was almost covered with the snow of a few days ago, and where bare, it was soft from the melting of it.

As for myself, and I think it was the case with the captain, I was so little surprised at the result of our search that I was scarcely annoyed at it; and upon a full realization of the situation I proceeded calmly and hopefully to consider the practicability of my participating with the La Noria Goose Club in the celebration of New Year's eve. The captain thought of going on to the San Antonio Pass, with a view to reconnoitering from there in the morning, but soon gave up the idea. So, as we stopped at Washington camp on our way back to the Mowry, Colonel Green stepped into his house to put on his ball suit, and I meanwhile got my toilet case and light shoes out of my roll of bedding.

We then cut loose from the column and, accompanied by Private T——, set out on the road to La Noria. The weather was perfection for a brisk ride, just cool enough for overcoat and gloves, which both of us had.

As we trotted though the oak-grove covering of the Patagonia footslopes towards the open bottom of the San Raphael Valley, we feasted our souls upon the grandeur of the Huachuca Mountains, whose heights were extrinsically signalized by the still conspicuous remnants of their winter mantle. We could see the *peñasco* of Captain Hatfield's camp, and over in Sonora the soft-hued San José, San Lazaro, and Cananea (Caanan) Mountains.

We passed a party of Mexicans cutting hay for our camp with a hoe, picking out tall bunches without regard to kind or quality, getting, of course, the rankest and poorest.

Arriving at La Noria about sunset, we proceeded with our host, Mr. Sydow, whom we met at the entrance of the town, to his principal store. Here our orderly put up our horses in the corral, and we were led through the kitchen where supper was being prepared, into the bedroom, between the store and the kitchen. I was told that I was to sleep in the bedroom with Mr. Sydow, who offered me his bed, he having a cot for himself. While we were talking around the bedroom fire, he happened to think of one or two Mexican acquaintances across the line whom he had not invited, and immediately despatched a mounted messenger to them with an invitation. Supper being announced, we adjourned to the kitchen where some eight or ten of us, guests and regular messmates of Mr. Sydow, sat down to a spread of cold fresh pork, and canned stuff of various kinds, of which I partook with the avidity to be expected of me after the riding and climbing that I had done.

About an hour after supper, having shown T—— the corner of Mr. Sydow's bedroom where he was to make down his own bed, and furnished him with a stock of cigars with which to see the new year in, I adjourned with Colonel Green to the ball room. Finding nobody there but the fiddler and guitar player we walked through into the little room at the back, used as office and bedroom by Mr. James, the custom house officer, where we joined the circle of talkers around the stove. About nine o'clock the pattering of feet and starting up of music in the adjoining room announced the arrival of the Señoritas; and about two minutes after I was putting my best foot forward to the sound of a "valsa." The room in which we danced was not the one used at the *baile* I attended here last summer. It was, however, very much like it. Both of the long walls of this room had shelves all the way up to the top on which were stowed cans, boxes, kegs, and other such commodities, the room being used by Mr. Sydow as a store-room. The building, of which it forms a part, was at the time of my last visit here the property of his mercantile rival, who had since had to sell out.

There were not more than eight or ten lady guests, and I was assured that the entertainment this evening had fallen short of that given on Christmas eve; a distinctive feature of which was, in the language of my informant, that the girls would "talk back at ye." This occasion proved sufficiently enjoyable, however, to be protracted until three o'clock in the morning, at which hour we adjourned to Mr. Sydow's for supper. The company there discussed, along with more palpable matters, whether the dancing should be resumed. The question being decided in the affirmative, we were starting to go out of the door, when the musicians, whom, it seems, nobody had thought of in connection with supper, made their appearance and calmly but firmly objected to playing any more without something to eat. It being then a quarter of four, sober second thought, thus unexpectedly occasioned, determined us to revoke our former decision and retire in search of rest.

The ladies from Santa Cruz having no other place to go to, Mr. Sydow, of course, offered them his room. So having waked up T——, whom I found coiled up in his corner, and moved him into the front room, I went off with Colonel Green in search of other shelter, which we obtained under the hospitable roof of Judge Harrison.

DISMOUNTED TROOPER, TENTH CAVALRY

IX

LA NORIA, ARIZONA, January 1, 1886.—We left the Harrisons before the family was up, and breakfasted at Mr. Sydow's. There I learned from T—— that his horse escaped from the corral during the night, and that he did not know where it had gone. Throwing his blanket over Colonel's Green's horse, he started off without an overcoat in the wind and rain, to look for it. He was gone over an hour, during which time I was haunted with a presentiment of a debit account with the quartermaster. He came back without the horse, but with the gratifying information that he had tracked it some distance in the direction of camp, and had no doubt that it had gone back there.

Shortly after breakfast, having taken leave of my host and the Señoritas, I repaired with Colonel Green to Judge Harrison's to pay my respects—having told T—— to join us there with the horses when he had breakfasted and saddled up. We drank to a happy New Year from the judge's excellent mescal.

Having business at the Blue Nose Mine, about three miles beyond our camp, the judge set out on his way there with me. I had now an escort of two men, a man having been sent to me from camp with T——'s horse, which had come in there early in the morning. The weather was the worst that I have known in Arizona, rain and snow storming after us all the way. As I expected of so old a frontiersman, the judge soon became impatient at my gait, and wanted to take up a lope. After considerately accommodating himself to my walk and trot for the space of about two miles, he politely inquired of me: "Is this your traveling gait?" Said I: "Yes, sir." "Well," said he, "will you excuse me if I go ahead? I can't stand this. I have very little over me, and am getting wet." Of course I gracefully acquiesced, and he went ahead at a good canter, I keeping on a steady jog trot. Having proceeded thus about four miles, or come to within a mile or so from our camp, I descried, some 100 yards ahead of me, the figure of a man on horseback, which I soon recognized as the judge's, and in a moment I had overtaken him. He could not understand, he said, how I had caught up with him. The judge had alternated in his gait between a canter and a walk, stopping at one time altogether to let an especially severe spell in the storm blow over; I, on the other hand, had not varied from a trot, and had made no halt. What was more to the point, however, I was riding an American horse, and the judge a Spanish or Mexican. The more I see of the horses of this part of the country the more satisfied I am as to the superiority for cavalry of the American over the Mexican, Texas, Colorado, or California horse. While these horses have certain excellent points not possessed by the American, they are all inferior to it when it comes to working under a load of from 200 to 250 pounds.

MOWRY MINE, January 2, 1886.— The ground is covered with snow from three to four inches deep. The horses, which are out on herd, will not get much for their hard picking.

I pity our poorly clad Indian scouts. They, however, keep up their spirits wonderfully well. Their torn and worn moccasins being no protection to them, they keep their feet warm by exercise, tracking rabbits through the snow and running them down with whoops and yells. It is only, I suppose, by thoroughly exhausting themselves that they are enabled to sleep through these freezing cold nights with their scant covering. Most of them, having no trousers, wear nothing on their legs but a pair of drawers. Several of them go barefooted.

LOCHIEL, January 3, 1886.—Feeling inclined towards a change of scene and some exercise, I resolved after breakfast to ride down here and see if I could not by hook or crook get across the line as far as Santa Cruz. I found Mr. Sydow in his store. He had intended going to Harshaw, but put off his business there to take me on my pleasure trip. After a light lunch we set out in his one-horse shay, and in about a minute were in old Mexico. Mr. Sydow pointed out to me, as we crossed the line, a group of water holes constituting the head of the Santa Cruz river, which we followed pretty closely on the road. Two or three miles from the line we passed an old *jacal,* or Mexican hut, standing out on the point of a mesa, which up to two years ago, I was told, was the resort of horse thieves. A band used to come down from the Huachuca Mountains, steal both horses and cattle about La Noria, and carry them off into the Patagonia Mountains, where they would keep them concealed until ready to venture out to sell them.

The Santa Cruz bottom, or the arable part of the valley, averages about a mile in width and is kept fertile by water running under it as well as through it. The stream is lined with fine old willows, the yearly clippings of which are used in hedging in the fields. The principal crops are corn and barley. Extending back to the Cananea Mountains on one side and to the Santa Ritas on the other are stony and rocky mesas and inclines, which are given over to ranging horses, burros and cattle. There was not as much snow, of course, in this valley as there is on the top of the Patagonias, but the air was not by any means balmy, and the Mexicans that we passed going northward on their scrubby ponies, held their *serapes* closely about them, covering their mouths for the protection of their throats. One of them was conveying a load of corn and *frijoles* on a burro, evidently intent upon smuggling.

Having made eight miles from La Noria we arrived at the Pueblo of Santa Cruz, which I had known thus far only by name and through its fair and its gallant representatives at *bailes.* It was about what I expected to find, a loose assemblage of mud houses that looked at a short distance as if they might have been conjured up, ready made, from the ground on which they stood. It numbers about 800 inhabitants.

In company with one of the leading citizens we made a visit to the church, a new building of adobe, with stuccoed facade, without tower or steeple, but supporting, nevertheless, three bells. The auditorium has a capacity of about 150 people. A few rush mats lying about the floor were the only seats at hand, the congregation, as a rule, bringing their own seats with them, or squatting down on the bare brick. The lower class of Mexicans rarely use chairs—that is, to sit on. They commonly keep one or two in the house to stand on, or to offer to guests, and if they have a table they may use them to eat from when the floor is crowded or wet, or the company at the table especially attractive.

About the altar were three old paintings, presumably of Spanish execution, that would have well graced any church. A singular church ornamentation to me was that of two angular arches, one in rear of the other, each formed of a string of little flags or banners, suspended at the middle from the middle of the ceiling, and fastened at the ends near the bottom of the walls. The little flags were of blue material, swallow-tailed, and bordered white, and bore alternately the legend, in plain white letters, *Maria Reina, Maria Purissima.*

In the sacristy we were shown banners, symbols, and other paraphernalia pertaining originally to an out-door procession, but now forbidden by law from going outside of the church. Nowadays a Mexican priest is not allowed even to wear his canonicals in the street, nor is the church allowed to maintain or govern even a private school. Such is Mexican reaction against church domination.

Having "done" the church we walked over to the graveyard, or *campo santo,* a few hundred yards from it. Here within an area of about one acre are the remains of some 500 people, more than half of whom, I am told, killed by Apaches. The sacred space is destitute of inclosure, even to a boundary line; and with a few cases excepted, the graves themselves are unmarked save by the loose stone piled into and over them to keep out the coyotes. On one only did I see a name. It was rudely cut in a black wooden cross, and underneath it was a simple request to the reader for a paternoster.

Before leaving Santa Cruz we gave ourselves the pleasure of a visit at the Montoyas, one of its families, where we would gladly have remained longer than we did but for its growing late, and dark and cold. We were asked to put up our traps and stay over night, which we were not at leisure to do, and as we shook hands to go, we were welcomed to return with the typically courteous expression of Spanish hospitality: "Aqui tiene V. una casa a sus ordenes"—here is a house at your command.

FORT HUACHUCA,[24] January 6, 1886.—Wanting an opportunity to see Fort Huachuca, I asked the captain a few days ago if he could not give me something to do there, and have in consequence been furnished with the following order:

CAMP TROOP K, TENTH CAVALRY.

MOWRY MINE, A. T. January 5, 1886.

ORDERS NO. 1.

First Lieutenant John Bigelow, Jr., Tenth Cavalry, with a non-commissioned officer and three men, will proceed to-morrow, the 6th inst., to Fort Huachuca, A. T., for the purpose of drawing clothing, etc., for Troop K, Tenth Cavalry, and Indian scouts. On the completion of said duty, he will return with his detachment to the camp of Troop K, Tenth Cavalry, at the Mowry Mine, A. T.

THOMAS C. LEBO,
Captain Tenth Cavalry, commanding camp.

Furnished with this order and my detachment, in which was included one pack-mule, I set out this morning at half-past eight o'clock for the Huachuca Mountains. Having to go across country, I let a man who knew the way go ahead as guide. In from one to two hours we were out of the wooded foothills of the Patagonias, crossing the open valley separating them from the Huachucas, which we entered about twelve o'clock. We found the snow thicker and the air colder as we rounded their northern point above the heads of their foothills. Our route, about thirty miles long, lay for the greater part on the estate of Mr. Colin Cameron, a son of Simon Cameron, and nephew of Don Cameron. His claim covers a tract sixteen leagues, or more, square; his title being that of an old Spanish grant. We did not see a human dwelling or human being, or a water course or source until we reached the Huachuca Mountains, in which we passed two or three houses near small streams and springs, with tracts of cultivated ground surrounding or adjoining them. The soil had the appearance of being soft and rich.

Fort Huachuca lies in what is called Huachuca Cañon, on the east side of the north point of the Huachuca range. We entered the post at its upper, or higher end, and passed through the outskirts of tents, huts, shanties and houses—the quarters of a few privileged soldiers, of certain civil employees, and of laundresses and other hangers-on, or camp followers—past the guard house to the parade ground, where in accordance with custom, the officers' quarters were ranged on one side, and the men's on the other. Not finding the adjutant at his office, I repaired to the quarters of the post commander, Colonel Royall, of the Fourth Cavalry. Having reported to the colonel, by whom my detachment was referred to the sergeant-major for assignment to a troop for quarters and rations, I proceeded to the quarters of Brevet General Forsyth, commanding the troops in the field, and reported to him. The General, who had kindly asked me to come to his house whenever I should come to the post, made me his guest.

FORT HUACHUCA, January 7, 1886.—Spent the forenoon attending to business, and to the vanity of getting myself shaved and shorn. The afternoon I devoted to looking over the military works in the general's library, most of them French and German, which he procured when abroad. Such an opportunity for professional reading does not present itself often on the frontier. It might and it should, however, present itself in the house of every officer.

The Arizona papers have it again that General Miles is coming to relieve General Crook. The officers do not know whether to believe it or not. They are divided, too, in opinion as to whether

General Crook has done the best that could be done in the campaign, or the worst.[25]

FORT HUACHUCA, January 8, 1886.—Spent a few moments this morning in the post library, where I found a pretty good collection of papers—though not as good as at Fort Grant—but no books. The Fourth Cavalry, whose headquarters this is, has, I am told, a good regimental library, but it is boxed up. I saw no indications of impatience on the part of the garrison to get at it.

I was shown by General Forsyth through the quarters of Captain Lawton's troop of the Fourth Cavalry, the only troop at present in the post. It is altogether the best set of quarters, as regards both plan and appointments, that I have seen in the army, and in its neatness and orderliness reflects the highest credit on its captain. On the ground floor are the following accommodations: A good-sized office for the first sergeant, a set of bathrooms with hot and cold water, a capacious dining-room and a kitchen. Up-stairs is a main dormitory, and, adjoining it, a small one for the sergeants. The corporals live with their squads. I was struck by the brightness and airiness of the rooms, such a contrast to the dinginess and closeness of the barracks at Fort Grant. A room on the ground floor is to be fitted up as a troop library and reading room.

After dinner I strolled over to the captain's new stables. They consist of a frame building roofed over, with an opening running along each side of the ridge-piece for ventilation. The stables in Texas and Arizona are ordinarily mere sheds. In these that I am describing, at the head of each stall is a placard of tin, bearing the following *data:* the number of the horse, its name, the name of its rider, and the number of its rider. Underneath this placard is a roller of salt, a patent arrangement for the horse to lick. The saddles, covered with a piece of canvas, are suspended on wooded hooks at the rear of the stalls. In each stall is a little canvas contrivance for holding a curry-comb and brush.

Similar stables are building for the other troops of the post. Between every two sets is a corral, formed by fencing them together at the ends.

MOWRY MINE, January 9, 1886.—Returned here to-day, a day, earlier than I wanted to, on account of the threatening appearance of the weather. Found Dr. Terrill in camp on his official visit.

MOWRY MINE, January 10, 1886.—The doctor set out to-day with Colonel Green to visit Santa Cruz. Before they had reached the Washington Mine the colonel's buggy broke down, in consequence of which they surprised us by coming back on foot. They soon set out again, however, on horseback.

MOWRY MINE, January 11, 1886.—A drizzly day, promising well for the grass. I wonder whether General Crook, now that water may be found practically in every hole in the ground, is not going to modify his plan so far as guarding the water holes is concerned. I am in receipt of a copy of the following circular:

HEADQUARTERS DEPARTMENT OF ARIZONA IN THE FIELD.
FORT BOWIE A. T., December 24, 1885.
Circular:

Hereafter all officers in reporting trails or movements of hostile Indians, will report number, whether they are afoot or mounted, the direction they are taking, and if possible, of what the party is composed (men, women, children). In giving location, care should be taken to give distance and direction from some well-known point. It should be remembered that all these particulars are of the utmost importance.   By order of
BRIGADIER-GENERAL CROOK,
C. S. ROBERTS,
Captain Seventeeth Infantry, A.A. D.C.

I take this as an indication that results are looked for at an early day from the operations of the two companies of Indian scouts in Mexico. They have been endeavoring to work their way to the rear of the hostiles, who are supposed to be fronting the line, and drive them up against our cordon of troops. They have been gone now about six weeks, and are rationed only for two months. Such at least is my understanding. It is hard to get any authentic information in regard to the campaign, everything being purposely kept as secret as possible.

The doctor returned this evening, not over-pleased with his trip. Owing to the bad weather he did not see the one sight of Santa Cruz, the church and cemetery.

MOWRY MINE, January 12, 1886.—Had a longer talk than usual with my Mexican neighbors. Don Sebastian is a deserter from the Mexican army, in which he served at the time of the French expedition.

He tells me that there is in every State of Mexico a military force consisting of an eight company battalion of infantry, numbering 1,000 men, and a complement of cavalry and artillery,— the whole constituting a brigade, and being commanded by a Brigadier-General. Four such brigades constitute a division, the command of a Major-General. There is in Mexico no General of the army, the Major-Generals being commanded directly by the Secretary of War. The privates in the Mexican army are paid every day. The term of enlistment is five years, as with us, but with this difference, that a soldier is not sure of his discharge at the end of it; in fact, he is pretty sure that if sound and able-bodied he will not get it. Desertions, which from this cause, among others, are very common, are punished with only five months' confinement, and compulsion to serve out the term of enlistment. Non-commissioned officers are reduced to the ranks. Don Sebastian deserted as a sergeant after three years' service. Mr. Rios hardly believed my assertion that the standing army of Mexico was larger than that of the United States.

MOWRY MINE, January 13, 1886.—For the last few days I have had a presentiment that we should receive official news before long of the state of the campaign, and that a change would shortly be made to a more active plan, but the mail that came this morning brought nothing to confirm it.

MOWRY MINE, January 15, 1886.—The paymaster, who arrived this morning, tells us that a detachment of Indian scouts

THE CAVALRY PICKET

out with soldiers of Captain Viele's troops, killed two of the soldiers and made off, undoubtedly to join the hostiles.

In my morning conversazione [*sic*] I learned that the Mexicans have a way of hardening a horse's hoofs by an application of mescal plant, crushed and heated. Mr. Rios tells me that he once took a horse to a blacksmith which, on account of the hardness of its hoofs, could not be shod; the nails bent so they could not be driven through the horn.[26]

The captain is at the present moment shaving, and having the spots taken out of his blouse in preparation for the ball this evening at Harshaw. It devolves upon me, as the last attendant from this camp at such an entertainment, to remain here to guard against the possible disorderly consequences of to-day's payment.

MOWRY MINE, January 16, 1886.—From the representations made to me this morning by Mr. Rios in regard to the Yaqui Indians, in whose country he has been, I gather that the latter are about on a par, in point of civilization, with our most advanced Indians of Indian Territory. The cause of the impending war between them and the Mexican Government seems to be the proposed opening of their dominion to settlement. Here is something for those of our people to ponder upon who regard the reservation as a causative peculiarity of Indian savagedom, and propose to regenerate the Indians by the abolition of the reservations and their establishment in severalty. The land that the Indians are now on in their tribal relation is theirs as far as anything guaranteed to them by our Government can be. Suppose that they want to continue in tribal relation. Having for generations been fraudulently debarring them from civilization, are we now to commence fraudulently imposing it upon them?

The establishment of our Indians in severalty—in consonance, that is, with the policy of their preservation and civilization—is dependent upon their acquiring a desire for it; and their evolution or development up to the point of this desire, which is the true Indian problem, has never been even seriously contemplated by our Government. Our Indian policy has ever been, in the main, a systematic evasion of it. The settlement of the Indian question without the solution of this problem, means nothing more nor less than peaceful, or forcible extermination.

MOWRY MINE, January 20, 1886.—There has not been a day without rain or snow or hail since the 11th of this month, neither has there been a day that the sun has not shown itself some time or other. Southwesterly winds are here unfailing harbingers of bad weather, and such we have had off and on now for several weeks, and they are not yet passed. February is a very uncertain month; the Mexicans call it *"El mes loco,"* the crazy month.

I expect to be at Fort Grant to-morrow night. I shall miss the sound of Spanish, especially Blasita's cheery greeting, *"Como le va, Teniente?"* and her old father's courteous invitation, *"Pase; pase V., Teniente, sientese."* The Rioses have had a hard time lately with the weather, having been prevented from sleeping at night by the rain dripping through their roof. They now have a huge piece of hide suspended at an angle over the bed, forming a tolerably good shelter. The mud floor, however, except under the bed, is all mire and puddle. The two children seem none the worse for all this. The little boy, José Juan, is continually eating. I hardly ever see him that he has not a tin cup in his hand, and is not either consuming or soliciting a supply of *frijoles.* He has usually nothing on but a plain linen shirt of so fine a texture that the complexion of his tough little body is discernible through it, and reaching very little below where his trousers ought to commence. Surmising a connection between his semi-nudity and voracity, I suggested to his mother the advisability, as it seemed to me, of proceeding with his clothing below the line where she had left off, and she took the suggestion in such good part that I had the satisfaction this morning of seeing the little fellow in a pair of trousers, if I may so call the primitive canton flannel garment to which I allude. It is cut looser than should seem necessary for comfort, and as short as is consistent with distinct bifurcation.

The mail not bringing me my leave of absence, I determined at the suggestion of the captain to go to Crittenden, in order to be ready to take advantage of it by to-morrow morning's train, should it come this evening, or to wait over until to-morrow evening, should it not come to-day. Accordingly, after the men had dined I had my horse saddled, and having done up a few things in a roll to take with me, set out with two men and a pack mule for the railroad.

I had hardly gotten out of camp when one of my men asked permission to stop behind to put the two men's rations, which he was carrying in a bag in his hand, on the pack mule. If there is anything a colored soldier can be trusted, under all circumstances, to take good care of, it is his rations. I granted the request, and afterwards regretted doing so, for I did not see either of the men again until an hour after I had arrived at Crittenden. They represented to me that they could not keep the pack on the mule; that the rope being wet, they had to stop repeatedly to tighten it, etc. I was disgusted with what I deemed their want of zest and pride, and rebuked them for it—I think, with good effect. They might as well have been in camp for all the protection or other advantage they were to me.

FORT GRANT, January 21, 1886.—My authority for a leave having come yesterday, I partook at half-past five o'clock of the "first breakfast" at the hotel, and at about seven o'clock boarded a train and settled down with my Spanish grammar and my papers and periodicals to their enjoyment from a spring-cushioned seat. At Benson, the junction with the Southern Pacific Railroad, I lunched at a Chinaman's at the small cost of twenty-five cents, and I think I know what I ate.

It brought me back to civilization to find myself, as I did at one o'clock, seated in a sleeping car opposite a young man in a close-fitting checked suit, carrying an extreme height of collar and sporting a varnished cane.

Stepping down on the platform at Willcox, at half-past two, I met Mr. M——, the father of the bride, on his way from Fort Davis, Tex., to attend the wedding at Fort Grant. There being no ambulance at the station we got into the stage, a very different conveyance from what the average eastern man would imagine. It was a rickety carryall, with the front seat taken out. Owing, I presume to this deficiency, the forward side-curtains reached only to within a foot and a half of the woodwork, leaving an aperture through which the cold air seemed to compress itself for concentration upon us. Fortunately we each had a blanket, but with two thicknesses of blanket over my legs, and my over-coat and cape about my body, I was not warm. There was no straw or rug in the bottom of the wagon; nothing to oppose the streams of air coming up through the half-inch cracks between the half-inch planks, or, on the other hand, to prevent our watching the congealing ground as it sped away beneath us. At half-past eight we drove up in a happy state of mind, though in a sad state of body, in front of the post-trader's store, where the mail was delivered, and I commenced shaking hands. Thence we rattled over to the officers' line. The stage had hardly stopped in front of my gate,—just inside of which I recognized the form of the most important personage to me in Fort Grant,—when I heard in a voice that I knew to pertain to it: "Is that you, John?" to which inquiry I answered not in words.

10th Cavalry Types

X

FORT CRITTENDEN, ARIZONA,
January 29, 1886.—The post has
been shocked by the news of the killing of Captain Crawford. In the
train this afternoon I was asked by
a number of persons manifestly affected by it, whether it was reliable,
and how the calamity occurred. I
could only say that the news was official and comprised no particulars.[27]

A miner from the Sierra Azul in
Mexico, with whom I had conversation, remarked, with reference to
the cause being accidental: "Them
Mexicans have no use for us except
to beat us out of all they can. What
them fellows wanted was to get our
camp outfit, that's the idea." This
man, when the Chiricahuas broke
out was with his family and three or
four Mexicans on his mine, and had
just got well started—getting out
carbonate of silver going $100 a
ton—when the Indians commenced

--◦◦{ 125 }◦◦--

killing Mexicans around him. Seeing a party one day passing near his camp, he thought it time to take his young wife and child and go away. He accordingly moved to Tombstone, where he has been ever since. "I had nothing to do there," he said, "and spent lots of money, and a man gets mighty worthless doing nothing; so I made up my mind I'd take my little lady and babe and go back to the mine, Indians or no Indians; and now if they come, I'll give them the best I've got, that's all." I could not but turn as he spoke, and take a look of reverent interest at the "little lady and babe," a seat or two ahead of us on the other side of the car.

MOWRY MINE, January 30, 1886.—Spent the night at the Crittenden section house, where I breakfasted with the early risers at half-past five. At half-past eight I set out on foot with Mr. Manning, the Justice of the Peace, to look at certain ancient remains or relics about a half-mile from the station. Crossing the Sonoita bottom and ascending a low plateau about 1,000 yards long and 100 wide, I found myself among bits of pottery and earthenware, some of them colored in bright stripes. Following the mesa lengthways we came upon a caved-in well, a circular hollow with blackish bottom, covered with long rank grass, the Mexican *zacaton*. Beyond this were the remains of a wall or foundation inclosing an area of two acres or more, the site apparently of a combined fort and dwelling, a sort of castle. Inside of the inclosure was another old well. This part of the plateau was more thickly strewn with pottery than any other.

From here we went across a gully to the burying ground on an adjoining plateau. The top of the latter was artificially leveled and the sides were cut down a certain distance, vertically making a rectangle of it, and a step all around it; on each side was a terrace constructed by similar leveling and trimming. All the graves, however, were on the top. I felt very much like expending a few dollars in Mexican labor for the purpose of getting into and under some of these mounds, especially a big one in the center, which I presumed to be that of a chief; but I feared that I might spoil them for some expert or connoisseur who should examine them after me.

From the evidence of architecture in the village and of engineering on the burying-ground, I am satisfied that this settlement was one of wild Indians, such as the Apaches of the present day.

I should state that among the relics on the first plateau were numerous broken *metates,* worn very deep, indicating long usage. A *metate* is a rude stone mortar, still used by the Mexicans to grind and crush corn, chili, coffee, etc. The population must have been of those prehistoric Arizonians, if I may so call them, who attained to a state of semi-civilization and left their traces in the ruins of Casa Grande, Pueblo Viego, etc., and various cliff and cave dwellings. But who those people were—Aztec, Toltec, or ancestors of the Pueblo or Village Indians of the present day, such as the Zunis, Moquis, etc.—is yet to be determined. There can be no doubt that they lived in fear of some formidable enemy and it should seem that they sought security in a social and military organization not unlike that of the mediaeval Europeans— the rich and powerful establishing themselves in castles, the poor and weak coming under their protection as vassals.

On our walk we crossed a quarter section, 160 acres, of Government land that had been taken up by Mr. Manning, but which he forfeited by failing to comply with the legal requirement that he reside with his family upon the land for at least six months and cultivate a few acres of it. It has since been taken up by Mr. Richardson under the "Timber Culture" act. According to this law, a patent may be acquired for a quarter section or a smaller tract of ground by planting one-fourth of it with timber, protecting such timber, and keeping it in a healthy growing condition for a period of eight years, the trees not being more than twelve feet apart in any direction. Comparatively little advantage is taken of this law, most land being taken up under the pre-emption law, which leaves the settlers free to plant and cultivate as he chooses. The availing himself of it on the part of Mr. Richardson was due, I am told, to his having exhausted his right of pre-emption.

One would expect, in this dry country, to see more trees planted than there are, and it would seem a wise measure to increase their cultivation by still further legal action. Their present neglect is due to a variety of causes, foremost among which is the failure to appreciate the influence of timber upon climate and agriculture. Another is the hard utilitarianism of our frontier populations, the lack of aesthetic sense and consequent blindness and indifference to the improving effect of timber upon the landscape. Another is the unsettled feeling and changeful mode of life common among frontiersmen, and the consequent disregard of permanent improvements. A large proportion of the people of this section have come as the Chinese come—to make their fortunes, but not their homes. Those even who come to stay, or who subsequently decide to do so, are more or less disposed to roam, through an original propensity that brought them out, or through attractions to new enterprise.

Another cause is the uncertainty of the tenure and ownership of much of the best land, owing to Indian outbreaks and Spanish grants. The settlement of the latter would contribute greatly to the prevention and repression of the former. Many of the vast tracts now held under Spanish titles as pasture land would, doubtless, be opened thereby to settlers, and secured against Indian raids by a population of comparatively small proprietors.

I set out from Crittenden at half-past nine, and traveling slowly, arrived in camp at three o'clock. Tonto Jim was in our tent with the captain to receive us. He did not stay long, as I offered him nothing to smoke. These Indians are greater smokers of cigarettes than the Mexicans. Not smoking now myself, I have discontinued keeping tobacco, and I apprehend that my Indian friends will fall off from me. They used to come in and make long visits on my tobacco-box, and would often ask me for tobacco and cigarette papers, of which I kept an extra supply for them. They never say "thank you," or anything that seems like it. I do not think there is any such phrase in their language. I once gave to one who asked me for tobacco, an unopened half-pound package; all he did was to grunt and stow it away in his breast pocket, and turn to me for papers. Their begging and sponging goes on all the same, whether they have money or not. Often as I have been to their tents and camp fire, never has one offered me a cigarette, or a taste of coffee, or anything else.

MOWRY MINE, February 1, 1886.—Made a special visit to the Mexican family, the Rioses, to present them with a few toys and articles of clothing, that I brought out with me from Fort Grant. The old man has not yet had his roof fixed, but he has given notice to his employer that if it is not fixed for him he will leave. He is determined not to fix it himself because it was in the contract that his *patron* should furnish him with a house, and in its present condition, the structure that he is living in, he claims, is not a house. His monthly pay and emoluments consist of thirty dollars, and forty pounds of flour and fifty of fresh beef. In return for this he keeps the stock within a certain range from straying off the ranch.

The month is opening with beautiful weather, still and balmy, like the late spring in the north. Mrs. Rios tells me that this is an *año bueno,* that last year was an *año malo.* Leap year, or as the Mexicans call it, *año bisiesto* (bissextile year), is regarded by Mexicans as a bad year, bringing death and sickness and troubles of all kinds to both men and animals.

MOWRY MINE, February 2, 1886.—Hearing that there had been a great *find* made at the Blue Nose, and that the mine was looking better than it had been for many months, I walked to it, a distance of three miles, and went through it. There are two ways into it, one a vertical shaft and the other a horizonal tunnel. My guide took me first to the mouth of the shaft, over which a large bucket dangled from a half-inch wire cable, and skipping into position on the rim of it, with one end of the handle between his feet, called upon me to "get on." I did so, but with less alacrity than he, placing myself over the opposite end of the handle.

Both of us being "on," he gave a signal to the man at the engine, whereupon I felt as if suddenly disembarrassed of my feet and perceived that I was making a rapid and accelerating descent. With that lightning quickness of thought that is said to come to drowning people, I conjured up a series of dreadful liabilities. I imagined the bucket striking something and suddenly tipping up, tumbling us both into it or off it; our clutching it and hanging to it for dear life; our being severed from it by a projecting beam or spike and held dangling while it sped on without us. Noticing that my guide, holding out one hand, gave the timbers an occasional tap that sent us out into the middle of the shaft, I loosened one hand and kept up an unsatisfactory attempt at shoving off at the right time from my side until passing through twilight and darkness, we sank into such utter blackness that I could distinguish nothing, not even my companion. Leaning forward, then, with a sway in my back, my both hands grappled to the cable, I dismissed the timbers and their perils from my mind and thought of the bottom. I wondered whether we should strike it at the rate at which we were traveling, and speculated as to its being water or rock; I even imagined its being a powerful spring-board. Suddenly, without having felt the slightest jar. I found myself at a standstill, and, looking about on the side of an approaching candle, perceived that our conveyance was on terra firma. Each of us taking a candle, we went to the end of a drift where two men were timbering up a *shoot,* an inclined passage through which to drop ore to a lower level. From here the ore is to be shoved to the shaft. Coming back to the shaft it was pointed out to me how the magnesian limestone was slaking and scaling off. Every morning an hour's work is done clearing the drift of the droppings. Returned safe and sound to the surface we proceeded to the tunnel, and, having followed it to the end, branched off through tortuous downward sloping passages to where the *find* was alleged to have been made. I had already learned that the latter had proven a very great disappointment, the ore not going, according to the assayers, over six dollars to the ton. It seems that the miners had mistaken *zincblende,* the resinous variety, for the waxy variety of *hornsilver.* I asked one at the mouth of the mine the name of a mineral that I brought out with me and was answered: "Them scientific cusses calls it *Rosa cobaltic,* we calls it *Rose Quartz.*" It was a variety of *Cobalt bloom,* the arsenate of cobalt. According to my guide this magnesian limestone is a poor rock to mine in, the veins rarely, if ever, being true fissure, and always running out as a small depth. The ore of the Blue Nose occurs principally in *pockets* or *kidneys.*

MOWRY MINE, February 2, 1886.—In the course of an after-dinner visit to Señor Rios, who lives here, I heard the sad story of the killing of her father's five brothers by Apaches. They were out with fifteen other men after cattle, and the whole party had sat down to lunch, when they were fired into, and all but one were killed. He alone had kept his horse saddled, and jumping on it, he got away with but a wound in his thigh. The *vecinos,* fellow villagers, came out at daybreak, and, putting the nineteen bodies in one wagon, conveyed them to the village. That afternoon—the graves having been laboriously prepared—the population, mournfully chanting and mutely sorrowing, accompanied the nineteen coffins to *Campo Santo,* each one borne on the shoulders of four men. The five brothers in their separate coffins were interred in one grave.

The tri-weekly drills (dismounted) which had been suspended on account of the bad weather, have been resumed, the First Sergeant commanding, as before. What a fine opportunity should present itself in a camp like this for instruction in fencing, signaling, estimating distances, etc. I have not seen a fencing-mask or glove in the army since I left West Point, and we did not see much of those implements there. If in the matter of fencing we are never to get beyond the slashing and thrusting at the air as laid down in Upton's drill book, let us spare the troops the carrying and polishing of a sabre, and put more of his time on whatever weapon is deemed his most effective one.

Assuming the sabre as done away with, the pistol is of doubtful advantage as a substitute for it. I am rather in favor of a long rifle, or longe-range carbine, for both mounted and dismounted firing, with a bayonet or attachable lance head for hand-to-hand work.

MOWRY MINE, February 3, 1886.—It is about time for the conference between General Crook and Geronimo. I doubt its resulting in the termination of hostilities, as I apprehend that Geronimo is not yet ready to make an unconditional surrender.

I see in the papers that there is a bill before Congress for the suppression of gambling in the army, and that a number of officers have written to its framer or backer, approving of it, and urging his pushing it through. I should not like to see it passed. It stands already enacted that: "Any officer who is convicted of conduct unbecoming an officer and a gentleman, shall be dismissed from the service" [61st Article of War], and that "All crimes not capital, and all disorders and neglects which officers and soldiers may be guilty of to the prejudice of good order and military discipline, though not mentioned in the foregoing articles of war, are to be taken cognizance of by a general or a regimental, garrison or field officer's courtmartial, according to the nature and degree of the offense, and punished at the discretion of such court" [62d Article of War]. These two enactments should answer every judicious purpose of the bill in question.

MOWRY MINE, February 6, 1886.—Private A—— is to be discharged for enlisting under false pretenses. Upon the expiration of his first enlistment, he was given what is called a *bobtail* discharge, a discharge without character; and he subsequently had one forged with the character "Good," and re-enlisted. When the battalion was at Lordsburg last summer, this man sold his carbine to a citizen, and pretended to have lost it through no neglect of his. The great difficulty, not to say impossibility, of preventing this sort of rascality, under our present system of discipline, is among the reasons of some of our officers for their disuse of the pistol in the field.

Three wagons arrived yesterday from Fort Huachuca with grain, and with provisions for the mess. This does not look like an early termination of the campaign. I am about equally likely, a week from to-day, to be at Fort Grant on the march towards the Sierra Madres, or here. If the campaign does not close with the impending meeting of Geronimo and General Crook, it will not do so for months, for the Indians will have decided to fight us or defy us to the bitter end.

MOWRY MINE, Sunday Morning, February 7, 1886.—Having just finished inspecting the troops, which leaves me free from duty until next Sunday, when I shall have the same fifteen minutes' occupation again. If those who are preparing themselves for a commission in the army appreciated the importance to an officer of intellectual preventives against idleness, ennui and dissipation, they would never begrudge the time spent in edifying studies unconnected with the military art.

The men of the troop, having spent or gambled away most of their pay, spend less time drinking and smoking in the two rum-shops near camp, and more basking in the sun, cracking jokes and playing tricks. While a colored soldier will stand more work and hardship without grumbling than a white one, he will exert himself less of his own accord. Gymnasiums, foot-balls, base-balls and bats, and such things, move him comparatively little.

MOWRY MINE, February 8, 1886.—The Mexicans are about as independent of doctors and apothecaries as the Apaches. They know the healing properties of a great variety of plants, and keep a stock of them on hand. Don Sebastian, the Mexican who lives with the Rioses, informed me to-day that he has a medicine that he does not think anybody else knows of, not even the Apaches, and telling me that it could be found in certain cañons of the Huachucas, brought it out and showed it to me. It is a black seed, somewhat larger than caraway. Two or three pinches of it, he says, is a dose. He told me that Mrs. Rios—and she corroborated his statement—was taken with a pain one night in her chest and shoulders, so violent that she could not turn over in her bed—she told me that had it lasted two minutes longer, it would have killed her—and that a dose of this *mochilita,* as he calls it, cured her instantly. He told of a tree or shrub in Mexico, called *cocolmeca,* of such virtue as an anti-rheumatic that carrying a cane of it is certain cure; adding, however, that a decoction is ordinarily taken along with the cane. Mrs. Rios brought out several of her vegetables specifics, *medicinas de las Viejas,* old women's medicines, as the Mexicans call them, done up in little bags and packages, and tied up in the corners of handkerchiefs, and discoursed on their nature and use to me. One of them was *tierra de encina,* earth of evergreen oak, which is taken out of the pith or from a hollow of that tree. How it forms there, whether in the process of growth or of decay, she did not know, but I presume in the latter. It is given for lung troubles. Among her other remedies were anise seed, peony and chamomile.

Old Mr. Rios informed me with pride that he had never taken an apothecary's drug in his life, and getting up from his chair, and raising himself to his full height of six feet or more, he beat his chest and slapped his arms, declaring himself sound and strong in every part.

Mr. Thompson, an American living in Harshaw, stopped at the Rioses this evening in a wagon in which he is tranporting his wife, a Mexican woman, who is thought to be fatally ill, to her home in Sonora. She is so weak that she can hardly speak, and her face and limbs are swollen from a cold, so the Mexicans say, contracted during a fever. I helped lift her out of the wagon in which she was lying on three thicknesses of mattress, and move her into the house, where she was placed on the only bed. I afterward had our cook take her over a can of peaches, the only nourishment she cares for.

No campaign news to-day, except a report communicated by the stage driver, that General Crook has gone down into Mexico to meet the Indians, coming up in a party of about forty (men, women and children), including Geronimo and other big chiefs.

MOWRY MINE, February 9, 1886.—Mrs. Thompson was better this morning. Mrs. Rios administered peony to her during the night, which alleviated a pain in her head, and gave her some sleep. At half-past nine, the party having breakfasted and the team being hitched up, I helped put the invalid back in the wagon, and then watched it start jolting up the stony road, over the divide. Mr. Rios rode ahead, his horse helping pull, by means of a lariat or picket rope fastened to the horn of his saddle and to the pole of the wagon. At La Noria, Mr. Thompson will borrow a conveyance that has paid the Mexican custom duty, and transferring his wife to it, will push on to cover, if possible to-day, the twenty-one miles from here to his destination.

As soon as his *patron* comes back from the East, and Mr. Rios has some money, he is going to send his little harum-scarum Blasita, who is growing up, as he says, like a coyote, to an American school at La Noria. Meanwhile, I am coaching her in her pot-hooks, with the more satisfaction, as it affords me a certain practice in Spanish. When I am at my books translating English into Spanish, or Spanish into English, I feel as if I were quite a Spaniard, but no sooner do I get among Mexicans, and one of them opens on me in idiomatic speech, that I feel like an ignoramus.

The language of border Mexicans is good enough Spanish for the professional purposes of an army officer. It will enable him to make himself understood among Spaniards anywhere.

MOWRY MINE, February 10, 1886.—Mr. Rios has just completed a fine horsehair cinch, and has promised to make me an especially handsome one to take East with me as a keepsake. He makes also, as most Mexican ranchmen do, bridles, reins. halters, lariats, whips, etc., of braided thong. I left him standing this morning on the sunny side of his house, absorbed in the occupation of paring thongs off an old boot top.

I hope when I go East to take with me some earthen cooking utensils, the main secret of the excellence of Mexican cookery.

MOWRY MINE, February 11, 1886.—Mrs. Rios informed me yesterday that she had a cow in the corral, and asked me to send my cook daily for milk, and this morning I witnessed for the first time the milking of a *bronco* or undomesticated cow. It was tied to the inside of the corral, and its hind legs were fastened together with a light rope just above the hocks. Its calf was allowed to come up and suckle it until the milk was well started, and then taken off and tied. Mr. Rios thereupon came up on its right side and held the pail, ready to jump and run, while Mrs. Rios, stealing up on the other, took the principal part in the performance.

As I was returning to my tent to take up my Spanish grammar and reader, I was pleasantly surprised to see Doctor Terrill ambling briskly into camp, followed by his orderly. I was expecting him to-morrow to go with the captain and myself to the ball at Harshaw. He came to-day in order to have time to recuperate after his thirty-five-mile ride from Copper Cañon.

MOWRY MINE, February 12, 1886.—We have gone back to three meals a day, having gone through the season of short days on two. Lunching at half-past twelve, and dining at five, I have now more time unbroken in the afternoon for exercise. I usually start out after lunch on a climb to some neighboring peak, in search of a new prospect, or to some mine that I have not visited, and get back in time to do about an hour's reading before our attendant, deferentially assuming the position of a soldier, announces to me: "Sir, Lieutenant, dinner's ready, sir."

We had the company at dinner, today, of Mr. James, the customs agent, and Mr. Philpin, the school teacher, going, like ourselves, to the ball. Shortly after the repast they went on their way, Mr. James sharing the seat of a buggy with a Mexican musician whom he had brought with him from La Noria; and Mr. Philpin filling a fine and comfortable-looking Mexican saddle. Our party set out about an hour later at the transition of twilight into a bright star-and-moonlight. A ride of about an hour and a half took us over the road familiar to the captain and myself, but new to the doctor, crossing the open summit of the mountain, and going down the broken declivity into the gradually narrowing cañon; past the Blue-Nose camp, where the sides are highest; and along the rocky-bottomed creek, where they are closest and steepest; and thence out through the expanding mouth into the pass in which Harshaw is situated. Upon arriving in town we were shown into the hotel, the interior of which consisted of a room fitted up with six cots and one washstand, over which we read the notice: *"Transients are required to pay in advance."* Being the first arrivals, we had the choice of beds, and a dry towel. Our final toileting done, we repaired to the ball-room where we walked in on the quadrille. We were introduced through the combined politeness of a number of persons, there being no one in the room, it is safe to say, whose acquaintanceship extended to all the ladies that we met. The guests had come from far and near in all directions, some from ranches on the Babacomori, forty and fifty miles off, whence they had ridden since morning. The attendance must have numbered about two hundred, and included many children whose parents, no doubt, believe in allowing them as well as themselves all the social advantages that their lonesome lives afford. The room danced in is ordinarily a school-room but has been disused as such for some time on account of the depletion of the county treasury. It was amply large and well lighted with lanterns and candles. The floor was everything that a dancer could wish, unless exception be taken to a few empty knot-holes in which a heel would occasionally catch—flaws, as it were, on the surface of perfection. The musicians, most of the time, were two violins, one guitar, and one accordion, who changed with others, now Mexican music predominating, and now American. The dances were the quadrille and the ordinary American round dances, two of the former to one of the latter. In accordance with frontier custom the dances were *called,* and not twice alike. The caller is an improviser, whose chief aim it is to perplex and confuse. It is, in fact, no small commendation of a caller that he can "tangle 'em up."

This was the first American ball outside of the army that I had been to on the frontier. I was surprised at the number of women, having no idea that there were that many within the social radius of this essentially masculine center. Many of them have grown up in their present homes since a community of sanguine prospectors laid the foundation of this once thriving and now lifeless mining town. There were no costumes presenting anything especially characteristic.

MOWRY MINE, February 22, 1886.—Dr Terrill's birthday coinciding with George Washington's, I set out this morning for Captain Hatfield's camp to celebrate both anniversaries, separately or together as might be arranged, but I got no further than La Noria. As I stopped in front of the store, Mr. Sydow came out with the remark:

"You have come just in time."

"Time for what?" I inquired.

"Why, haven't you heard the news?"

"No."

I was informed that last Friday morning a party of Indians killed three American prospectors and a Mexican who was with them, also a Mexican vaquero near Genovérache Ranch, about sixty miles east by south from La Noria, and fifteen from Captain Hatfield's camp; that the Indians numbered from thirty-five to forty; were *muy arreglados* well equipped, and were making westward towards Milpias in the Cananea Mountains. Thinking it more than likely that Captain Hatfield was out of camp, and the doctor with him, and not knowing but that there was an opportunity for K troop to get on the war path, I gave up my trip to the Huachucas; and, sending back one of my two men with a note to the captain, settled down to waiting for further news, or confirmation of what I had received. Messengers were expected from Santa Cruz, where men were arming and organizing, while others were scouring the country for trails,

NO TIME TO LOSE

looking out for dust and signal smokes, and warning isolated ranches and mining camps.

In the course of inquiries among Mexicans, I met a man who was wounded in a fight at Limpias last summer, and was for three weeks in the hospital at Fort Huachuca. According to him the Indians in that affair were not Apaches, but Indians of Mexico serving in the Mexican army, or deserting from it. Much of the robbing and killing along this border that is charged to the Indians is done by Mexicans.

I remained at La Noria until three o'clock in the afternoon, when having learned nothing further, and trusting to the citizens for notification in case of developments, I went back to camp. My messenger had rejoined me with word from the captain that

he would have the command ready to move, and upon my arrival
in camp I found the horses in the corral, rations weighed out, all
ready to pack, and extra ammunition issued to the men.

"WE STOPPED AT THE RANCH"

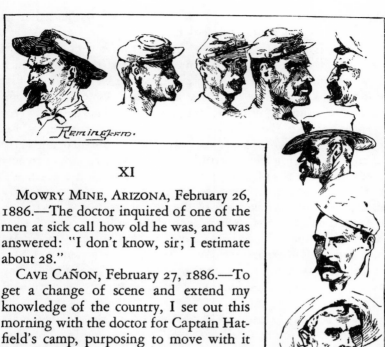

XI

Mowry Mine, Arizona, February 26, 1886.—The doctor inquired of one of the men at sick call how old he was, and was answered: "I don't know, sir; I estimate about 28."

Cave Cañon, February 27, 1886.—To get a change of scene and extend my knowledge of the country, I set out this morning with the doctor for Captain Hatfield's camp, purposing to move with it to-morrow to its new site on the east side of the Huachucas. It had rained all night, but the roads—a mixture of sand and clay, absorbing and hardening readily—were not generally heavy. The light mountain air, coursing through the shining wet trees and bushes on our way, broke upon us in refreshing compensation for the already ardent sunshine.

We stopped at the ranch of Mr. Campini, eight miles from Cave Cañon. His

SKETCHED AT ROLL-CALL.

house, situated in the bottom of one of the numerous gullies that we had to cross, is prettily shaded, and set off by a neatly fenced-in yard. From what I heard here I judged that the killing reported lately at La Noria was done by cowboys, and that its one victim was a Mexican horse-thief.

We arrived at Cave Cañon, in which the captain is now camped, at about four o'clock. As we entered the camp, which is so shut in that we were almost in it before we saw it, the first thing that I noted was the rustic horse-shed, which affords efficient protection against the sun, and sufficient, perhaps, for cavalry horses in the field, against wind and rain and snow. Beyond it we passed the line of common tents of the men, and came upon the towering sibley occupied by the captain. About twenty yards up the arroyo from here is a dug-out used as the officers' kitchen and dining-room. The camp is prettily watered by a brook running past the front of the line of tents, and separating it from the troop kitchen and tents of the Indian scouts. A little while after our arrival the captain came riding into camp. He had been out most of the day with the department engineer officer, who is taking notes for the perfecting of the military map of the Territory. This does not look like an early cessation of hostilities.

ASH CAÑON, February 28, 1886.—Before the sun was over the mountains the first call for reveille roused me from my cot, or rather the doctor's, which he had hospitably surrendered to me. Partly because of the extra earliness of breakfast, and partly because of the discomfort of a cold bed, our party was prompt to answer the twanging summons; and in the time it took me to get on my first-in-order of outer garments, my companions had raised themselves to sitting postures and gone so far toward dressing as to re-identify themselves and one another, and exchange morning salutations. The captain, who had slept on a camp cot with nothing under him but the canvas and one thickness of blanket, had dreamt of himself as on ice, and not as an oyster or as a corpse, but as a conscious human being.

Before we sat down to our breakfast the men had finished theirs, and were striking their tents and putting them in the wagons. At half-past eight the troop was formed in line ready

PACKER HITCHING UP A CINCH

to mount and march, and at the command of the captain it broke into column and started up over the side of the arroyo toward the road. The pack-train of five mules trotted close about our rear and flanks, their drivers galloping around and among them to keep them from straying too far, and occasionally dismounting to adjust a load or tighten a rope. The three heavily loaded six-mule wagons labored along some distance in our rear. About three miles from camp the head of the column was halted. We were close to the Mexican line, which we had to cross to make the bend of the road, and the captain, though authorized to cross by the Mexican custom agent, thought it well to take the precaution before doing so, of closing up. Our three wagons would have been a more tempting prize for a party of piratical Mexicans than was the camp outfit of Captain Crawford. We crossed and recrossed the line without knowing exactly where. In the course of the three miles made on the territory of our sister republic, we saw no indications of humanity other than the road, which in one sense, at least, is more American than Mexican. Halting again inside of the line to water the horses, we proceeded along the eastern base of the Huachucas, overlooking the broad, smooth valley of the San Pedro, to Ash Cañon. We are settled here on the fertile and beautifully located ranch of Mr. Emanuel—the officers under the hospitable roof of the homestead, the men in a grove near the house, where they are getting their tents and effects ready to be put up and arranged in the morning. The horses and mules are down toward the bottom of the valley picking over the bunches of dead grass. The ranch is watered by a spring about a quarter of a mile up the cañon from the house, which forms a pond of almost tepid water that never freezes over, encircled with a dense growth of watercresses. The water is distributed by a system of ditches, or *acequias,* through fields of grain, vegetables, vines and fruit trees, out of which it runs past the house down into the pasture, for the stock to drink from.

FORT HUACHUCA, March 16, 1886.—About half-past nine this morning I set out with the doctor and my two men for this post, where we arrived at about one o'clock. Our route lay, like yesterday's, at the top of the long foot-slope of the mountain, and afforded an extensive view of the russet-colored, undulating plains, with their long, graceful sky lines, and their streaks and dots and patches of wintergreen darkening in the distance to a blackish hue, of earth and rock-tinted cones and mounds; and of serrated mountains, rough and forbidding in form, but soft and alluring in their delicate coloring of snow white and purple gray.

Upon arriving and reporting to the post commander, Colonel Royall, I reported to Major Forsyth, commanding the troops in the field, and at his kind invitation, put up at his house.

MOWRY MINE, March 4, 1886.—The evening of my arrival at Fort Huachuca, the officers and ladies of the post were treated to a musical performance, a cantata, by a young Swiss, a general-service clerk. The next evening I went to a garrison hop. What with this dissipation and dining out, and the excitement of having a tooth pulled, I was variously and abundantly entertained. I learned nothing in regard to the campaign, except that, according to the latest *on dit,* General Crook is to meet Geronimo on the 15th of this month.

Camp-life seems drearier and emptier than ever. I try to reconcile myself to it as a wholesome discipline in preparation for the intervals of inaction in real war, but it is hard to imagine this inanity in real war.

MOWRY MINE, March 10, 1886.—Since the 6th instant, the men have had another experience of ephemeral opulence, which terminated, I believe, last night in a ball. Our soldiers are paid every two months. Having been six or eight weeks without a nickel, they suddenly find themselves in possession of from $25 to $50—often where there is no spending money except at the sutler's store, and without their having a need to supply or, outside of enjoyment, a want to meet. No wonder they go into excesses and crowd the guard-house. To pay them every month would be to double the evil. To pay every week would hardly be to mitigate it. To pay every day would be impracticable to our present pay corps. This latter course involves either a large increase of the corps, or a radical change in its methods of disbursement and accounts, besides the entailment of additional work and responsibility on other officers. It seems, on the whole, however, to be the best way out of the pay-day difficulty.

MOWRY MINE, March 11, 1886.—After blowing and blustering two or three days, it snowed all night, and the country is now covered with a layer two or three inches thick, as heavy a fall as we had during the winter. The sun is out, however, and the air is balmy.

PAY DAY

The contributions to the *Army and Navy Journal* relative to the Manderson bill for the reorganization of the infantry, have impressed me anew with the need of a consolidation of opinion among our army officers. Much might be done toward its accomplishment through the influence of some class or other of officers of notable professional spirit and intelligence, say the prize medallists of the military service institution. The institution would add greatly to its present usefulness should it regularly procure and publish the views of these officers on the most important military measures before Congress; such as the Manderson bill and the Logan bill of the present session.

MOWRY MINE, March 14, 1886.—Coming in from a walk this afternoon, I was accosted by a couple of Mexicans, one of whom handed me the following communication:

SEÑOR CELADOR [Mr. Sheriff], I enclose to you a list composed of some inhabitants of the *celaduria* [*county*] under your charge, which I require that you enlist for me this evening, in order that to-morrow at seven o'clock in the morning they may join a force which this *ayuntamiento* [magistracy] is organizing to go in pursuit of Indians.

I earnestly beseech that you take the greatest pains to enlist them, as it is a matter of great importance.

LIBERTY AND CONSTITUTION!

Santa Cruz, March 13, 1886.

The document, sealed and stamped, was signed by the *Presidente,* or Mayor, of Santa Cruz. I was told in explanation of it that the day before yesterday a party of ten Indians, all mounted, were seen on the east side of the Cananea Mountains, making for San Lazaro; that one of the party was killed that day by an American, and the sum of $200 found on him, besides a gold ring; and that the force of volunteers organizing to go in pursuit of the remainder numbered ten men from La Noria and twenty from Santa Cruz. Upon the return of the captain, I communicated to the messengers that he would like to have further news in regard to the matter, and that for the present he could do nothing for want of provisions. Our regular supplies will be exhausted to-morrow, after which the troop will have nothing to subsist on but its savings, which include no coffee, bacon or sugar. I am sorry to miss an opportunity of going into Mexico. There will be numerous volunteers, however, for the expedition, as the finding of $200 on one of the Indians will lead to the supposition of a good sum of money on some of the others.

MOWRY MINE, March 18, 1886.—It is now three days since General Crook was to have met Geronimo, but we have not yet heard of his having done so.

The Indians reported making for San Lazaro have doubled back, and the volunteers of Santa Cruz are not going out.

A party of visitors has arrived at the Mexicans', consisting of the mother and the eldest son of Mrs. Rios, the latter a boy about five years old, and a nephew, younger than he. They were brought here from Magdalena by Mr. Rios, and traveled from Nogales on burros, crossing the mountain by the rough trail that I followed last summer. Being told this by the lady-traveler herself, I abstracted myself for a moment from the conversation, to consider whether she took the burro up the hill or the converse. She is about six feet tall, and as ample in figure as in height. Her straight black hair; sharp, close eyes; slightly aquiline nose, and rather small, thin-lipped mouth, bespeak her of Indian blood. She wore an unstarched white dress of light material, similar to our cheese-cloth, which was soiled and torn through the vicissitudes, no doubt, of cross country traveling. There are now nine people living in the two rooms of the little hut. There they cook and sleep and eat. I have figured out in regard to their sleeping arrangements that Mrs. Rios and her mother, with the two smallest children, and maybe the one hen with part of her family, occupy the stronger of the two beds, while Mr. Rios with the other two children occupies the other bed; and that the remaining members of the household, Don Sebastian and a middle-aged son of Mr. Rios (by his former wife), sleep on the floor in the other room, where the family cook and eat.

The chickens of the Rioses are the best provided for of the Mexican families that I know of. They have a box fitted up for their accommodation under the bed, but if any of them are restless or discontented, they wander forth in search of food or of a new resting-place, and will soon cackle the whole house up if interfered with. The head of the family, with a companion of his own sex, roosts outside on the saddle-rack, where the two together share the responsibility of the watch-dog. In case of a good rain the feathery portion of the household have the house pretty much to themselves. The women and children have to go to bed, and while the men are out attending to their work, the old cocks, and hen and all, feast undisturbed upon the splashy, miry floor. If any of the featherless ones get up, it is probably not for long, only for time enough to drink a cup of coffee and eat a plate or two of beans. Meanwhile, the gallinaceous family may explore the beds. I hate to think of their finding anything there, but I have seen the older ones pecking at the sheets, in a way that satisfied me that it was not for nothing, and I cannot believe that it was for exercise. If the owners of the house assert their rights with force, they repair, skipping and chuckling, to the richer feast that awaits them out of doors. Before retiring for the night they make a visit to the dining-room, to partake of the leavings of supper, consisting of dish-water, coffee dregs, cigarette stumps, and other such tid-bits. The hen and the chicks then file off into the bedroom, where, having made the rounds, to see that nothing is overlooked, they assemble for rest and digestion in their special apartment. If they have a thought of heaven, it is the hope that it may rain, and no matter how hard, seeing that all heaven cannot leak through that roof of theirs.

While this is going on, the two old cocks come strutting out in front of the house. After making their way as unobtrusively as possible, through the evening gathering, they go fluttering up, first one and then the other, to their roost, where they blink irrelevantly at their startled lords while shifting and adjusting themselves into comfortable security.

While upon the lookout this afternoon, I watched for some-time a great volume of faintly colored smoke rising from a mountain range over in Mexico, which I judged to be about sixty miles from here. It was too large for camp or signal fires and probably came from burning grass or timber. If caused by Indian deviltry, we shall probably soon know it.

About ten o'clock this evening, as the captain and I, sitting up later than usual, were comforting ourselves with a good growl and a mescal punch, I heard a horse's step in front of the tent, and looking out descried in the darkness the form and countenance of our friend the doctor. His orderly being referred to the corporal of the guard, he was taken in and treated to the cheer before us, and to something more nourishing. In return he imparted to us, as officially reported from headquarters, that General Crook was on his way to the line to meet Geronimo, and that the latter and the other Indians were going to surrender, with the exception of Mangas, who cannot be found. He is thought to have cut loose from Geronimo, with a few followers, to carry on a campaign of his own.

TEVIS RANCH, March 20, 1886.—Came here with the doctor, traveling pretty straight across country. We had to dismount a number of times and lead our horses up rough narrow trails. I wished several times for my little camera. Looking back in our ascents, we commanded a slanting, grassy terrace at the head of the Santa Cruz valley, the smooth, even bottom and rugged sides of which we over-looked to beyond La Noria. The Huachuca peaks are almost clear of snow, and the grass in the valley is just tinting itself with a fresh growth.

About five o'clock, having crossed the divide and the broken decline beyond, we came around the point of an intervening hill upon the homestead of Tevis Ranch. It is a strikingly large adobe building, with a capacious arched entrance, and most advantageously situated at the head of the Barbocomari, within a few feet of the railroad. From a spring at the back of it a stream runs in a narrow ditch completely around it, watering a number of young cottonwood trees. We were received by a male "help," who informed us, to our great regret, that Mr. Tevis had gone to Fort Huachuca, but that the two other gentlemen of the house, Mr. Bruce and Dr. Perrine—who were known to the doctor but not to myself—had only gone down the track and would soon be back. While waiting for them to return, I learned from this acting major-domo that the estate numbered 37,000 acres, and sustained 16,000 head of stock; that the stock

ARRIVAL OF THE DOCTOR

was owned in equal shares by four persons, the three gentlemen
mentioned and one other, and that the land was wholly the
property of Dr. Perrine.

The sun having sunk pretty low and no one having come to the house, the doctor and I got on our horses and rode down the track. About half a mile from the house we came upon Mr. Bruce—who, I had heard, was an excellent sportsman—shouldering a shot-gun, and behind him Dr. Perrine carrying a dead duck. We needed no pressing to agree to spend the night with them. Upon arriving at the house our two orderlies were sent to the stable with the horses, and the doctor and I taken inside, where, it being near dinnertime, we proceeded to our much needed ablutions. The interior of the house was no less striking to me than its exterior. Such furniture, such pictures and plaques, and especially such books—in short, such taste and refinement, I had not expected to see in my excursions from the Mowry mine. After a dinner which combined the acme of city with that of country fare—in which ducks from the waters of the Barbocomari, and beef from its grassy banks, fresh vegetables and pure California wine, dessert, etc., were served by a shining, spotless Chinaman—we gathered around the fire in the sitting-room. There I learned from Mr. Bruce that he and I had been fellow students at the University of Berlin, which I thought justified me in referring to the trite observation on the smallness of the world.

MOWRY MINE, March 21, 1886.—This morning the doctor and I parted from our hosts with many assurances of our disposition to renew our visit, and about half a mile from the house he branched off toward Fort Huachuca, while I continued on my way to the Mowry. He said that he would probably be out at our camp in a week, but I do not expect to see him again that soon.

There is no room for doubt now that General Crook has gone to the line to meet Geronimo, and it can hardly be long before the troops will be going back to their posts. This time last year I was packing to move from Texas to Arizona, and I have been pretty constantly in camp or on the march ever since. When I consider the little professional advantage that this roughing it is affording me, I am satisfied with the prospect of a return, without honor or distinction, to my garrison home.

NOGALES, A. T., March 24, 1886.—Having lain awake almost all night with an aching tooth, I set out early this morning in quest of such dental treatment as I might ascertain to be available. Stopping at Harshaw, where I had heard there was a farrier or horse-doctor who could pull teeth, I was told that there was no relief for me there, but that there was a doctor at Crittenden who was a good tooth-puller. There I learned that the doctor was away, and that it was not known when he would be back. Though my ailment had now almost left me, I was determined, being on the railroad, not to turn back until I had seen a dentist; so, waiting for the evening train, I came down here, the nearest point, according to my information, where I could find one. Upon my arrival about nine o'clock, I walked over to the Nelson House, in company with its traditionally "genial" proprietor whose name it bears, and feeling tired, went at once to my room and to bed. Upon putting out my candle I became deeply absorbed in a most strange phenomenon. Each black wall of my room, except the outside one, was set off with vertical stripes of luminosity about half an inch wide and a foot apart, extending from floor to ceiling. Recollecting my being told at Crittenden that the partitions between the bedrooms were nothing but planks with wide cracks between them, which statement was annoyingly corroborated by my ears, I readily accounted for what I saw without having recourse to the supernatural, but for a long time afterward the talking in the hall and neighboring rooms prevented my wholly dismissing it from my mind.

NOGALES, March 25, 1886.—Out of respect to my fellow-boarders I went before breakfast to the nearest barber-shop and was shaved. Having breakfasted, I stepped over to the office of the dentist, a few doors from the hotel, and finding that he had not come from his house, strolled about the town. I was ciceroned by a gentleman who struck up an acquaintance with me on my uniform. A short distance from the hotel, as we turned to leave the main street, my attention was directed to a pile of loose stone, about four feet high, on the inner side of the pavement, which I was told was an international boundary monument. A few steps from here a sort of booth, or covered counter, was pointed out to me on the curb of the sidewalk: "There," said my cicerone, "is the place to get Mexican cigars." As I was about to ask him how that was done, seeing nothing there but this bare and apparently empty structure, and no one near it, I was asked: "Do you see this store?" and my attention was directed to a liquor store opening on it.

"Yes."

"Well, that store is in the United States, and this booth is on the line. Now, you ask in that store for a Sonora cigar, and the keeper will come out and take you on the Sonora side of the booth, and open a box in it, and sell you your cigar at the Mexican price."

From this interesting American curiosity we passed into the Mexican part of the town, smaller than the American by about a half. It includes the station and most of its dependent structures. Crossing the railroad we walk across the decent-looking plaza and out through a tolerably clean street radiating from it, at the corner of which the salutation of my companion is acknowledged with Spanish gravity by an inflexible and resolute-looking custom officer. A few steps farther and we pass the first Mexican store, the only one that struck me as comparable to the better stores across the line. Wandering through the suburbs around back to the United States we see several hackels and even a dug-out, but the principal houses are gable-roofed and have quite an Americanizing effect. On the whole I find Nogales-in-Mexico a far neater and more inhabitable looking place than I expected.

The American and Mexican towns together number about 12,000 inhabitants. The only industries that I can learn of are brewing and soda working—making soda-water, ginger-beer, etc. A smelter about completed is expected to commence running about the 1st of next month, relying mainly upon Mexico for custom.

Besides the *Occidental*, at which I am staying, there is an hotel called *The Delmonico,* while a third American hotel, to be called the *International,* is in course of erection. There are also several Mexican hotels, or inns. Considerable building is going on, and it is thought by many residents as well as outsiders that the Nogales people are "overdoing their town." It was founded about three years ago, as the railroad reached here from Benson. Its name is the Mexican for walnuts, which are said to have abounded here at one time.

On my way back to the dentist I was accosted, to my surprise, by a certain non-descript of a practitioner, who, through his bungling and fraudulent work at Fort Grant and at Fort Huachuca, was the cause of my visit here. I thanked him for his invitation to call at his office. The resident dentist to whom I immediately went, found, upon examination, a prong remaining from the back tooth which this quack had undertaken to pull. Having tried upon it all modes and methods of extraction, he proceeded to what I may call the operation of ejection, or prying out. This involved a course of trial and experiment for the securing of the right hold with the right instrument, my apprehensions of which were hardly ameliorated by his expressions of sympathy and commendation of my nerve.

I spent part of the afternoon in the photograph gallery receiving instruction, which I mean to turn to especial account in taking views. They are hard to buy in Arizona; the photographers rarely take them, as they do not pay as well as likenesses.

To have a reminiscence of Nogales, I bought a little Mexican dog. It looks somewhat like a Spitz, but has a more pointed, foxy face, and softer hair and disposition. It wags its tail almost like a prairie-dog. I should not wonder if it were a cross between a prairie-dog and a coyote. Its owner's price for it being ten cents, I paid twenty-five, allowing fifteen cents compensation for the little girl who procured it for me. *Dime* shall be its name.

THE DOG OF NOGALES

Most of the evening I sat on the bench in front of the hotel enjoying the soft, still air and conversation with the hostler and other strangers. There is little formality out here about making acquaintance. One cannot travel far in uniform without being spoken to by someone who has worn the army blue and feels his heart go out to every wearer of it that he meets. To such old soldiers I owe many a pleasant and profitable interview, despite their occasional wearisomeness, endeavoring to convince me that there never was and never can be again such campaigning as they participated in.

MOWRY MINE, March 26, 1886.—For about an hour after going to bed last night I was kept awake by a chattering of Chinamen in the kitchen, the window of which was directly opposite mine, and about six inches from it.

I was waked at a quarter-past four, and, half an hour later, without having breakfasted, I was walking over to the station with my baggage, consisting mainly of a pair of new shoes, which I carried in a box under my arm, and *Dime,* whom I toted in a grain sack. Soon after I got in the train it was boarded by a custom officer, who, however, made no inquiry or examination as to my traps. The matter of custom duty had not before occurred to me. When, after the second visit from the same official the train started, I congratulated myself on my happy escape or immunity from taxation. The train had hardly advanced one hundred yards, however, when it stopped, and in walked an American official on tour of inspection. He satisfied himself by inquiry that my box did not contain cigars, and, by giving a dig at *Dime,* that I had not misrepresented the contents of my bag.

It was just light enough as we moved out of the station to observe the country, which darkness had prevented my doing on my way hither. The immediate environment of Nogales could hardly be more uninteresting, consisting of treeless hillocks, shutting out all prospect short of the distant mountains. Leaving the smelter on our left we were soon among the green trees and fields of the Potrero, a small stream rising about six miles south of Nogales. About nine miles from Nogales we passed the town as it is called, of Calabasas, the terminus of a projected railroad from Tucson, and crossed the grandly sylvan Santa Cruz at the point where the Sonoita Creek runs into it, when it is running. A few miles farther we emerged through a cut from the valley of the Santa Cruz, upon the embowered permanent stream of the Sonoita, which we followed from there on more or less closely.

Upon arriving at Crittenden I put *Dime* in a box, and nailing him in securely, entrusted him to a man going up to our camp in a wagon. I then breakfasted at the German restaurant with the relish that I was entitled to by a fast of four hours since getting up. It was my intention to go after breakfast into the Santa Rita Mountains to look at a mining prospect which I was recommended to have recorded, but the horses with which I was to be driven out could not be found, and I did not go.

MOWRY MINE, March 30, 1886.—The doctor, who arrived this evening, tells us that General Crook has met Geronimo, and is now on his way back to Fort Bowie with him and his followers. It looks as if we were indeed near the end.[28]

MOWRY MINE, March 31, 1886.—Being unable to procure any hyposulphite of soda, which chemical is indispensable to the prosecution of my photography, I decided yesterday, having the promise of the doctor's company, upon riding over to Nogales to-day to buy or beg it.

We set out from camp on the Mowry trail at twenty minutes past seven. After about an hour's travel we reached the edge of the mountain-top where we stopped for awhile to take in the view. A line of bright green foliage standing out in refreshing contrast against the prevailing dull colored prospect marked the winding course of the Santa Cruz, across and beyond which, half way up the rumpled and wrinkled side of the valley, a few straggling houses enabled us to locate Nogales.

This Mowry trail is called by Mexicans the *Guajalote* trail. *Guajalote* is the Mexican for turkey, which form of game once abounded here. *Chiricahua* is the Apache for turkey.

Having dismounted and slipped and slid and stumbled down to the footslopes, we got on our horses, and picking our way into the bottom of a ravine, took up a jog-trot for the Santa Cruz, which we struck opposite Courtney's Ranch. It is a very different sight from what it was when I saw it last summer, being now about fifteen feet across and a foot deep. Its magnificent cotton-wood trees, the largest, I think, that I have ever seen, are in full foliage. From a point about half a mile below Courtney's, where we ran up against a wire fence that extended across the river and out two or three hundred yards on both sides, we turned back to the house to inquire the way. We thereupon followed a good road in a pretty straight course westward, catching a glimpse now and then of the rippling waters meandering on our right, from which we afterward branched off to wind our way up the gently sloping base of the Atascoso Mountains into Nogales. We stopped at the Nelson House to dispose of our horses and then walked over to where I had got my Mexican pup, for the doctor to try to get one like it, which, however, he did not succeed in doing. We lunched at the *Dos Republicas,* a Mexican restaurant. The national dish, frijole beans, was served up in the vessel in which it was cooked, a sort of compromise in earthenware be-tween a cup and a saucer. A Mexican aliment served to us, of which we partook but sparingly, was *enchilada.* This consists of corn pancake strewn with bits of egg, onion, lettuce, olive, chili, or red-pepper, and I don't know what, and seasoned besides with oil, vinegar, salt and pepper.

About half-past two o'clock, having attended to our business, we got on our horses and turned their heads again toward the Santa Cruz. After crossing the river we had some trouble keep-ing the right course among the sharp, steep spurs of the Pata-gonias, and, having got into the wrong ravine, came near missing the trail over the top. However, we got well up on it in time to watch from a commanding position the disappearing of the sun behind the other side of the valley, and about an hour later, as it was growing uncomfortably cool and awkwardly dark, we dismounted in front of our cheerful tents.

A SIX-MULE GOVERNMENT TEAM AND WAGON

XII

FORT GRANT, ARIZONA, May 10, 1886.—About noon I was informed by the commanding officer that he had orders to send me out in the field. I have been in the post since the 10th of last month. In that time General Crook has been replaced as commander of the department by General Miles, who has initiated a campaign in which the troops are put forward to do the fighting, and Indians are employed only in small numbers as scouts and trailers. The following order indicates the spirit of forthcoming operations:

> HEADQUARTERS, DEPARTMENT OF ARIZONA, IN THE FIELD,
> FORT BOWIE, A. T., April 20, 1886.

GENERAL FIELD ORDERS NO. 7.

The following instructions are issued for the information and guidance of troops serving in the southern portions of Arizona and New Mexico.

The chief object of the troops will be to capture or destroy any band of hostile Apache Indians found in this section of country; and to this end the most vigorous and persistent efforts will be required of all officers and soldiers until the object is accomplished.

To better facilitate this duty, and afford as far as practicable protection to the scattered settlements, the territory is subdivided into districts of obervation as shown upon maps furnished by the Department engineer officer, and will be placed under commanding officers to be hereafter designated.

Each command will have a sufficient number of troops and the necessary transportation to thoroughly examine the district of country to which it is assigned, and will be expected to keep such section clear of hostile Indians.

The Signal detachments will be placed upon the highest peaks and prominent lookouts to discover any movement of Indians, and to transmit messages between the different camps.

The Infantry will be used in hunting through the groups and ranges of mountains, the resorts of the Indians, occupying the important passes in the mountains, guarding supplies, etc.

A sufficient number of reliable Indians will be used as auxiliaries, to discover any signs of hostile Indians, and as trailers.

The Cavalry will be used in light scouting parties, with a sufficient force held in readiness at all times to make the most persistent and effective pursuit.

To avoid any advantage the Indians may have by a relay of horses, where a troop or squadron commander is near the hostile Indians, he will be justified in dismounting one half of his command and selecting the lightest and best riders to make pursuit by the most vigorous forced marches, until the strength of all the animals of his command shall have been exhausted.

In this way a command should, under a judicious leader, capture a band of Indians or drive them from 150 to 200 miles in forty-eight hours through a country favorable for cavalry movements; and the horses of the troops will be trained for this purpose.

All commanding officers will make themselves thoroughly familiar with the section of country under their charge and will use every means to give timely information regarding the movements of hostile Indians to their superiors or others acting in concert with them, in order that fresh troops may intercept the hostiles or take up the pursuit.

Commanding officers are expected to continue a pursuit until capture, or until they are assured a fresh command is on the trail.

All camps and movements of troops will be concealed as far as possible, and every effort will be made at all times by the troops to discover hostile Indians before being seen by them.

To avoid ammunition getting into the hands of the hostile Indians, every cartridge will be rigidly accounted for, and when they are used in the field the empty shells will be effectually destroyed.

Friendly relations will be encouraged between the troops and citizens of the country, and all facilities rendered for the prompt interchange of reliable information regarding the movements of hostile Indians.

Field reports will be made on the 10th, 20th and 30th of each month, giving the exact location of troops and the strength and condition of commands.

By command of Brigadier-General MILES:

WM. A. THOMPSON,
Captain 4th Cavalry, A.A.A.G.

SULPHUR SPRINGS VALLEY, May 11, 1886.—I set out this afternoon with thirty-five dismounted cavalrymen, all the available cavalry in the post, for Willcox, on Southern Pacific Railroad, under orders to proceed to Calabasas, about nine miles north of the Mexican line, and report from there to Colonel Royall, Fourth Cavalry, at Fort Huachuca. I had my private horse, which I rode, and a wagon in which I transported twenty days' rations, the horse equipments of the men, and a supply of camp equippage and cooking utensils. There being no water between the post and Fisk's ranch, twenty miles distant, I was accompanied by a water-wagon with a supply for the night. An hour or more after dark I went into camp, about eighteen miles from the post. The men were pretty tired and footsore, but only one fell out, and he came into camp with the column, riding on top of the water-wagon. There was not a bush within foraging distance, so there was no cooking, and men were soon through with their cold supper of hard tack and canned beef, and ready to turn in. At nine o'clock I had the trumpeter quiet the last lingerings of after-supper hilarity by sounding taps.

CALABASAS, A. T., May 12, 1886.—At break of day a livelier performance of the trumpeter brought the men to their feet, and at the first appearance of the sun over the horizon—our slender breakfasts being disposed of and the wagon packed—we turned again into the dreary, dusty road to Willcox. The men were so stiff from yesterday's march that we traveled slowly, making little more than two miles an hour.

While waiting at Willcox for the train, the men dined at a restaurant at a cost to the government of twenty-one cents per man, the sum allowed me to each one for three pints of coffee. They were given all the coffee to take with them that they wanted, and, for their evening meal, they had besides coffee, the remainder of the canned beef and hard bread of their traveling ration, issued for to-day, but part of which they ate yesterday for supper.

About half an hour after time the train arrived, and my men set to work putting their horse equipments, tentage, rations, etc., into a baggage car assigned to us. I had intended that in the loading of the horse equipments, the detachment should file past the door of the car, and each man put in his own bundle in turn. But at the command for this operation to commence my whole line broke, and every man made a dash for the door. After a dignified and, of course, ineffectual attempt to check this disorder, I contented myself with looking on in contemplation of the brawn and vigor that it brought into play. The men being thereupon filed into a passenger car, the train started. A straight pull up the gentle slope of the Sulphur Spring Valley, a spurt across Dragoon Summit, a tortuous descent into the valley of the San Pedro, and we are at Benson, where the New Mexico and Arizona road branches off to the Mexican border. Here we change cars and transfer the baggage, the latter operation being executed with the same zest and vigor as the loading at Willcox. At Huachuca Station I met a number of acquaintances; among others, the Adjutant of the post and Dr. Terrill. The former gave me an order from Colonel Royall, in command of the Southwest District, directing me to report at Calabasas to Captain Lebo, my troop commander. I learned from the doctor that he had come in for a portion of the active service that I had missed, having assisted at the amputation of Corporal Scott's leg. The brave corporal, I was grieved to hear, is in a very critical condition. At Crittenden I had a talk with Lieutenant Clarke, who was with the captain in the recent fight. A party of Indians prepared an ambush for our troop, which was on their trail, but the captain was too sagacious to go into it. Seeing this, the Indians opened fire upon his column as it was turning their ambush, whereupon the troop deployed and attacked. The Indians held their ground and made an attempt to get our horses, which was frustrated by a covering force and a detail sent to drive the herd to the rear. Each side in the fight numbered about thirty men. Three Indians were seen to fall and to be dragged back out of fire, a pretty sure indication that they were killed or mortally wounded. Our casualties were one man killed and one wounded.

"INDIANS WERE SEEN TO FALL AND BE DRAGGED BACK OUT OF FIRE"

At eight o'clock we arrived at Calabasas, where I met the captain at the station. Leaving my baggage, with the exception of the men's bundles, in the baggage car, which was switched off here, I put my men into camp and then repaired to the hotel where the captain is staying, and took a room.

CALABASAS, A. T., May 13, 1886.—At seven o'clock this morning I was at the railroad station to telegraph my arrival here to Colonel Royall. While writing my despatch, a message went through to Fort Huachuca from Nogales to the effect that a party of forty Mexicans and some Papago Indians had been ambushed about seventy-five or eighty miles southwest of Nogales, and every man killed. This report, however, was not confirmed this evening, and is therefore not to be believed. Later in the day we received various reports by telegraph of engagements across the line, probably all different versions of the same affair. Sifted down they indicate that there has been an engagement somewhere in the State of Sonora, and that the Indians had the best of it. Captain Lawton, of the Fourth Cavalry, is understood to be on their trail. Has a force of eighty soldiers (infantry and cavalry) and twenty Indian scouts, with rations for about ten weeks; also a fund of $1,000 in silver.

I have had my detachment pitch their tents on a *mesa* adjoining the flat on which the town and station of Calabasas are situated. I heard before coming here that this was a very malarious locality, and have heard here, of course, that it is no such thing. The Calabasas people admit that there was more or less malaria here before the introduction of cattle, but claim that the stock now in the country, eating up the rank vegetable matter, prevent the germination of all such diseases.

Calabasas consists in the main of a loose array of about a dozen poor-looking houses and shanties, facing at respectful distance the two-storied brick hotel, with its porch and veranda, as if to do homage to its lonesome stateliness. The hotel is named the Santa Rita. It was built about four years ago in the expectation that the railroad would be built to connect this point with Tucson, and that the road then building, the New Mexico and Arizona, would locate here the elements of civilization with which it started Nogales. The house throughout is well furnished, carpeted and wall-papered. There is water in every room, forced from a tank in the garden; also an electric bell, and the end of a gas-pipe. To look out from the front veranda of the Santa Rita, over a foreground of rank grass, animated now and then by a careening jack-rabbit, upon the adobe huts, constituting the bulk of the town, and then with the impression thus obtained fresh in one's mind to contemplate upon a wall-map in the hotel reading-room, the blocks and squares, and parks and avenues of the *Townsite of Calabasas,* is singularly instructive.[29]

CALABASAS, A. T., May 14, 1886.—I sent off two detachments to take post, the one at Peck's ranch, the other at the Santa Rita.

Indians are now reported about five miles West of Imuris on the railroad, forty miles south of Nogales. Captain Lawton and Lieutenant Davis will keep them stirred up, and may drive them this way.

General Miles arrived here this evening with his aide, Lieutenant Dapray, and a general service clerk.

CALABASAS, A. T., May 15, 1886.—Sent out three detachments of four men each as ranch guards reading to them the following instructions:

CALABASAS, A. T., May 15, 1886.

The detachments of dismounted troops are located where they will give protection to the exposed settlers, and where they would be likely to intercept the movements of any band of hostile Indians.

The men will be instructed that it is their duy to discover the Indians before being seen by them. They should be constantly on the watch, and will fire upon any number, and the closer the range, the better.

They can frequently go out before day and take favorable position for observing the adjacent country, and make it their business to hunt for any hostile Indians in the vicinity.

Should Indians be discovered, reliable and definite information will be sent to the commanding officer at Calabasas, by any citizen whose property is being protected.

By command of Brigadier-General MILES:

J. A. DAPRAY,
Second Lieutenant, 23d Infantry, A.D.C.

The general went this evening to Nogales, accompanied by Captain Lebo.

CALABASAS, A. T., May 16, 1886.—Telegraphic information went through here this morning to the effect that Captain Hatfield's troop, while carrying off booty from an Indian camp, which it had "jumped," was ambushed with disastrous effect, losing most of its horses, and two men killed, and two or more wounded. Lieutenant Clarke has been ordered to join Captain Hatfield with our troop from the Mowry Mine.

READING THE ORDERS

Tubac, A. T., May 17, 1886.—About four P.M. yesterday it was reported to me by an excited American, coming at a gallop into Calabasas, that at a ranch about six miles down the Santa Cruz, a house and fence were burning that were supposed to have been fired by Indians. As soon as possible I set out at a gallop with thirteen men and ten days' rations, guided by the aforesaid American. About three miles from camp we were met by a Mexican riding leisurely toward us, who stated that he had just come from where we were going, and that there was nothing the matter there. A number of Mexicans who had attached themselves to us since we started were satisfied by this man's representation that there was no use in going any farther, and turned around and went back. Rejecting the suggestion of my guide to go on "just to see," I turned my column about, and while the sergeant walked it back to camp, I trotted ahead to contradict any false report that might have been wired to General Miles.

In the evening I had an interview with a party of Americans who had just come from the ranch, and learned from them certain particulars which made me desire to go there and examine the situation for myself. Accordingly, at four o'clock this morning I set out with my detachment of yesterday—all the men I could mount—and after an easy walk of about six miles, arrived at the ranch in question, the Palo Parado (stake in the ground). Leaving my men on the road, I walked over to the house on the other side of the dry bed of the Santa Cruz, and interviewed its inmates, four or five men and a number of women and children. One of the former showed me, about two hundred yards to the right of the house, the smoldering ruins of an old hut, from which a track of two human feet—one moccasined and one bare—led down into the bed of the river; also, back of the house, the ashes of the fence where a stretch of about a hundred yards had been burned to the ground. The government guide that I had with me failed to find any tracks or other signs about the fence that looked at all suspicious, and after trying to follow the track that we found at the hut, gave that up too. As the latter seemed to continue down the bed of the river, I decided to follow the river along the road as far as Tubac, on the chance of getting on the track again, or of learning something further in regard to it. We had not gone far before we found it in the road, and soon afterward we were given to understand that it was made by a Mexican deserter, footing it to Tubac. Keeping on, however, as I wanted to see the country, we passed a number of fields lying fallow from want of water, which were formerly irrigated from the river, and caught a glimpse through the tops of cotton-wood and mesquite trees, of the white dome and walls of the ruined Mission of St. Joseph, of Tumacacori. The latter, as well as the town of Tubac, is described in Wilkie Collins's "Black Robe." I acquired much interesting information in regard to both from Mr. Lillie T. Mercer, the justice of of the peace at Tubac, where we arrived about noon; and what I shall state in regard to them, I rest mainly on his authority.

THE GOVERNMENT GUIDE LOOKING FOR TRACKS

The mission[30] was established by Jesuit padres in 1752, and finally destroyed by Apaches, in 1820. It effected the conversion of the Papago Indians, who supported and enriched it by their labor in its fields and mines. They had to bring in each week a certain money's worth of ore, for which they obtained one alamo (about sixteen pounds) of corn. If they failed of this contribution, their rations were cut down.

Since the Americans first came here in 1850, thousands of prospectors have worked in these mountains in search of what is called "the great Tumacacori Mine," and books and maps have been published purporting to locate and describe it. There is a legend that if one stands at the mission door, and faces due north-east, one can look into the mouth of the mine; and accord-

PAPAGO INDIAN

ing to an old Mexican legend, if one stands on the *camino real*, royal road, opposite the mission, and watches where the sun sinks on the 15th day of July, one will find the mine immediately below where it disappears.

In 1876, an old Mexican—by name, Cayetano Marquis—made a trip to Alamos, in Sonora, to see his mother, and while there, happened to bring up the subject of the Tumacacori mine. His mother, who was about ninety years old, and was born and had lived many years in Tubac, looked at him curiously for a while, and then said, "Why, my son, you don't believe in that story of the Tumacacori mine, do you?" He replied: "I neither believe it nor disbelieve it; but as there is so much talk about it, I do not know but that there is something to it." At this, the old lady, who was of an hysterical turn, went off into such a fit of laughter that it was actually thought she would die. Seeing the effect of this topic on his mother, Don Cayetano did not bring it up again during his stay with her. Before he departed, however, the good woman did so herself. "My son," she said, "I don't want you to waste your time or money looking for a Tumacacori mine, for any particular Tumacacori mine never had existence. The whole story is a fable, gotten up by us residents of Tubac in order to obtain money from the American trains coming through during the winter on their way to California. Their earlier route had been due west across the plains, but they had experienced so much death and suffering that during the winter months they came instead through Northern Texas, Chihuahua and Sonora, to the present town of Santa Cruz, and followed the Santa Cruz River to the Gila, whence they proceeded westward to California. When they first began to come here, we had no knowledge of the value of money, and would not exchange our commodities for any amount of it; but finding after a while how we could use it at the trading-posts, we learned its value, and then our only object was to obtain it, no matter how. Wagon after wagon, train after train, would come in, and from each one would come the inquiry whether there were any rich mines in the neighborhood. Being answered that there were none, they would pay out a little money for our products, and pass on. A few of our older heads got together one day to see if they could not get up a scheme for keeping the trains here longer, that we might make more off them; and so it happened about this time that some one conceived the idea of a rich Tumacacori mine. It was tested upon the first train that came along, and it took at once. The travelers were retained two months, at the end of which their funds were so low that they had to go on, leaving with us almost all their money. The trick was played upon train after train, until hens, and eggs, and corn, and grain, and everything else that we had to sell was sold, and we had to send out to surrounding towns and settlements, mostly in Sonora, for provisions. Whole trains would come in loaded down with them.

"Not less than 5,000 men have thoroughly searched—at least, as they thought—all the mountains in the vicinity of Tubac, and failed to find the Tumacacori mine. Yet the story is thoroughly believed by some people to this day, and parties come every now and then from long distances to look for it."[31]

It is not four years since such a party came from San Jose, California, claiming to have maps from the existing mission there. It is needless to say that the party was disappointed.

The little cluster of dilapidated mud houses, constituting the present town of Tubac, is the remnant of an old frontier settlement of no mean size and importance. According to Hinton's Guide-Book, Tubac was the seat of a Spanish mission in 1720. In 1840, according to a Mexican authority, the Mexicans had a garrison here of thirty men, the town containing a population of 400. In 1858, according to S. W. Cozzens, it numbered a population of 800, principally miners. I visited the ruins both of the old mission church and of the *presidio*, or fort. A portion of the latter, still intact, is occupied by several Mexican families. I also looked in at the district schoolhouse, little frequented just now, the reason for which was suggested by the inscription, sloping up in large school-boy hand over the center of the blackboard: *The Apaches are out!*

CALABASAS, A. T., May 18, 1886.—At a quarter of five this morning I was on my return march to Calabasas by way of the Tumacacori mission. After a somewhat leisurely ride along the flat bank of the river, through a wild shrubbery of mesquite, I halted in front of its carved facade and dismounted for a half-hour's rest and sight-seeing. Through its doorless entrance I stepped into the body of the church. It is almost wholly un-roofed, but its bare walls and earthen floor are damaged more by pick and spade than by the tooth of time. Its most curious and notable features now are its defacements. To the right of the altar is a hole in the wall which, previously to 1855, was the depository of a hidden treasure. About that year there arrived in Prescott a priest, come directly from Rome, who with some difficulty procured for himself a guide to the Tumacacori mission, for a consideration of $40 a day for twenty days, and also a number of men as escort for $10 a day. Arriving with his party safely at the mission, he walked at once to the altar, and, after making certain measurements from the altar and floor, took some heavy object, and breaking through a shell covering, opened this hole in the wall and drew from it, in gold and bul-lion, $80,000. Impelled by this incident, stories of silver bells, etc., Slavonian Jews and other vandals have torn up the floor, and undermined and gouged out the walls, reducing the struc-ture to a dilapidated condition.

From the nave I walked out through the sacristy into a rec-tangular space back of the church, inclosed on its three outer sides by a high adobe wall, whose empty niches were once occupied no doubt with shrines. About the center of this inclosure is a circular stone mortuary containing a number of plain graves. It must have been pacing around this melancholy memorial, under the gaze of saintly effigies, their thoughts alternating between the salvation of souls and the exploitation of the earth, between the beauties of religion and the power of money, that the sturdy missionaries of St. Joseph held their sweet and deep meditations.

Close around the front and sides of the church are the remains of rude metallurgical works, the ruins and bare foundations of the residences of priests and laborers, and traces of old acequias, or irrigating ditches, through which the adjacent fields were brought under cultivation.

There is in the Santa Rita mountains a mine called the Salero (salt-cellar), from a legendary association with this mission. Some hundred years ago, a bishop on a visit from Alamos, in Sonora, to the different churches in his diocese, being honored at Tumacacori with a feast, allowed himself to remark, as he surveyed it: "You have everything here except a salt-cellar." The brothers thereupon dispatched to the mine a number of Papagos, who procured some silver, worked it into a salt-cellar, and brought it to the mission in time to present it to his holiness before he got up from the table.

From Tumacacori's lone relic of Romanism, we pursued our way in due time across the Santa Cruz, and along the hot, dusty road beyond it, to the embryo of American civilization at Calabasas.

Here I found the captain and the paymaster. Indians were reported this evening crossing the railroad at Agua Zarca, twelve miles south of Nogales.

CALABASAS, A. T., May 19, 1886.—The captain received the following despatch this morning:

NOGALES, A. T., May 19.

Two Mexicans killed eight miles below on railroad last evening—other on trail to Barnett's ranch. Bodies brought here for burial. Two American prospectors and three Mexicans reported killed in same vicinity.

W. J. PARKS,
Late Captain Duncan Rangers.

We are ordered to keep a sharp lookout for Indians going north pursued by Captain Lawton.

The following despatch was received this afternoon:

FORT HUACHUCA, May 19.

Captain Lebo, Calabasas:

Lieutenant Johnson, with Clarke's troop and twenty packs, should be at Calabasas to-night; also Tisdall's Co. C, First Infantry. Lawton is behind Indians and expects to have Wood with strong force south and west of Indians before daylight to-morrow. You can take an effective force and strike west and south wherever you think you can strike the hostiles. Miles, Commanding.

The captain will await the arrival of Lieutenant Johnson to get the pack-mules coming with him, and hopes meanwhile to learn something further by which to direct his movements. I have made arrangements for leaving my things in safety and taking the field. As it is a sultry afternoon, threatening rain, and we are liable to travel at night, I shall take my overcoat with me on my horse. My bedding is thrown in a corner of my room ready to be rolled up and put on a pack-mule; my pistol is cleaned and cartridge belt replenished; my maps, postal cards, etc., are laid out to be put in my saddle pockets, and my riding trousers and heavy boots are where I can jump into them at a moment's notice.

I am satisfied now that the fires at the Palo Parado ranch were a device of people on the ranch for drawing soldiers to it.

SHANAHAN'S RANCH, May 20, 1886.—General Miles went through here last night on his way to Nogales. On the same train with him were Captain Wood, Fourth Cavalry, referred to in the general's despatch of yesterday; Captain Tisdall, First Infantry, with the greater part of his company; Lieutenant Dapray, the general's aide; Dr. Terrill, who is going with Captain Wood into Mexico, and a troop of the Second Cavalry, with its horses. The troop is to go through Nogales to-night if the general can get the custom-guard to let it do so. It is a stringent rule of that body to allow no train to cross the line after nine o'clock. General Miles expressed the apprehension that the Indians would turn around and go south before we should be ready to head them off in that direction.

Lieutenant Johnson not arriving, and the captain having decided not to start until morning, I turned in last night at ten o'clock, and slept until four this morning. Having breakfasted in camp and attended to the final arrangements of getting off, I walked over to the station to meet the 5:15 train from Nogales, and learned that last night's train had been allowed to cross the line.

An American who came up here this morning from Nogales, tells me that the two Mexicans who were killed there, as reported in yesterday's telegram, were brothers. One of them was killed at the first fire, having been struck but once. The other had evidently made a fight of some duration from behind a tree, his death attesting his indomitable courage. He must have hurt some of the Indians, for besides being shot many times, he was stabbed in several places; and the Apaches do not ordinarily mutilate their victims unless hurt by them.

According to the same American, a party went out from Nogales yesterday in search of five men who are missing and supposed to have been killed. Nogales is frightened into a state of siege.

Leaving in reserve at Calabasas the troop that arrived in the night under Lieutenant Clarke, the captain set out at 8:50 this morning with the remainder of his command, consisting of troops D and L, without having heard anything further in regard to the Indians. Our two citizen guides, riding at some distance ahead of the column, led us by a good road to Owen's ranch, in the foothills of the Pajarito mountains, and thence by a plain, but in many places narrow, treacherous, path into the heart of the range, where we are now camped.

About a mile from here we found a small horse or pony, saddled and bridled, lying down resting. The saddle was of Mexican type, and the blanket under it of army pattern, marked B 18. We supposed the blanket to be one of Captain Hatfield's, captured in his recent fight. To the saddle were hanging about five pounds of beef, cut Indian fashion into strips, to dry; also a piece of cowhide, presumably for soling moccasins. At this point of our march we stopped for half an hour to allow the guides to hunt up trails. They found tracks of about six ponies going in three different directions. Thinking to learn something regarding the main body of the Indians, the captain pushed on

A MEXICAN MADE A FIGHT FROM BEHIND A TREE

for Shanahan's ranch. We had proceeded about one hundred yards, when I was startled by an exclamation ahead of me; and looking up, I saw the guide nearest the column jump off his horse, and, pointing to the top of a hill that we were circling, bring up his Winchester to cock it. The captain called out to him to hold on—not to fire, that it was one of our men. Having meanwhile seen a man in a white shirt and without hat disappear suddenly behind the very top of the hill, I was not so sure myself as I should have liked to be that the captain was right. Almost immediately after disappearing, however, this man returned, accompanied by another, wearing a soldier's blouse, and the two stood together looking at us, neither having a gun. Satisfied then that they were soldiers, the guide went up to them to see if they had any news. They had none. These men were from the infantry outpost at Shanahan's ranch, about half a mile

"WE FOUND A SMALL PONY, SADDLED AND BRIDLED, LYING DOWN"

ahead of us. They had allowed us to come within a hundred yards of them without seeing us, and had not seen the horse that we picked up about two hundred yards from them, directly in their front. At the post, we found a sergeant with eight men, including the two on the hill. The principal duty of the detachment

"BRING UP HIS WINCHESTER TO COCK IT"

is to keep Indians away from the water, and to notify the command at Calabasas of any movements of Indians that they may detect.

The ranch, marked only by the hut in which the guard is living, is abandoned by its regular occupants.

SHANAHAN'S RANCH, May 21, 1886.—At about a quarter past three this morning, a courier arrived from Calabasas with the following despatches:

NOGALES, May 20, 1886.

To Lieutenant Clarke:

Captain Lawton reports Indians camped last night about five miles north of Planches de Plata, about twenty-five south-west of this point. Trail indicates moving north. Send word at once to Lebo. I want your command to prevent their moving north; and *strike hard* at first opportunity. About thirty Indians, men and squaws, some on foot. Have infantry and dismounted men at all stations, to be on the watch and destroy as many of them as possible   MILES, Commanding.

NOGALES, May 20, 1886, 6 A.M.

To Lieutenant Clarke:

Send word to Lebo at once; also, about report of thirty Indians at Town's ranch.   MILES, Commanding.

Planchas de Plata (Plates of Silver), so named from the remarkable specimens of native silver found there, is on the Mexican side of the line, about fifteen miles southwest of here and Town's ranch, about half that distance southeast. We understand, therefore, that there are Indians to right and to left of us, numbering, all told, about sixty, or the same as ourselves. On reading the despatches, half an hour before daybreak, the captain had the cooks aroused, and at half-past five the horses had been groomed and were being saddled. Meanwhile the courier who had come from Calabasas, a citizen guide, was sent off to notify the outposts to the west of us of what we had learned, and enjoin upon them extra caution and vigilance. Another guide went over to a ridge about a mile north of camp in search of Indian signs. The captain sent a guide last night to Oro Blanco, the headquarters of the outposts, to get what news there was there.

It is highly probable that the horse picked up yesterday afternoon, as well as another brought into camp in the evening, belonged to an advance party of the Indians reported to us early to-day. It looks as if they went through here yesterday morning, and catching sight of the infantry, at once jumped off their horses and took to the hills.

From half-past seven to half-past ten we lay observing the country in a position about a mile back on our route of yesterday. Having made nothing thereby, apart from the capture of two more horses, we returned to camp, and having watered, moved to shade and grass a few hundred yards beyond it. There we are now waiting with horses saddled, for a report from Owen's ranch, that we may know whether any hostiles have passed in our rear.

BARTLETT'S RANCH, May 22, 1886.—About two P.M. yesterday we set out from Shanahan's ranch. We marched in and out of cañons and up and down divides past Bartlett's ranch, where there is a post of eight or nine infantrymen; and also McClenahan's where there are four dismounted cavalrymen. Between the latter, as we passed them and the column, there was a very lively interchange of greetings. The poor fellows at the ranch, not having a house within sight, have built themselves a little stone redoubt commanding the spring.

About two miles beyond here, as my troop was about to go down into a ravine out of which the column, which was dismounted, was ascending on the other side, I was abruptly informed, by mounted messenger, that there were forty Indians at the place where we camped last night. I sent the report forward to the captain, and, turning my troop about, waited for his action. He marched us back on our tracks, but upon conferring at Bartlett's with another messenger by whom he was there met, he put us into our present camp. It appears that the forty Indians reported at Shanahan's are the eighteen or twenty scouts of Captain Lawton, who has come in there with his command, on a trail of from twelve to fifteen hostiles. After marching about twelve miles, and a large part of the way on foot, we are camped within two miles of the place where we camped last night.

Bartlett's ranch is at the head of the Sycamore cañon, a frowning chasm, lined with blocks and columns of basalt, interspersed with hardy rooted oak. Three or four weeks ago, a man was killed by Indians a few hundred yards from the house, and another wounded while taking aim from the doorway at an Indian on the hill that we are camped upon.

Owing to the roughness of the trail, there was a good deal of falling out this afternoon to have horseshoeing done. The old shoes had to be used over again as our new ones are not "set" or prepared to be put on. Until we get to a forge the latter are so much old iron that we are carrying about in our saddle-pockets. It would be well if our horseshoes were issued with large enough holes in them to admit a nail.

Tubac, A. T., May 23, 1886.—At 8:20 this morning, the captain having returned from a visit to Captain Lawton, the command was put on the march for Tubac. Captain Lawton thinks that the Indians he is following are hard up for horses, a number of their women and children being afoot. His scouts, under Lieutenant Finley, were out this morning examining tracks, with a view to determining where they came together. Captain Lawton's especial function is to keep the Indians on the go, following their trail though it should number but three tracks. Ours is to keep them from getting north of here.

Through a confusion of rounded hill-tops, broken here and there by projecting rock, but generally well covered with grass and timber, we made our way to the long, narrow cañon called Hell's Gate, and proceeded slowly and with difficulty through it. Parts of it were as uncanny as the name would imply, and strongly suggestive of an ambush. We had advance guard of about six men accompanying the guide, but could not afford to send out flankers, and had therefore to take the chances of being fired upon from the bluffs on either side. We passed Peck's ranch, where Mrs. Peck was killed and her twelve-year-old niece was taken captive by Apaches, the 27th of last month. I will tell the story as I heard it. Having been out back of the house, her little niece came up to Mrs. Peck, who was sitting on the bed holding her child, and told her that there was an Indian outside, behind the chicken coop. Mrs. Peck replied that it could not be, and got up and went out. She had hardly crossed the threshold when she fell dead from a bullet, dropping her infant from her arms. The girl was then secured, and the baby killed by a blow on the head.

A fresh trail that we followed into the cañon turned out of it before we came to the house.

Emerging from the cañon we descended along barren *hog-backs* into the valley of the Santa Cruz, and followed in a downward direction the dry bed of the stream, shaded by magnificent cotton-woods and willows, and strewn with huge trunks and limbs in all stages of decay.

About half a mile from Tubac we went into camp in the river's grateful shade, an acequia affording us water for man and beast.

From a couple of Mexicans, who witnessed our camping with evident satisfaction, we learned that about half a dozen Indians left here at daybreak this morning with six head of stolen stock.

Coming back from an after-dinner stroll over to town, I fell in with a citizen of Tubac, who is said to have lived some twenty-five years with the Apaches, and to have been with them on many a raid. Some say he is a Mexican who was captured by the Indians when a boy fourteen years old; others, that he is an Apache, and was captured by the Mexicans when a child, and subsequently recaptured by the Apaches. I asked him the meaning of a certain sign that we had found on the march to Shanahan's ranch—a strip of white linen or canvas tied to the branch of a bush. It meant, he said, that the Indians were taking captives along, and he informed me that when they kill a captive they indicate it by drawing a circle in the trail. I could not but think of the girl taken from Peck's ranch, and wonder about her fate.

About ten o'clock to-night we got our blacksmiths out with the spare horseshoes—every man carries two, one forefoot and one hindfoot—and had them go with a civilian blacksmith to his shop, two miles from here, to work at his forge. About midnight our horses, which had subsisted on grass since leaving Calabasas, were given a feed of barley-hay, which it had taken a Mexican from sunset until that time to fetch from his ranch, about two miles from here.

XIII

Santa Rita Mountains, Arizona, May 23, 1886.—We were up at daylight to make an early start in pursuit of the thieving Indians reported to us here. A few miles to the north lay the slopes, and ridges, and buttes of the southern extremity of the Santa Ritas, overlooked from the direction of Mount Wrightson, or "Old Baldy," by a succession of cones and peaks. Owing to the difficulty of trailing among the horse and cattle tracks about Tubac, we made straight for the mountains, where we knew the Indians had gone, and skirting the southwest point outside of its grand headland of bare rock, *picacho diablo*— devil's peak—took up the trail before we were well around on the west side. We followed it the rest of the day along the western footslope of the mountain. The march was an easier one than I had expected. There seems to have been no thought on the part of the Indians of availing themselves of the rough country near-by to put their pursuers at a disadvantage. From this, one of three things is to be supposed:

1. That for some reason, such as the difficulty just now of stealing stock, or the poorness of such as they might steal, they are uncommonly careful and considerate of what they have; or

2. That they want to be pursued in order to cause the withdrawal of certain troops form their present station; or,

3. That they are pressed for time. Thus they may be trying to make some squaw-camp, or ammunition cache, before the dark of the moon, which is now on the wane.

The three or four ranch-houses, or huts, that we passed were abandoned, and no doubt had been before the Indians came, as we found no dead body at any of them. One of these had evidently been pillaged, its floors being strewn with broken trunks and chests, clothing, eating and cooking utensils, and some bedding and furniture. Toward evening we stopped at the Bulldozer mine, also abandoned. There being no place here to water, we moved on, after having the canteens filled, to a ranch close by, which our guide had reported to be occupied. There being nothing here for the horses to eat, we got a ranchman to guide us to grass about four miles farther, where we went into dry camp after dark.

GILL'S RANCH, A. T., May 24, 1886.—At a quarter of six this morning we set out without breakfast for a ranch in Davis' cañon, at the northern end of the Santa Ritas, where we expected to get forage and eat breakfast. The persons in charge of it refused to sell any of their grain, on the ground that they needed it all for planting; and they had no hay. So, having watered the horses, we pushed on to the nearest point at which the command could be subsisted, Pantano Station, on the Southern Pacific Railroad, where we arrived at noon. Here we found K troop in camp under the command of Lieutenant Clarke. We have been on no trail to-day, but have kept in the general direction of the one that we followed yesterday. Before taking it up again the captain will await telegraphic instructions from General Miles.

Upon our arrival here, the horses had to go half a mile or more, to a muddy creek, for water, and on account of their weariness, I had mine led instead of ridden, hard though it was on my men.

After a double meal of breakfast and dinner at the eating-house or hotel, the officers repaired to the station, where they had the satisfaction of visiting two of the passenger trains, and of reading several despatches from General Miles. One of these was the following:

Captain Lebo, Pantano: WILLCOX, May 24.

Sergeant at Benson states Mexicans have Indians in rocky country two miles from Tres Alamos. Have your strongest mounts there as soon as possible.   MILES.

Troops D and K were selected for compliance with this instruction. Just before starting out with them the captain received the following supplementary despatch:

WILLCOX, A. T., May 24, 1886., 5:40 P.M.

Captain Lebo, Pantano:

Davis' troop remain where it is. Use your command against these Indians and make every effort to capture. Get these Mexicans to go with you. They can have four dollars per day and two thousand dollars if they get Geronimo. Wilder's troop is here now.

MILES, Commanding.

We were on the march an hour before sunset, and about nine o'clock had made our way northeastwardly up the foot-slope of the Rincons and around their southeastern extremity to Gill's ranch, where we are now camped.

LLOYD'S RANCH, May 25, 1886.—The Mexicans at Gill's ranch told the captain last night that there was a trail of from fifteen to eighteen animals within a mile and a half of the house, and that they would go out in the morning and put him on it. This morning not one would do so, all having to go back to their families. Our guide soon ascertained, however, by examination of the ground, that there was no such trail as they had told of. About six o'clock we were on the way to the San Pedro River. The captain's object was partly to see what truth there was in a report of Indians in its vicinity, and partly to get a better camp than we had last night. We had already learned that the reported surrounding of Indians two miles from Tres Alamos was a falsehood. About midway to the river the captain was overtaken by a Mexican with the report that Indians were fighting with Mexicans at a certain point in the Rincon Mountains. While far from crediting the report he turned the column about and proceeded toward the alleged scene of hostility. What became of the Mexican I do not know. I only know that he was not around when the captain found out at Page's ranch, a few miles from where he turned back, that the report was utterly false.

187

"WE FOUND A GROUP OF MEXICANS WITH THEIR HORSES SADDLED"

From Page's ranch our march was directed back upon Pantano, but we were not to get there to-day. Arriving at the ranch where we camped last night, we found a group of Mexicans, with their horses saddled, standing in front of the house, who told us excitedly that a man had been killed by Indians about nine o'clock this morning on the *camino real* (royal road), not more than four miles from there in the direction of Pantano. Meanwhile our guide, whom the captain had sent to Pantano with a despatch, rode up from that direction and reported that there were Indians at a house a mile and a half from where we were. There was no cross-questioning of the guide, who was known to us as a cool, sensible, and trustworthy man. The command "Attention," brought back the men that had gone to fill their canteens and straightened up those reclining in the shade of their horses. "Prepare to mount—mount! Forward—march!" and we are off at a brisk trot, which soon breaks into a gallop. Arriving at the house referred to we find it deserted, but bearing unmistakable signs of having been visited by Indians. The guide and the Mexicans pushed obliquely up the mountain, the command moving meanwhile along its base to opposite the point on the road where the dead body lay. Here the command halted, while the captain went over and made sure of this sad matter, and wrote a despatch to General Miles. A party of citizens came meanwhile from Pantano and took the body away.

The man killed was an American by the name of Robert Lloyd, who was living temporarily for safety at Pantano. He was on a visit to his ranch to let the calves out of his corral, and perhaps to attend to a few other matters, when his murderers, skulking behind a bush or rock by the side of the road, put a bullet through his back. From his blood-tracks it appears that he rode several hundred yards after being shot before he fell from his horse, and that he was then dragged some distance off the road before he was rifled and robbed by his captors, who took his horse, and gun, and ammunition.

While we have done no killing or capturing, we have accomplished something by to-day's operations in learning—first, that there is in these mountains a party of from fifteen to thirty Indians; second, that a Mexican report about Indians is not necessarily false.

We went into camp here to await instructions from General Miles, to whom the captain has recommended the employment of Indian scouts in the mountains.

In the course of the afternoon a party of men came out from Benson in a buckboard for the dead body, and, finding that it had already been taken away, made us a short visit and went back. Shortly after their departure, a detachment of our men, coming in from Gill's ranch, reported that they had passed these men and been told by them that they had exchanged shots with a party of five Indians at the house this side of Gill's ranch—

"HE WAS DRAGGED SOME DISTANCE OFF THE ROAD"

the one to which our guide had led us—and had taken a gun
from them, showing a gun as the one they had taken. A party of
citizens by whom we were subsequently visited, vouched for
the veracity of the Benson men, and testified to the significant
haste with which they had made for Gill's ranch. This other
party has been out all day visiting probable objectives of Indian
depredation, looking up trails and other signs for our information.

If there were more men in the Territory combining their fear-
lessness, energy, and knowledge of country, with their interest

"THEY HAD EXCHANGED SHOTS WITH A PARTY OF FIVE INDIANS"

in the work of the soldiers, the campaign would be a considerably easier and shorter one than it promises to be.

These Rincon Mountains are a mass of rock fashioned by plutonic and atmospheric forces into every variety of shape and form—an imposing exhibition of blocks and boulders, bold bluffs and promontories, broad, slippery slopes, peaks, domes, and crests, and jagged and serrated ridges. In their dazzling, reflected sunlight, they are anything but an attractive prospect to a traveler. We are told that the summit is, in the main, even and level, grassy and well-timbered, and that near the highest point is a good-sized lake; also, that there are few people well enough acquainted with the topography of the range to guide us through it.

RINCON MOUNTAINS, May 26, 1886.—Captain Lawton arrived at Lloyd's ranch with his command about noon, and after he and his officers had taken a little lunch with us, his Indian scouts were started up the mountain. Captain Lawton will drive the hostiles through the range, while Captain Lebo marched by Gill's ranch around the east side of the range, entering farther into the foothills. An hour before sunset I was detached with my troop to a gap known by the Mexican name of *El Puero*.* By dark I had my command in position, supper cooked, and fires out, and my men disposed with a view to forming an ambush. If the Indians are pressed to-day by Captain Lawton, they are likely to come through here some time between moonrise and sunrise. The captain has not troops enough to guard all the outlets of the range. He may, however, be able to watch them. On account of their women and children, the Indians are not apt to scatter, and thirty of them together will make a pretty plain trail.

RINCON MOUNTAINS, May 27, 1886.—Learned from a despatch to General Lebo and conversation with citizens that the trail on which we put Captain Lawton has turned down the mountain southwestward, but that it is likely to turn up again upon passing a certain ranch or two, which the Indians have probably searched for cartridges and provisions.

About eight o'clock this morning, while I was superintending the work of digging for water for my stock, a report came from the picket that a party of horsemen was approaching our camp. The men responded with alacrity to my call for them to get their guns, but before they had all complied with it the sergeant of the guard called out: "Tell them they are soldiers." In the course of fifteen minutes they came into camp and turned out to be, not soldiers, but Mexican volunteers from Tres Alamos, a motley,

*A narrow road through a mountain.

"THEY WERE A MOTLEY, HARD-LOOKING SET"

hard-looking set. They were armed with government Springfield
rifles, calibre 45 and 50. One of them carried an old rusty sabre
fastened under his leg. After resting a while under our shade,
they made off, with the purpose of rounding up fresh horses. If
they were regulars, they would be lying in camp, waiting for
their horses to rest.

About eleven o'clock an order came from the captain for me
to rejoin him. I had to throw away a mess of beans that was
being cooked for the men, the third that has been thus lost since
we started from Calabasas. Our army should have a field ration
that can be eaten without being cooked, for not only is it often
impracticable in the field to do any slow or lengthy cooking, but

it is often necessary or advisable to dispense with fires altogether.

We made our way by a rough trail, on which we had to dismount, from our camp down into the bottom of a cañon; and,
having followed it some distance into the range, proceeded
lengthwise to the latter, into Happy Valley, directing our march
upon the one bright spot that I could see in it, a square patch of
green, marking a ranch. While my horses were being well
watered at the house, I was presented by Mr. Mathews, one of
the owners, with a sack of *jerky*—jerked beef—which I gave to
the men.

Mr. Mathews accompanied me from here, guiding me by a
dry river-bed and winding, shadowy gullies and ravines, up
the side of the mountain to the captain's camp.

RINCON MOUNTAINS, May 28, 1886.—Our fires were all
out yesterday before dark, and were not started again before
daylight this morning. Having breakfasted, we resumed our
march up the mountain, and after a steep march of about a mile,
followed by a steeper walk of about two miles, we found ourselves on the top, at a large spring, surrounded by tall, fresh
grass, and overshadowed by fine old pines. We were in condition to relish the water, which seemed to us almost ice cold, not
having filled our canteens before starting, and the pine needles
under foot making the walking especially difficult. The banks
of the spring being too steep for the horses to drink from, we
moved to a small creek a few miles off, on the other side of the
summit, and there went into camp. While making this last
stretch two of my horses gave out, and had to be abandoned. As
I have but one spare horse, this puts one of my men on foot.

Our camp is as pleasing to the eye as it is restful to the body.
From the ridge on which the officers have established themselves
I look down upon the two rows of saddles of the two troops,
each with its cook-fire at one end; and, beyond, the sparkling
creek by which they are flanked, upon the steep backbone or
watershed of the mountain. Retiring over a springy sward, a dis-

"THIS PUTS ONE OF MY MEN ON FOOT"

tance of a few yards, I overlook a broken timbered declivity, and, extending out from it a dry, dusty plain. In my front are the hazy Tucson Mountains, near the foot of which I descry the shimmering town of that name; on my right the glaring, frowning Catalinas, and on my left, separated by a valley, the purple Whetstones and Santa Ritas.

Their canned provisions having given out, the officers commence to-day subsisting on soldiers' rations. An American soldier is allowed for his daily food: ¾ lb. of bacon or 1¼ lb. of fresh beans; 1⅛ lb. of flour or 1 lb. of hard bread; 0.15 lb. of beans or 0.10 lb. of rice, 0.10 lb. of coffee, 0.15 lb. of sugar, and a certain quantity of salt, pepper, vinegar, and yeast powder. He receives no liquor. With occasional exceptions, especially as regards bread and bacon—of which he has not always his full allowance—a soldier gets all he asks for of the nourishment provided for him. The rations are issued at intervals of about ten days to the company commander, who disposes of the savings for the benefit, as far as practicable, of all the men alike. They are ordinarily sold, and the proceeds expended for the improvement of the table fare or for means of amusement.

TANQUE VERDE, May 29, 1886.—While on a visit to the herd at break of day, I was informed by the sergeant of the guard that one of his sentinels had allowed several mules to get away during the night, without making proper effort to prevent it, and that he—the sergeant—had taken his belt from him and put him under charge of the guard. An investigation satisfied me that the delinquent deserved to be punished, and I accordingly had him make to-day's march on foot, leading his horse. Our march did not prove much harder, however, on him than on the rest of us, as officers and men had to walk about three-fourths of it.

Coming down the northern point of the mountain and out westward into the plain, we transferred ourselves in a few hours from the temperate to the torrid zone. In the foot-slopes we passed through an ardent grove of giant cacti, called by Mexicans *Sahuaros,* some of them fifty feet high. Among these prickly horrors grew a variety of lesser ones, more or less closely related to them. On the edge of the plain we stopped at the adobe house of Terris' ranch, at whose duck-pond we watered the horses. Being unable to procure forage here, we pushed on to Tanque Verde, about two miles farther, over a road so dusty that I could not see the troop ahead of me, and, at times, could hardly catch breath.

We are camped on the road between two fences lining it; an *acequia* affording us a slender stream of muddy water, which does for the horses. We get our drinking water from a well.

My first sergeant has reported to me that he has not bacon to last after to-day, and that his flour will last only to include breakfast the day after to-morrow, whereas he should have rations to last six days after to-day. I have, consequently, placed him in arrest.

We have learned here through despatches from General Miles that a portion of the Indians that we have been after are down in the Santa Ritas, and that they have committed depredations west of Crittenden, killing a man two miles from Greaterville. The general wishes us to find the rest of them, and to catch these should they return here, as he thinks they are liable to do after procuring fresh mounts.

We have no grain, but plenty of good barley hay. The men have fresh meat, the captain having bought a beef for sixteen dollars and had it divided between the two troops. The officers had a spread this evening of roast duck, bacon, greens, potatoes, onions, bread, and coffee.

NORTH OF PANTANO, May 30, 1886.—Before breakfast I walked, over fields and fences, to a farming Chinaman, and bought from him thirty-four pounds of flour for the troop. The wells at Tanque Verde afford the same clear, cool, soft water that we drank in the mountains; they are the secret, no doubt, of the successful farming done at Tanque Verde under irrigation.

If our command is to be in condition to follow a trail, it must rest now for several days. It is in need, too, of new accoutrements for the horses and clothing for the men.

Our column would be a curious sight for a European officer. Most of the men ride in their blue flannel shirts, their blouses strapped to their saddles; one big sergeant wears a bright red shirt, and looks not unlike a mounted fireman; some of the men take off their blue shirts and ride in their gray knit undershirts. There are all sorts of hats worn, of American and Mexican make, the most common being the ugly army campaign hat of gray felt. Some of the men wear over their blue army trousers, the brown canvas overalls, intended to be worn only on fatigue; some wear blue civilian overalls. There are few trousers not torn or badly worn, especially in the seat. Here is a man with a single spur; here one without any. The carbines are variously carried; some according to regulations, hung by a sling over the left shoulder, the muzzle steadied in a socket behind the right leg; some in a boot or holster under the leg; some strapped, muzzle downward, to the cantle or the pummel of the saddle; some loose in the hand in front of the body. I should state, however, that in K troop the carbines are all carried according to regulations. In my troop the non-commissioned officers are armed with a Colt's revolver, in addition to the carbine. The trumpeters in both troops are armed like the privates, and have no trumpets. The men's feet are some in shoes and some in boots. Each man wears a woven cartridge belt around his waist, holding from forty to forty-five cartridges, and carries about twenty additional cartridges in his saddle pockets. This ammunition is all that we have.

Left Tanque Verde for Pantano this afternoon, and marched again among the *sahuaros* at the base of the Rincon Mountains. At Teya's ranch, where we watered the horses and filled the canteens, I was pointed out the cañon in the Rincons from which a child was stolen by Indians about a week ago. When its mother tried to save it, the Indians pelted her with stones, presumably for want of ammunition. The child subsequently got away while its captors were pillaging a ranch, being surprised by a party of Mexicans. There being no grass at Teya's, we went two miles beyond it to make our present dry camp.

PANTANO, ARIZONA, May 31, 1886.—At break of day the cooks were waked, and at daylight the men were feeding and grooming, forage having just arrived in a wagon from Pantano. As soon as the horses had eaten—the horses are the primary consideration in a cavalry command—the mules were ordered to be packed, and this being accomplished, the horses were saddled and the command mounted and started for breakfast. Stopping only at the Mountain Spring ranch to water, we arrived at this dreary place at half-past ten.

WATERING AT TEYA'S RANCH

Two of the officers have got away for about three hours by taking the train to Benson. The men are mostly dozing in the shade of the station-house or enlivening the bar-room.

PANTANO, ARIZONA, June 1, 1886.—I had the satisfaction this morning of seeing for the first time a *Gila monster,* an ugly reptile peculiar to Arizona, and, as its name implies, most common along the Gila River. It is a sort of cross between a lizard and an alligator, roughly striped black and white. The specimen that I saw, which was found in camp under a saddle, was about sixteen inches long. When prodded with a stick, it hissed and thrust out its heavy forked tongue, raising its head menacingly, but scarcely moving otherwise. Its bite is often fatal, the effect of it depending more or less upon the state of the animal's temper and the depth of the wound. One of our guides tells me that he has seen a chicken killed experimentally by the hissing of one in its face.[32]

A freight train passing westward this morning left a party of Papago Indians here—men, women and children, with bag and baggage. I tried to talk with them but without success, as they understood neither Spanish nor English—at least, as I speak it. They were on their way from a hunt or an herb gathering in the country about Benson. These Papagoes travel a good deal as dead-heads on the tops of freight-cars, between Tucson, which is near their reservation, and points east and west of there.[33] They are a living refutation of the assertion that there is no good Indian but a dead Indian. Every fall they go out and gather acorns in the mountains about Tucson, and are feared by no one unless, as it sometimes happens, they are taken for Apaches.

This afternoon there was a scrub race of two hundred yards beween a Mexican pony and an American. The crowd that gathered to see it—composed mainly of soldiers and Mexicans and American ranchmen—is probably the largest that there ever was in Pantano. The Mexican horse was a supple, wiry animal, seemingly all nerve and sinew; the American was somewhat larger and comparatively heavy built. Both were ridden under a heavy Mexican saddle. The Mexican was the better jockeyed and led almost from the start, coming in a good length ahead. The stakes were five dollars a side. This event was followed by a race between an officer's pony and an American citizen's. The former was ridden by a soldier, the latter by a Mexican boy; the representative of the army under a folded blanket, the citizen horse barebacked, with a surcingle strapped around the rider's bent knees keeping them well up and fast to the horse's sides. Both riders were lightened by the removal of their boots. The army was beaten again, for the victory was to the citizen.

Received rations to-day to include the 19th of the month. I sold the candles, all but one pound, at the rate of ten cents a pound, thus raising $1.50, which will just repay me for the flour that I bought at Tanque Verde. I also exchanged twenty-five pounds of bacon with a Mexican ranchman for fifty pounds of beef, making a quarter of a pound of beef on every ration of bacon, or eight and one-third pounds altogether. I can

THE RACE

make one day's meat for my thirty-eight men (including myself), by thus bartering 142½ pounds of bacon.

PANTANO, ARIZONA, June 3, 1886.—It has not been so hot here as I expected. The officers have their beds made down under a sort of arbor at the house of a railroad employé, where they spend most of the day reading and sleeping.

I have made out a list of the clothing and equipment required by my men, in order that when we go into a post, I may at once make requisition for them. It would be most unreasonable to expect of our troops, campaigning on the frontier, the trim appearance preserved by European troops on a campaign. Our marching is done mostly away from roads, and largely through woods and thickets, and among prickly shrubs; our enemy leads us ordinarily over the roughest country that he can find, such as to a European army, as equipped in Europe, would be utterly impracticable: our men when not on the march, lie in the open air, or in bivouac, while European troops, as a rule, are established in cantonments, or quartered in houses: ours do not pass daily through towns and villages under the friendly or hostile scrutiny of the populations, with incidental opportunities of refitting and repairing; and, finally, owing to the unsoldierliness of our garrison service on the one hand, and the ingloriousness of Indian warfare on the other, our men have not the pride in their uniform of soldiers engaged in regular civilized war.

One rarely sees a frontiersman—be he ranchman, miner, guide or hunter—at his vocation in a suit of cloth, without its being protected by an outer suit of leather, buckskin, cotton or canvas. With slight modification our canvas fatigue dress would be a more suitable one for the field than is our regular uniform.

PANTANO, ARIZONA, June 4, 1886.—The captain received this morning from the Acting Adjutant-General at Willcox, the following copy of a despatch from Fort Lowell:

"Signal fires have been seen in Rincon Mountains the last two nights. A party of eight Indians was seen in San Pedro Valley last night. To-day Mr. Davis was killed at three o'clock, four miles east of Vail's ranch. Lieutenant Weaver and fifteen scouts leave here to-night for the scene of killing. These Indians have evidently been in the Rincon Mountains for the last two weeks."

These signal fires are doubtless the burning woods that have been observable to us ever since we came here. I cannot believe in the Indians in the San Pedro valley, as long as I know nothing as to the persons reporting them. I do not question the killing of Mr. Davis, but think it quite as probable the work of a Mexican or an American as of an Indian.

WHETSTONE MOUNTAINS, June 5, 1886.—About one o'clock this morning the captain was waked up by Mr. Mathews and informed that Indians had been at his ranch at six o'clock yesterday evening, and had taken from it seven or eight head of stock. Consequently, about an hour and a half after daylight, Lieutenant Clarke and myself set out with troops K and D respectively, he toward the west and I toward the east, to look up a trail and follow it.

I directed my march upon Mathews' ranch. Just beyond the Puerto, where I camped a few nights ago, I came upon three Americans that had followed the trail from the ranch, who, having put me on it, kept on following it ahead of me. It led down a cañon, and, turning out of it, circled the point of a spur on our right. A couple of citizens who there left me to go to Pantano, took a note from me to the captain, in which I reported that I was on a trail of from fifteen to twenty animals heading for the Whetstone Mountains. About an hour later I was joined by the two Mathews brothers.

"SIR, THEY ARE IN SIGHT"

XIV

W.HETSTONE MOUNTAINS, June, 1886 (*continued*).—With my regular guide, and three citizen volunteers to help him keep the trail, I push steadily along at a good four-and-a-half-mile walk. Suddenly the trailers halt. They are pointing ahead of them, and looking that way and at each other, evidently conferring about something.

The soldier charged with keeping up communication with them comes galloping up to me and, saluting, reports:

"Sir, they are in sight."

"What's in sight?"

"The Indians, sir."

"How far off?"

"About a mile and a half, sir."

By another question I ascertain that they are standing still. After making a few remarks to my men upon my intended tactics, I set out in two platoon-columns of fours at a brisk trot. About a mile from my objective point, I halt to let the men tighten their girths, and then push on, alternating between a trot and a gallop, across the railroad track in the bottom, and up the long, rolling slope fringing the point of the Whetstones. As I surmount the swells in the ground, I strain my eyes to distinguish the figures, or perceive some movement of the enemy. I make out nothing but a fixed, glistening line, as if of gun-barrels resting on the ground, and to the right rear of this what seems to be a herd of horses. But if that glistening is of fire-arms, that knoll marked out by it is no position to go galloping up to on horseback. So ordering my second platoon to open the

"BY PUTTING A CARBINE BULLET THROUGH ITS BRAIN"

action from an advantageous position, I started off at a gallop on a detour, to get at the enemy's flank and rear. Before this maneuver, however, is fairly under way, there arises a suspicion in my mind that my enemy is but an optical illusion, and when near enough to have secured my advantage over him, I perceive that his line of gun-barrels is a surface of smooth rock, and his herd of horses a clump of small trees.

Going through the foothills of the Whetstones we found two horses abandoned by the Indians, one a dead mare with a Mexican brand, the other a broken-down government horse, which was readily recognized as one of the two horses that I abandoned in the Rincons. Its gaunt frame and festering backbone, apart from evidencing impressment by the Indians, made me reproach myself strongly for not having shot it. I had a sergeant dismount and make the best amend possible under the circumstances by putting a carbine bullet through its brain. Proceeding westward around the point of the mountain, we came, in the vicinity of Kinnea's ranch, upon three head of cattle killed by the Indians. One had been cut open for meat; the others had only been stripped of a piece of their hide, presumably for making horse-shoes. These Indian horseshoes serve not only to protect the hoof, but also to make its impression less distinct. At Kinnea's we watered our horses—they had not drunk since yesterday evening—and filled our canteens. The trail led from here along the mountain-side to a creek, and followed it to its head. Here we found the body of a man shot through the heart. From papers lying near him and from his appearance, I judged him to be a German. He was evidently camping here, cultivating a small vegetable garden. Not far off lay his dog and *burro,* or Mexican donkey, both dead. We found his gun, an old smooth-bore, percussion-cap musket, and by it a bag of shot, and an old-fashioned horn powder-flask. The gun had been discharged, from which we inferred that he had made something of a fight, though it was plain from the exposed position in which he lay, that he had been taken by surprise. The rammer of his gun was stuck in the bore so that none of us could pull it out, but whether it became so in his own hands or in those of an Indian, we could only conjecture. While my guides were looking up the tracks of his murderers, I had a party of men take his pick and shovels and hastily inter him. I noticed on the top of his head a raw, white

"SHOT THROUGH THE HEART"

circle about the size of a dollar, which showed him to have been
scalped.

The trail took straight up the side of the mountain to the edge
of the top, where we found an abandoned camp. The little fire
where the wily marauders had cooked their stolen beef, and

around which they had discussed their day's work and planned the morrow's, was still warm. Off about ten yards from the fire and close to an abrupt fall or bluff, was the lookout from which they had scanned the country below for indications of pursuit.

As the trail was found to lead from here down a slope steeper and rougher than the one that we had come up, to continue apparently across the rough foothills, the three citizens decided not to accompany me any farther. It was an hour or two of sunset, and their ponies were all but worn out. The flanks of one jaded animal were bloody from the prodding they had sustained from a pair of huge Mexican spurs. I was sorry to lose my volunteers, who had already been of great service to me. Whenever the trail was lost they would scatter out on both sides of the column, and it would not be long before one of my four trailers would give his arm an upward and forward swing, calling out cheerily: "Here she goes!"

Coming down into the foothills one of the pack-mules turned a somersault, smashing our coffee-mill and losing twenty-five pounds of coffee. Upon a slight delay from this mishap we crept along the base of the mountain close behind our one guide, who, with the assistance of only one of the men, had a good deal of trouble keeping the trail. As the sun was sinking below the horizon, making further trailing impossible, we halted on an open space at the edge of a cañon, and went into dry camp. Having bread already cooked, we had a supper of bread and bacon, with water from our canteens to wash it down.

Two canteens, or six pints, of water will last one on a trip like this about one day. A man may be depended on for one day without water. Hence, the canteens may be calculated to carry the men along for two days, which is about as long as their stock will last without drinking. Six pints of water may seem a good deal to drink in a single day, but it will not to any thoughtful person who has had the experience of scambling up a barren mountain under an Arizona sun.

I estimate the distance marched to-day at forty-five miles.

"ONE OF THE PACK-MULES TURNED A SOMERSAULT"

BUCKEYE RANCH, June 6, 1886.—At the first sign of day the mules were brought in and packed. There was practically nothing for breakfast, as bacon could not be eaten without water, or bread cooked without it, and we had no hard bread. I had bacon cooked and given to the men, in order that they should have something to eat when they should come to water, and that I should not have to stop during the day to cook. Owing to the incompetency of one of my packers, I did not get off as early as I meant to, but was on the march within an hour after sunrise, with the guide and a soldier coadjutor well ahead on the trail. Just beyond camp we had some scrambling and sliding, which cost me 200 pounds of flour, sixty pounds of bacon, a half-dozen mule shoes and one manta, or pack cover—these articles having to be abandoned to lighten up the packs. I have lost, yesterday and to-day together, two days' supplies for my command. About ten miles from camp we came upon a path, or beaten trail, which led us to a point called Barrel Spring, the site of a Mexican wood camp. The water comes out of the steep side of the hill into an excavated basin about the height of a horse's chest. As two of our horses drank the basin dry, and it filled up very slowly, I decided not to wait here to water. I had my guide, however, go into an examination of the locality, which detained me nearly an hour. He found the tracks of a wounded man pursued by a man on a horse. It is presumable that the man on foot got away, as his trail led through a woody, rocky ravine, and, where the guide left it, was unaccompanied by signs of pursuit. A few hundred yards from the spring, on the road skirting the base of the mountain, stood a two-horse wagon loaded with wood; its driver or the Indians had doubtless made off with the horses. About a mile from this point, where the road turns into the mountain toward Mescal Spring, we passed another abandoned wagon. Perceiving beyond here that our trail led out of the mountain, as if to take across to the Santa Ritas, I dispatched my trumpeter, whose horse was lame and another man whose feet were sore from footing it among rocks and stones in canvas shoes, into Fort Huachuca, with a note from me to the commanding officer. The trail soon afterward turned from its eastward course toward the south, and led us around the western point of the Mustang Mountains down into the Barbocomari bottom, across the railroad, and, in a due south course, up a long, even slope ahead of us. Before we reached the rocky divide at the head of the San Rafael valley, the guide lost the trail, and, instead of telling me so at once and going back to look for it, kept on in the expectation of cutting it. As soon as I ascertained that this was the case, I halted the command and had my three trailers—there were two soldiers assisting the guide—undertake a thorough search for the trail. Having followed them around for nearly an hour among sharp and slippery rocks, and not knowing how long it might be before they would put me on the trail again, I determined upon taking the command to water, and accordingly, leaving the trailers to continue their search, with instructions to join me upon finding the trail or night coming on, directed my march upon Buckeye Ranch, about four miles off.

My horses had not drunk since the evening before and my men had, with few exceptions (I presume), consumed the water that they got at Barrel Spring. One of my packers had warned me that if the mules did not get water to-night they would go crazy. Said this alarmist: "You won't be able to do nuthin' with 'em, sir; they'll go plumb *loco,* that's what they will."

But here we are in the smiling valley in which we are to camp. What a satisfaction, upon unbridling at the creek, to see the dusty noses plunge into it, and hear the steady gurgling along the line of down-stretched throats! About dusk the guide came into camp and reported that he had been unable to recover the trail. I was exceedingly provoked, but had nothing to say. Guides and trailers are only human. They get tired and thirsty like other men and then think more of finding water than of finding Indians.

We have corn on the cob for the animals. Marched to-day, forty miles.

SANTA CRUZ, MEXICO, June 7, 1886.—At "crack of day," as the sergeant of the guard expressed it, the stir of camp was started by waking up the cook.

I sent two men, one a sick corporal and the other a useless packer, into Fort Huachuca, giving the corporal a note to the post commander, in which I reported my movements up to the time of writing, and stated that having heard of a need of troops below Santa Cruz, I was going that way in the hope of getting back on the lost trail, and requested in regard to the packer, that he be relieved from duty with my troop, stating my grounds for doing so.

I marched by road out of the Huachucas into the San Rafael valley, and down over Cameron's ranch to La Noria. As I passed Cameron's house an infantry sergeant came out and informed me that a party of fifteen Indians was reported to have been near Red Rock, and to have presumably passed between Harshaw and the Mowry Mine this morning.

Arriving at La Noria, I learned that Captain Wood, of the Fourth Cavalry, had gone through with his troop about two hours before, making for the Mowry Mine, to investigate the killing of a man at Peck's Mine, a mile or two beyond the Blue Nose. Intending to rest here until night or the following morning, I put the horses in a corral and had the cook put on a mess of beans. About two hours later Captain Wood came back, having learned this side of the Mowry that Captain McAdams, with his troop of the Second Cavalry, was on the trail. Captain Wood's is the first troop that I have seen with horses all of one color. His are gray, and fine large grays these horses were! Their light, active riders, moreover, bore the stamp of trained and seasoned soldiers. Advance guard and main body, followed by pack train and rear guard, swung past us in succession to the rhythmic measure of horses' feet, stamping out four and three-quarter miles an hour—both men and horses covered with dust, but with heads up, on a race with the Indians for the Penito Mountains.

While at La Noria, I replaced, by purchase on receipt, the rations that I lost and abandoned in the Whetstones, and likewise fitted myself out with horse and mule shoes. I also hired an additional guide. The usual pay of a guide or trailer is five dollars a day.

The shoes not being *set,* and there being no means of setting them at La Noria, I moved this afternoon to this place, where I was told there was a blacksmith. I went into camp about dark in the corral of Señor Alvino Aguséne, from whom I obtained barley hay.

Having arranged with the blacksmith for the use of his forge, I spent the remainder of the evening at the Montoyas', where I heard some harp and guitar playing, and singing, both Spanish and English. Young Mr. Montoya, the interpreter at the San Carlos reservation, at present Chief of Scouts for Captain Lawton, was one of the company. He left, however, before it broke up, having to join Captain Lawton by morning, in the Penito Mountains, with a party of twenty Mexicans raised here. Marched to-day thirty-one miles.

QUITACA, MEXICO, June 8, 1886.—My farrier and blacksmith worked until one o'clock this morning at the forge, and before breakfast the blacksmith was busy shoeing.

Having resolved on a move to the south and west, with a view of heading off the Indians or taking up their trail should they make past Captain Wood, I marched southward to San Lazaro, and, having rested there about an hour, giving my stock another feed of grain—their last, I presumed, for some time—proceeded to the Cajoncito de Quitaca, following it up to the smelter. The Cajoncito is a narrow cañon with high, rocky walls, whose only inhabitant is an American in charge of the works near which we are camped. The Indians commonly water in it on their way to the Cananea Mountains. San Lazaro is a ranch covering four square leagues, in the plain between the Santa Cruz Mountains and the Penitas. It is managed by four owners of a league each. Marched to-day thirty miles.

QUITACA RANCH, MEXICO, June 9, 1886.—Moved here, four miles from the smelter, to a safer camp, with better grass. The ranch is but a name. There is nothing left of it but the posts of an old corral, the crumbling walls of the *hacienda*,* and a tumbled-down hut. The latter I have taken as quarters for myself and guides, the men having the shelter of large oak trees.

BACANUCHI, June 10, 1886.—Just as the troop ceased grooming this morning, a mounted man was reported coming up the road, who, upon his approach, turned out to be a Mexican. He represented to me that the Indians were making east, pursued by a party of fifteen Mexicans. While I was talking with him, two more Mexicans arrived, one on foot and the other mounted, the latter delivering to me the following despatch:

CALABASAS, ARIZ., June 8, 1886.

Lieut. Bigelow, near Santa Cruz, via Nogales, Ariz.:

Captain Lawton is reported close to Indians this morning, base of Penito Mountains. It is believed his force is sufficient for that band. Unless your command is in close proximity to Indians, you had better move up toward Mowry Mine and be prepared to intercept a band of Indians west of Fairbanks that have been committing depredations to-day, and will doubtless be driven south by Lebo and Weaver.

MILES, Commanding.

On the back of the envelope was written in pencil:

"Opened by Captain Lawton, A.M. 9th, who is on trail of band, who have crossed into the Azuls."

So Captain Lawton's force had not thus far proved itself "sufficient for that band;" and the band was not coming my way, the Sierra Azul being to the south of the Cananeas. From the Mexicans, however, I gathered that these Indians were probably making for the Sierra Madre, and that if so, they would doubtless turn northward and come to Quitaca or Tinaja de Agua, twenty-one miles east of Quitaca, for water. Never having been in this lonesome country before, and having no map of it ade-

*Farm-house, homestead.

"SURPRISED BY A PARTY OF MEXICANS"

quate to my purposes, and no competent guide, I allow myself to
be governed to a large extent by the inhabitants that I meet.
Hence, deeming it too late to gain anything by going back to the
Mowry Mine, I decided to move to Tinaja de Agua, hoping by
thus placing myself between the Indians that Lawton was following and those coming from Fairbanks, to intercept one or the

other paty, or by patrolling the road between Quitaca and Tinaja, to get on one of their two trails. I thought it likely that the two bands were endeavoring to effect a junction somewhere about Tinaja.

Having saddled and packed and given a note to the messenger for General Miles, I set out, accompanied by the other mounted Mexicans. About three miles out we came to the only water short of Tinaja, called Ojo de Pino. My Mexican staying behind here, I had a couple of men go ahead to keep track of my two guides, who, I understood, had gotten the route from the Mexicans. Coming out of the the valley in which we had camped, over the south spur of the Cananea Mountains, we headed gradually southward into a shallow cañon, in which we accomplished a totally different march from what I had reckoned on. Not until we had gone thirty-five miles from where we camped last night did we get to water, and then we had to make five miles to this point for forage.

Bacanuchi is a ranch; sometimes it is called the Pesqueira ranch, having been the property of the late Governor Pesqueira, of Sonora. It is now held by his widow, who is desirous of selling it and retiring, I am told, upon the proceeds, to Los Angeles, California. The governor owned, besides this immense estate— twenty-four miles square—one adjoining it, called the Cananea ranch, of the same size—of which, however, he sold a portion. The consolidated estate is at present stocked with 15,000 head of cattle, and herds of horses and sheep.

Our camp is in an enclosed field, a few hundred yards from the *hacienda.* This is a substantial one-story adobe building, with an interior court, or *patio,* and a portico shaded by plain white cotton curtains, which in warm weather are sprinkled with water. The windows are all iron-barred. Around this mansion are the humble dwellings of the employés, down to the squalid huts of the *peons,* mostly of one room, with one door and no window.

For years Governor Pesqueira was the autocrat of Sonora, during which period he profited handsomely, it is said, through connivance with smugglers.

BACANUCHI, MEXICO, June 11, 1886.—Spent the day here in rest, relying for Indian news upon the *vaqueros* of the ranch. It was reported early in the morning that a couple of Indians had been seen somewhere about two miles below here, but these turned out, upon investigation, to have been smugglers. My hope of being invited to the *hacienda* was disappointed, and I wished for the days of the genial, hospitable old governor, who is said to have had an especial kindliness for Americans.

JARALITO, MEXICO, June 12, 1886.—To make sure that the Indians were not crossing my trail behind me, I set out about three o'clock this afternoon for Tinaja, twenty-one miles north of here (Bacanuchi is about fifty miles from the line by the road). I was accompanied by the Mexican that started out with me from Quitaca. He has been a major in the Mexican cavalry, and custom officer at San Pedro, and is now Inspector of Mines —a Federal officer, charged with assessing the value of mining property, and seeing that the work is done on it that is required by law, for in Mexico the mines are practically owned by the government. He was attended by a *peon,* or servant. Before we started he presented me with a lunch of hard-boiled eggs and *tortillas* done up for transportation on my horse, also a little bag of *pinole. Tortillas* are the ordinary Mexican bread, unleavened pancakes about one-sixteenth of an inch thick. *Pinole* is the staple diet of Mexican travelers and soldiers. It is ordinarily made of corn, roasted and crushed and slightly sweetened, the most common sweetening being *panoche,* a crude sugar. To prepare it, put a few teaspoonfuls in a cup of water, and let it stand until the grains have settled and swollen, then sweeten to suit the taste.

I had six men dismounted this afternoon on account of their horses' backs being sore. Having footed it fifteen miles, I let them ride the remaining ten to where we camped.

I passed Tinaja in the dark, my guides having branched off to it without leaving any one to bring me after them, and I pushed on here rather than go back. Citizen guides often prove unsatisfactory from the ignorance of the wants and methods of a military command, especially as regards the saving of time and horseflesh. They are not apt to appreciate, unless they have had experience with troops, the annoyance to a cavalry officer, arriving at an intended camping-place, to find his guide watering his own horse or conversing about the weather and the Indians, without having ascertained anything in regard to the approaches to water for the command, or the situation of grass or wood, or the supply of grain or hay.

It was well that I did not go to Tinaja, as it turned out to be an ugly hole at the end of a box cañon, with but one way in and out; but the place that I am at now is not much better for a camp, being dominated by a bluff on one side and commanded by steep hills on the other. Making camp after dark, I had the horses *side-lined* and the guard posted on the side of the herd from camp, with orders to look out for camp-fires and have an ear to footsteps, of horse or man. In a troop of cavalry there are ordinarily two sentinels over the horses if they are herded or *lariated* out, and one if they are on a line; none over the men or baggage. The wariness and superstition of the Apache Indian are ample security against his entering the body of a camp at night. To explain a couple of professional terms: "Side-lines" is the army substitute for hobbles. They connect a fore and hind foot, and consist in the main of two leather leglets joined by an iron chain. On account of their aptness to hurt the feet they are used as little as possible. A lariat is a rope about thirty feet long, and half an inch thick, used for holding a horse when he has to graze, and cannot safely be herded or turned loose. In the army it is furnished with an iron picket-pin fifteen inches long.

PINAL, MEXICO, June 13, 1886.—In order not to run short of rations, and having to make short marches on account of my dismounted men, I am working gradually back toward my base at Calabasas. To-day's march of eleven miles around the north point of the Cananea Mountains to this old and nearly extinct mining settlement was, for the greater part, over a dry, rolling country; we are now among rocky hills, and creeks and rills, and noble pines.

A courier from Captain Wood's troop of the Fourth Cavalry came into camp this evening with a note for Captain Dorst, understood to be near Ojo de Agua, twenty-six miles from here. As he had traveled forty miles yesterday, and twenty to-day, and, moreover, did not know the way, I took the note from him, and sent it on by a courier of my own. No grain last night or to-night, and the grass here is scant and poor.

SAN LAZARO, MEXICO, June 14, 1886.—Marched by a fairly good road, up a winding, rocky ravine, flanked on both sides by pine-covered heights, to the Copper King mining camp, near the top of the Cananea Mountains, and thence by the Quitaca Smelter, here. At the smelter I left the road and took the trail, which is said to be a short cut. On this trail I lost three horses without gaining appreciably in time, but with a lasting gain, I hope, in my distrust of short cuts. I had the dismounted men take their horses at the Copper King Mine, and ride from there on.

Our marches of the last ten days add up as follows:—June 5, 45 miles; 6, 40; 7, 31; 8, 30; 9, 4; 10, 40; 11, 0; 12, 25: 13, 11, and 14, 29—255 miles. They thus average a forced march, the regulation march of cavalry being from 15 to 20 miles.

I am told that the day after I passed through here going east, a party of Indians, numbering thirty-seven, crossed the road some twenty-five miles below, tesifying to their hot pursuit by eating raw meat. It is some comfort to reflect that if I had been there to receive them they would probably have known of it, and changed their course, perhaps to the very one on which I was looking for them.

LA ESPERANZA, MEXICO, June 15, 1886.—About the middle of last night the courier whom I had sent to look up Captain Dorst came into camp on foot, carrying his blanket. His horse

A "SIDE-LINED" HORSE

had "played out" about ten miles from here. He had not found
the captain, who, as I have since learned, has gone into Fort
Huachuca.

Marched six miles to this point on the Santa Cruz. Three of
the dismounted men had to foot it. The fourth, a packer, whose
services I could ill dispense with, I allowed to ride a pack-mule,
for which there was no load.

We have a good road from here to Calabasas, down the valley
of the Santa Cruz. The gratefulness to us of thick foliage and
rippling water can hardly be appreciated by one who has never
lived and traveled in this arid region. There is no town or village

on our route. La Esperanza, like San Lazaro, is a ranch. Back of its hacienda is a fine orchard and vegetable garden, watered by an acequia. The river has a width here of about six feet, and a depth of about as many inches, and runs the year through. I am told that apples, which I thought were a northern plant, grow better here than any other fruit.

BUENA VISTA, MEXICO, June 16, 1886.—This ranch is close upon the line, part of it being not improbably in the United States. Its name, *Fair View,* is that of an old Mexican ranch, whose ruined hacienda tops an eminence on the south side of the river, nearly opposite the modern hacienda on the north side. How the old ranch came to be abandoned is not known, but it is supposed to have been depopulated by Apaches not less than a hundred years ago. There are a few houses about here, forming a little settlement. I spent part of the afternoon at the one from which I drew my forage, where I heard some Mexican singing. I was told by the señoritas that their voices would have been accompanied by a guitar but for the mourning of the performer, a young girl in a neighboring family, for a brother killed by Indians about a month ago. He died, they said, a brave man, having fought to his last cartridge; he was found with his head crushed to a jelly.

The dismounted men came into camp in pretty bad shape. Several are badly chafed, and most of them have sore feet, due mainly to the bad state of their boots and shoes. One is quite sick, and will have to be allowed to ride. They have asked permission to start out to-morrow before breakfast, in order to get as far on their way as possible before the heat of the day. I have informed them that they will be started immediately after getting their breakfast.

CALABASAS, A. T., June 17, 1886.—My guide set out this morning on his mule about an hour after my dismounted men, intending to overtake them and show them the way; but he did not catch sight of them until he came to where they had stopped, pursuant to my instructions, to wait for the troop, ten and a half miles from where they set out, and about two miles from Calabasas.

A mile beyond the point where we passed our foot contingent, the road led between two notable ruins opposite sides of the river; one, old Fort Mason, abandoned about fourteen years ago; the other, the residence of the once Governor Gandara, of Sonora. All that one sees of the fort is a scattering of foundations, the superstructures of which have been destroyed by time, or removed by the neighboring population, to put into their own dwellings. The residence shows thick, solid walls, thus attesting that it was a more substantial structure than the so-called fort.

Have learned since my return here that the Indians reported west of Fairbanks, on whose account General Miles had directed my proceeding to the Mowry Mine, had existed only in the excited imagination of a certain ranchman.

FORT GRANT, A. T., September 20, 1886.—A day or two after my return to Calabasas I marched my troop to Crittenden, and turned it over to its regular commander, Captain Keyes, 10th Cavalry. Remained thereafter in camp at Calabasas until September 12th when troop K commenced its march to Fort Grant. The order from General Miles prescribing this movement was the first official intimation that we received of the close of the campaign. We were not altogether unprepared for it, however, having then for several weeks been discussing rumors of approaching peace.

NOTES

1. There was a place called Baily's on the Camp Thomas-Solomonsville road, a short distance west of the latter town and a trifle northeast of Camp Grant. It is shown on a map of Arizona prepared by Lieut. Fred A. Smith, 1879. Whether this was Bailey's Wells, I cannot say. No mention of the place is made in W. C. Barnes' *Arizona Place Names.*

2. Fort Grant, first established in 1859 as Fort Breckenridge, at the junction of San Pedro river and Arivaipa creek, Arizona. This post was abandoned in 1861, re-established on the same site as Camp Grant in 1862. It was again abandoned in 1866. New Fort Grant, the post to which Lieutenant Bigelow refers, was founded Dec. 19, 1872 at the base of the Graham Mountains, a short distance from the famous Sierra Bonita Ranch owned by Henry C. Hooker, and twenty-five miles north of Willcox, Arizona.

3. Canned vegetables were introduced in the United States from Europe as early as 1818. The tin-plated can was patented by Thomas Kensett in 1825 and by the 1880s canned vegetables as well as oysters, fish and lobsters were being shipped all over the world; hence the officers and soldiers at the frontier posts were able to supplement their monotonous army diet with vegetables, oysters and fruits—provided they had the money with which to buy them from civilian stores or the sutler's canteen. See May, Earl Chapin, *The Canning Clan,* N. Y., 1937.

4. Debates and arguments of the relative merits of the sabre and pistol versus carbine or rifle for field equipment of the cavalry on the frontier raged unchecked for many years following the conclusion of the Civil War. Many officers, who had seen service during the War, felt that the pistol or revolver was the only sensible weapon for mounted troops, other than the carbine, while others were equally vehement in their preference for the sabre. Protagonists of the latter weapon urged sharpening of the blade, which as a rule, was not done. There were those who preferred using the sabre as a point and others who thought the slash was more effective. As a rule, however, most cavalrymen voted the sabre a decided handicap, both as a dead weight and as a weapon, consequently the sword was seldom seen, except in the garrison and as a parade accessory.

5. Riley's, Reilley's or Reiley's Ranch as it was variously spelled was located in T. 12, S., R. 22 in the Winchester Mountains, south of Camp Grant and immediately adjacent to Hooker's Ranch, according to the map of 1879. Barnes (*op.*

NOTES

cit.) states that the ranch, a mountain and a canyon in Cochise County were all named after a frontier rancher known as "Well-digger Riley." (See *Place Names of Arizona*, by Will C. Barnes, Tucson, 1935.)

6. This Cedar Springs was an historic spot in Graham County, Ariz. During the 1880s it was headquarters for Norton & Stewart Cattle Co. (according to Barnes, p. 84-85). Near the springs, as mentioned by Lt. Bigelow, Geronimo and his band, after leaving San Carlos for Mexico, attacked a wagon train, Oct. 2, 1882, within sight of the stone house on the ranch. Bales of calico, sacks of flour and sugar were destroyed by the raiders. During the attack four or five troops of the 6th Cavalry arrived, and a pitched battle ensued. The Apache withdrew at nightfall. The fight was a draw.

7. Lt. Bigelow has now moved south, close to the Mexican border. The area in which he and his troop K, of the 10th Cavalry (the "Buffalo Soldiers" as the Negro troopers were called by the Plains Indians) had penetrated, is rich in mines.

8. This was Dr. Leonard J. Wood who, during World War I, became a Major General and during the greater part of 1918 was in command of Camp Funston, Kansas.

9. Lochiel is a small village in southern Arizona, about twenty-six miles southeast of the town of Patagonia, and is almost on the Mexican border.

10. The Mowry Mine was one of the most famous silver mines in the Patagonia Mountains in southern Arizona. As mentioned by Lt. Bigelow (p. 51 and 53) Sylvester Mowry had been an officer in the United States army prior to the Civil War. Letters written by Lt. Mowry from Fort Yuma and elsewhere during the 1850s indicate that he was, to say the least, a "full blooded man" and not averse to boasting about his amorous accomplishments. He purchased the silver mine, which bore his name, for the sum of $25,000 in 1860. Mowry invested heavily in equipment and goods. Two years later, June 8, 1862, Mowry was taken prisoner by order of General James Carleton, charged with giving aid to the Confederacy. The mine and all personal property were confiscated by the Government, and Mowry carried prisoner to Ft. Yuma. On November 14, 1862 Mowry was unconditionally released, but he never recovered his property which, along with machinery, buildings, etc., was sold at public auction by the U. S. Marshal and Mesilla, Dona Ana County, New Mexico July 18, 1864. Today the Mowry Mine is in other hands, but is not being worked. The buildings at the mine which were erected by Mowry have long since vanished, along with the tall brick chimney mentioned by Lt. Bigelow, the bricks of which were converted into walks and small retaining walls around the houses and other structures built within the past few years. The mine can be reached by a winding mountain road some fourteen or fifteen miles south of Patagonia.

11. Lt. Bigelow's "government No. 8's" simply meant regulation shoes or boots.

NOTES

12. Camp Crittenden was established on the Sonoita Creek, March 4, 1868, a short distance from the site of old Fort Buchanan. The buildings were of adobe and stone and the ruins of the post stand in the fields on the north side of the highway approximately 12 miles north of Patagonia. The post was broken up in June 1872. By 1874 it was described as "a useless ruin although the buildings and reservation are still in charge of Mr. S. Hughes." Lt. Bigelow was probably at the village of Crittenden about six miles from the old post, where a post office had been established June 11, 1873.

13. This was a mine on the east side of the Patagonia Mountains on Harshaw creek. It was named for David Tecumseh Harshaw, who settled there in 1875. Originally this place had been called Durazno or "Peach" by the Mexicans. A post office was established here April 29, 1880 (Barnes, p. 199).

14. Lieutenant Charles Henry Grierson graduated from the United States Military Academy, June 13, 1879 and entered the 10th Cavalry as a second lieutenant the same year. The old war horse, Col. Benjamin Henry Grierson, was in command of the 10th at this time. Lt. Grierson was promoted to first lieutenant July 6, 1886 and served in the regiment in various capacities through 1897. He became Lieut. Colonel of Volunteers, commissary of subsistence, May 9, 1898 and was honorably discharged March 17, 1899. (Heitman, Francis B., *Historical Register and Dictionary of the United States Army*, Washington, 1903, vol. I, p. 478.)

15. This town was the county seat of Greenlee County, Ariz. Bigelow in making a surmise at the origin of the name was not alone in his guessing game. Barnes (p. 99) cites various versions. One is that Clifton was named after Henry Clifton, recorder of the Hassayampa District, who, in company with four other prospectors, located copper mines on the San Francisco river upon which the town of Clifton was later established. However, two other men, W. A. Smith and Charles M. Shannon, said that the name came from the cliffs. Shannon, whose uncle founded the district, often related the facts of first camping under the huge cliffs and later called it "Clifftown." I cite this as an example of how place names are given, and how often the truth about their origins is obscured.

16. General George Crook was noted for his informality of dress and his independence of action while in the field. During the campaign of 1885-1886, H. W. Daly who was chief packer of the column penetrating Mexico east of Lt. Bigelow's area, described Crook at his famous meeting with Geronimo at Cañon de los Embudos (Canyon of the Funnels) in Mexico south of the border town of San Bernardino. Daly said: "General Crook, at this time wore a light brown canvas coat and overalls, a pair of Apache moccasins, and a low, double-crowned cork hat (*i.e.*, sun helmet, A.W.) and on his hands a pair of buckskin gauntlets. His long whiskers were braided in two plaits, as he always wore them when in the field." (Daly, H. W., "The Geronimo Campaign," 2 pts., *Journal of the United States Cavalry Association*, July and October, 1908, p. 97, Pt. I.) Usually General Crook, the "Gray Fox" as he was known to the Apache, rode a mule,

NOTES

carried a double barrelled shot gun (he was an ardent hunter) and rolled up in his blanket wherever night overtook him on the trail. He was an old campaigner, and a soldier's soldier.

17. Barnes, p. 415, states that this town in Graham County was named after I. E. Solomon, who opened a store there in 1876. Some maps have it Solomonsville, and it is alleged that William Kirkland, mail carrier between Clifton (approximately thirty miles northeast of Solomonville), named it after his friend Solomon.

18. Again Lt. Bigelow is guessing at the origin of a place name. Hodge, F. W. (*Handbook of the American Indian*, BAE 30, Pt. I, p. 492) believed it stemmed from the name of an Apache settlement west of Socorro, New Mexico, and the word Gila had been applied by Mimbreno and Chiricahua Apache to the extreme headwaters of the river as early as 1630.

20. The long Springfield rifle carried by the Apache scouts, or in fact any long muskets or rifles were designated as "Long Toms." This same term was used for certain cannon on shipboard. In fact, there is a distinct possibility that "Long Tom" originally was more vulgar and was transferred from one source to the other as a slang expression. (See Partridge, Eric, *A Dictionary of Slang and Unconventional English,* London 1937, p. 492.)

19. Masked dances among the Apache and their kinsmen, the Navajo, were held at various times, and had different significances. The Apache referred to the masked figures as "Mountain Spirits" which in white man's parlance became "Devil Dancers." These men assume the character of the Mountain Spirits and appear at Apache gatherings, sometimes at the girls' puberty rites, in healing ceremonies, and formerly in war rites. Or, they might simply dance to provide entertainment for the crowd. Four masked figures, accompanied by a fifth who is the clown, usually take part in the rituals. The masks and head adornments described by Bigelow indicate that his scouts were both providing entertainment and warding off any evil that might come to the party.

21. General Crook instituted the system of issuing these tags to the Apache who were on the reservations in his charge in 1873. The tags were in the shapes of crosses, triangles, diamonds, squares, crescents, and disks. Each form signified the band to which the wearer belonged and the number on it represented the owner whose name appeared opposite it on the agency roster. Thus untagged hostiles were quickly spotted if they attempted to mingle with their more peaceful brethren, and scouting parties encountering Apaches wearing tags, yet away from their reservations and without passes, could make the tag bearers give an accounting on the spot. In setting up this system General Crook had been anticipated by the first settlers of Virginia, who in 1661-1662, issued official silver and copper disks to the Indians in nearby villages, and compelled the leader of all bands visiting Jamestown and other Virginia settlements to wear the tag issued to his particular band. Those disks were in effect the first official "dog tags" used in the New World. General Crook was nearly two centuries late in applying the idea to

NOTES

the Apache. (See Bourke, John G., Capt., *On the Border With Crook*, N. Y., 1891, p. 219, and Henning, Wm., *The Statutes at Large of All the Laws of Virginia*, 1619-1660, and Vol. II, 1662-1680, Richmond, Va., 1810, pp. 141-142.)

22. At the present time there is a small adobe building standing alongside the road on part of the property which was once part of the Mowry Mine. Local tradition says that this was once an "old store," but other than this there is no evidence to tie it in with the grog shop opened by the ex-troopers of the 10th Cavalry. There is an old safe in this building, but I am of the opinion the safe was used elsewhere and brought to the structure at some later date.

23. General George A. Forsyth rose to fame from the ranks. He served through the Civil War, receiving promotion after promotion, from private in the dragoons to brigadier-general of volunteers. After the war he continued in service and gained undying fame for himself and his small band of scouts at the Battle of Beecher Island, Sept. 17-20, 1868. He retired from the service, Mar. 25, 1890. (Heitman, *op. cit.*, p. 430.)

24. Camp Huachuca was established at the mouth of Central Cañon, Huachuca Mountains, in Cochise County, Arizona, as a temporary post in 1877. However, so important was the garrison to the mining area in which it was located, the fort became a permanent one in 1881. Although its other contemporary and more famous posts were abandoned once the Apache troubles were settled, Ft. Huachuca continued to be a more or less active garrison. Troops were trained at Huachuca for both World War I and World War II. In 1949 the fort and buildings, including a reservation of some 12,000 acres, were transferred to the State of Arizona, but in recent years it is once more a busy area, reactivated by the mounting interest in air activities. Here at Huachuca the last of the Apache scouts served out their days of active service doing garrison duty.

25. Although General Crook was by far the best man to handle the Apache tribesmen, he ran headlong into trouble when he tried to deal fairly with the Indians as human beings, particularly with those civilians who trespassed upon the lands set aside for the Indians. Crook hated the petty, grafting white men who cheated and robbed the Apache of their cattle and rations. Crook knew that the continual encroachment upon the rights of the reservation Indians would eventually bring about more bloody outbreaks, and he fought to avert these troubles, but in vain. General Crook, unable to keep his word pledged in the name of the United States, because of political machinations in Washington, resigned his command of the Department of Arizona in 1886, and General Nelson A. Miles came in. The appointment of Miles pleased the citizens of Arizona. They presented a gold-mounted sword to General Miles for *his* work in cleaning up the Apache situation. When General Crook died on March 21st, 1890, and news reached the Apache Reservation, his ancient enemies and friends wept for the loss of a good friend and an honest warrior.

26. Another method of hardening the hoofs of horses, mules and burros, practiced by the Mexicans and Indians in Arizona and Sonora, was that of mix-

NOTES

ing the liver of a deer with ashes or lime and making it into a paste. This was applied to the feet of the animals and allowed to dry. Then another layer of the mixture was applied and so on until a thick crust had formed. It was alleged that this coating became rock hard and kept the animals from getting sore feet. The Apache also cut rawhide into pieces just large enough to fit around the horses' hoofs and then tied the hide on with thongs. These crude coverings also proved effective. One of them is preserved in the museum of the Arizona Pioneers Historical Society in Tucson.

27. The tragic and useless death of Captain Emmet Crawford, wounded January 11, 1886 near Nacori, Sonora, Mexico, deprived General Crook of a most valuable officer. Daly (*op. cit.,* p. 85), paid Crawford this tribute: "He was the bravest among the brave; gentlest among the gentle; he forgave and overlooked the faults and frailties of others, while being the most chivalrous and gentlemanly officer and man that I have ever known in or out of the service. His loss to all those who ever knew him, and particularly to General Crook, was irreparable."
    Captain Crawford was shot down deliberately by a Mexican rifleman belonging to a militia outfit known as the *Seguridad Publicos,* organized by the Mexicans to get in on the kill of the Apache under Geronimo. The Mexican troops jumped Crawford's camp of Apache scouts early in the morning, probably under the mistaken idea that they were the renegade Indians. Although the Mexicans were informed by the American scouts in Spanish that the Americans were friends, the fire did not cease. Captain Crawford, in company with an Apache scout "Dutchy," scrambled up on a boulder in plain sight of the Mexicans, and Crawford waved a white flag. A moment later he fell, struck by a rifle bullet fired by a Mexican not much over twenty-five yards distant. Dutchy then killed the Mexican. Mortally wounded, Crawford was transported from the scene of the skirmish, and died, on the 18th of January. Four days later he was given temporary burial in the little Campo Santo at Nacori. Some time later his remains were sent back to the home of his brother in Kearney, Nebraska, and there buried. (See also Shipp, Lieut. W. E., "Captain Crawford's Last Expedition," *Journal of the U. S. Cavalry Association,* Dec. 1892, reprinted in the *Journal,* Oct. 1908. Lt. Shipp, a member of the expedition after Geronimo in 1885-86, was killed in action at San Juan, Santiago, Cuba, July 1, 1898.)

28. See notes on Geronimo's surrender in Daly, *op. cit.,* and Bourke, John. G., *On the Border with Crook.*

29. This elaborate townsite of Calabasas, like many other real estate speculations, never materialized.

30. Lt. Bigelow errs in his dates for the establishment of Tumacacori Mission. Father Eusebio Kino first visited the Indian village near the site of the present mission ruins in 1690. By 1695 the place, called San Cayetano de Tumacacori, was a Jesuit stock farm, where sheep and goats were kept. Two years later the Indians had built an adobe house, roofed with earth, for the use of the visiting padres. In 1701 Father Juan de Martin included Tumacacori in his district. The

NOTES

Franciscan missionaries took over the Jesuit missions in 1767. In 1772 Father Antonio Reyes reported that there was a church and priest's house at Tumacacori, but the buildings were bare of furniture and ornaments. Twelve years later it was flourishing. By 1822 a new church of adobe was finished. Tumacacori however became the target of Apache raiders, (they attacked the mission in 1769 and later). By the late 1840s it was a roofless ruin. It is now a National Monument, and the National Park Service has partially restored the old building. The present structure is Franciscan in origin.

31. The Southwest is rich in lost mines and buried treasures. Every old sheep corral and the ruins of weatherbeaten adobe huts have been probed and dug into by seekers of easy wealth. The region around Tumacacori and Tubac has attracted more treasure hunters than almost any area in southern Arizona. In March 1935 I was sent to Tumacacori as consultant on some archeological work being done at the Mission by Archeologist Paul Beaubien, who did an excellent job laying bare the entire area around the buildings. In the course of this work huge holes were found inside and outside the mission walls which had been dug by treasure-mad, ignorant vandals. In his book, *Tucson, Tubac, Tumacacori, To Hell,* Col. Gil Procter relates some entertaining yarns about the lost mines and the "Treasure of the Padres," all of which are of the conventional type. I believe this naive explanation related by Lt. Bigelow concerning the origin of the extensive search that has been conducted for such loot since the 1840s is probably the most truthful account that has yet been rendered. Over a century has passed since the villagers in Tubac began circulating the rumor of the "lost" Tumacacori mine, but the lure is as strong today as it was in the 1840s and 1850s. The same technique was used by ranchers and other residents in Arizona to keep the military in regions where the need for troops had long since passed, by the simple expedient of circulating false rumors concerning alleged or impending Indian uprisings, in order that the promoters of such legends might harvest a sure crop of golden eagles from Uncle Sam's quartermasters by selling forage and farm produce to the troops. For that matter the Chambers of Commerce today use the same pressures to prevent the abandonment of lucrative army bases in their neighborhoods, regardless of the best interests of national economy.

32. So far as I am aware this is one of those legends which surround the ugly gila monster. These lizards are poisonous, but are not as dangerous or deadly as the folklore of the region say they are.

33. When the Southern Pacific pushed its tracks eastward across Arizona, beginning in 1877 and reaching New Mexico in 1880, the railroad granted special privileges to the Indian tribes such as the Pima and Papago, who were entitled to ride free. As a result these Indians made the most of it and rode freight and flat cars between Yuma and Tucson, carrying baskets and pottery, which they sold and traded to both whites and Indians. The Yuma Indians also came in for free transportation and they too rode back and forth, visiting their friends. However, one head man didn't like the idea of riding on freight cars, and protested that he should be given first class passage, but to no avail. He was told if he wanted to ride the cars, he would have to travel as the rest of his tribesmen—which he did.

INDEX

INDEX

INDEX

INDEX

INDEX